GOD'S OTHER CHILDREN

MARIAM, AGE 16

MARIAM, AGE 30

GOD'S OTHER CHILDREN

Personal Encounters with Faith, Love, and Holiness in Sacred India

BRADLEY MALKOVSKY

HarperOne
An Imprint of HarperCollins*Publishers*

HarperOne

Sanskrit Pronunciation Key from *Bhagavad-Gītā: The Beloved Lord's Secret Love Song* by Graham M. Schweig. Used by permission of HarperOne, an imprint of Harper-Collins Publishers.

HarperCollins books may be purchased for educational, business, or sales promotional use. For information, please e-mail the Special Markets Department at SPsales@harpercollins.com.

HarperCollins website: http://www.harpercollins.com

HarperCollins®, ♦®, and HarperOne™ are
trademarks of HarperCollins Publishers.

FIRST EDITION

Library of Congress Cataloging-in-Publication Data

Malkovsky, Bradley J.
God's other children : personal encounters with faith, love, and holiness
in sacred India / Bradley Malkovsky. — First edition.
pages cm
ISBN 978-0-06-184068-5
1. Malkovsky, Bradley J. 2. Spiritual biography. 3. India—Religion.
4. Religions. 5. Christianity and other religions. I. Title.
BL73.M355A3   2012
261.2092—dc23   2012033661

13 14 15 16 17 RRD(H) 10 9 8 7 6 5 4 3 2

To my wife, Mariam, and my mother, Betty Malkovsky,
the two people in my life who most perfectly embody
the selfless love of God

Contents

PART II

Prologue

At a Spiritual Crossroads

I don't think we really understand where we have been until we have finally arrived at our destination.

When I was thirty-one years old, after having completed thirteen years of wandering in various parts of America and Germany, I had reached a point in my life where nothing was settled. I had just earned a graduate degree at the University of Tübingen, but I did not feel called to teach. Nor was I looking to get married and start a family. Years earlier I had spent almost a year in a remote mountain monastery in the United States, but I did not feel a call to the monastic life. I had also done volunteer work at a soup kitchen in a desert city and in a hospital in urban Germany, but I did not discern that either of these places would be my life's calling. While all these activities—studying theology, living in a monastery, serving the poor and the sick—were good and wholesome and had taught me much about myself and God, there was still a restlessness inside me, a longing for something more that I did not fully understand until I went to India. And so when my time in Germany came to an end, I followed my instincts and headed off to India with very little money in my pocket. It was only after I arrived there that I began to understand how everything in my life had been a preparation for India.

Officially I was in India to do research for a doctoral dissertation, but deep down I knew that the more important reason I was there was to continue a spiritual quest that had begun many years before.

This book recounts a number of episodes of my journey into different religions. Its focus is on India, the land where, in my encounter with Hindus, Buddhists, and Muslims, I was forced to rethink everything I had previously held about God, the world, and myself.

When I first arrived in India, I did not expect to learn about Islam or Buddhism. I had come to study a particular branch of Hinduism called Advaita Vedānta. My goal was to study the Sanskrit language and do doctoral research on Śaṅkara (ca. 700 CE), one of Hinduism's greatest thinkers, and to place his teaching in dialogue with Catholic teaching. I originally thought I would stay one year in India and then return to Germany to finish my doctorate, but I ended up staying five years. There were two reasons for this. First, I soon learned that I would need to stay a lot longer than one year to study Śaṅkara. In fact, one could spend a whole lifetime studying his writings and still not fully plumb the depths of his teaching. The second reason was family life. I met and married my wife in India in an unexpected and wonderful turn of events, and our first two children were born there. Marrying into a Sunni Muslim family led to new and enriching interactions with a great many Muslim relatives and friends that often diverted me from fully concentrating on Hindu studies.

It was also around that time that I discovered the power of Buddhist meditation and took up seriously the practice of yoga. So I wasn't just reading books all the time or working on my dissertation or interacting with Muslim relatives. How could I pass up the opportunity to investigate the other spiritualities that were all around me? And so my first visit to India ended up lasting much longer than I had originally planned. What I experienced and discovered about the value of Hindu, Buddhist, and Muslim spirituality during that time and on subsequent visits to India has far exceeded all my expectations. India and its religions never cease to amaze me. They have a way of shaking us loose from our parochial preoccupations and getting us to see the world and God and ourselves with new eyes.

The stories here recount experiences that taught me an unexpected spiritual lesson or deepened my awareness of the riches of another religion or broadened my understanding and appreciation of the mystery of God. There are times, as will be seen, when I do not quite know what to make of what I experienced or what conclusions I should draw from my Christian perspective. Christian theology does not always provide ready-made answers to new questions and new experiences.[1] But sometimes we act as if it does. Too often, as one Asian Christian theologian has put it, Christians, in their encounter with people of other religions, have suffered from "teacher complex."[2] We have been only too ready to teach and proclaim what we believe as Christians, but we have not always been good at listening and learning from others. Perhaps the time has come for us not only to give witness to Christ, but also to start learning what God is teaching us through other religions. Fortunately, the age in which we now live provides us with greater opportunity to interact with people of other religions than during any other time in human history.

By profession I am a Catholic theologian, since I have degrees in Catholic theology, and I teach theology at a Catholic university, but, truth be told, most of the time I feel like I'm just a beginner. There is still so much in my own rich theological and mystical heritage that I need to learn. The main reason for this has to do with spending most of my time learning about other religions and trying to keep up with new developments. I don't have time to examine my Catholic tradition as much as I'd like to these days, even though I've already spent years doing it. And so when I'm lecturing at my university on the relation of Christianity to other religions, it sometimes strikes me that I'm really just a student inside a professor's body. I'm very aware of the boundaries of my knowledge. I'd like to know more about what people in other religions have come to experience and understand about the supreme reality, and I wonder how all our understandings fit together, if indeed they do. Even after years spent studying Hinduism, Buddhism, and Islam, I feel like I'm still taking my first baby steps in exploring those religions. One thing I have learned along the way, though, is this: those other traditions are every bit as deep and rich as my own. They are absolutely brimming with wisdom and insight. And they have the capacity to lead their followers to holiness, a holiness that is recognized as holiness by Christians from within their own tradition.

As to Islam, I can proudly say that by virtue of my marriage I have many Muslim relatives in the city of Pune, India: aunts and uncles and cousins and other assorted relatives of various stripes, most of whom are wonderful and decent people. I mention this because in these very disturbing times, it is important to remember that along with some very real disagreement we may have with Islam, there is also much that unites Islam and Christianity theologically, spiritually, and humanly. And it is a characteristic of the post–Vatican II Catholic approach to other religions[3] that we seek out similarities and commonalities before we discuss our obvious differences.

In this book I set out to do three things. First, the stories I tell—whether they involve the practice of Buddhist meditation, visits to shrines of Muslim saints, or the experience of being healed by a Hindu physician—are intended to give the reader a sense of the value of other religions and their power to heal and transform our lives. This is not something easily assumed by a Christian. It is one thing to believe that people of other religions are sincerely seeking the Divine; it is quite another to discover just how much God has already given them.

Second, by connecting these stories to the lives of real people I hope also to avoid making sweeping generalizations about other religions, of making the mistake of presenting them as if they were unified mono-lithic entities. Over the years I have come to appreciate more and more just how complex and how varied each of the great world religions is. This should not surprise us. Religions, after all, consist of people re-sponding to the divine presence and call, and people invariably display a wide range of beliefs, dispositions, temperaments, and capacities for spiritual growth and understanding. This book, then, offers no aca-demic introduction to the history and thought of the different religions I will be presenting. But I do give witness to my firsthand experience with people of other faiths, of their beliefs and practices, of their holiness and flaws, and that experience, though limited, has become authoritative for me as I try to sort out theological issues pertaining to the relation of Christ and Christianity to other religions.

Putting a human face on other religions is especially important in regard to Islam, because so often Islam is presented in the West as essentially violent, intolerant, and opposed to humanistic values. I hope to counter that caricature by showing a different side of Islam, one that I know is true from my experience of having lived among Muslims.

By focusing on the human dimension of religion rather than on doctrine alone, I hope to bring the reader to a deeper appreciation of just how much we all share as human beings in our spiritual striving, regardless of our religious affiliation. By the end of the book I hope the reader will come to recognize the validity of referring to people of other religions as children of God.[4]

Third, this book raises questions about the relation of Christ and Christianity to other religions. In a world of many saints and savior figures, how are we to understand Christ? How can we who are Christian affirm the value of other religions and spiritual paths without relativizing the significance of Christ? How do we understand his salvific work? How has my own thinking about Christ and God changed through my growing knowledge of other religions? How do other religions help me come to a deeper understanding of who Christ is and his significance for our world today? How have other religions helped me to rethink the mystery of God, of who I am, and of the final goal of all our questing? These are some of the questions that were in my mind as I wrote this book.

I came to the conclusion many years ago that not only is my faith in Christ a gift from God, a mystery that I do not entirely understand, but that the people I meet are equally gifts of God, each manifesting the presence of the divine mystery in their own unique way. When I think of India, I find that this is especially true. Encounters with Muslims, Hindus, and Buddhists in India, and also with fellow Christians who live there, have enriched my spirituality and thinking in ways that I could not have begun to imagine when I first arrived there. I am grateful for having come to know such people. This book gives but a small glimpse of that experience. So much more must be left unsaid for now.

Part I

I

Return to India

The air is hot and soupy even at two o'clock in the morning as my wife, Mariam, my daughter, Karina, and I leave the Mumbai airport terminal. Our two nephews Abid and Tahir appear and walk up to us shyly. I have not seen them since they were small boys; now they are in their midtwenties, dark haired and grown up. "Hello, Uncle," says Abid, the elder brother, in perfect English, extending his hand to me. *"Asalaamu alaikum,"* I say in Arabic, the standard Muslim greeting around the world, which means, "Peace be upon you." Abid smiles broadly that I, a Christian, would greet him so. *"Walaikum asalaam,"* he replies, "and peace upon you." The exchange of greetings is repeated with Tahir with the same cheerful effect.

Though India is a predominantly Hindu country—approximately 81 percent of a population of 1.1 billion—it is also the home of the third-largest Muslim population in the world; its 14 percent translates into more than 150 million Indian Muslims. Only Indonesia and Pakistan are home to more Muslims than India. In fact, there are more Muslims living in India than all the Middle East combined. It is because of such large Muslim populations in the south and southeast of Asia, in countries such as Indonesia, India, Pakistan, and Bangladesh, that more than 80 percent of all the world's Muslims do not live in lands where Arabic is the first language. In India, Arabic is spoken only by scholars and imams, that is, those formally trained in the Islamic textual and ritual traditions, whereas the great masses of Muslims use Arabic in limited fashion, either as a greeting to fellow Muslims or to recite formal prayers. In daily conversation they speak a multitude of local languages. For example, even though my nephews have returned my greeting in Arabic, they understand very little of the language; their mother tongue is Urdu-Hindi.

In India the languages spoken are mostly region based. Here in the southwestern state of Maharashtra, bordering on the Arabian Sea, the preferred language is Marathi, but Muslims who have immigrated from outside Maharashtra tend to speak Hindi or Urdu-Hindi, or whatever other language from their homeland, and know very little Marathi. Both these languages, Hindi and Marathi, are derivatives of ancient Sanskrit, as are north and central Indian languages such as Gujarati, Punjabi, and Bengali. And broadly speaking, the higher the level of education, the greater the likelihood that the Indian citizen has mastered English in addition to speaking one or two or even three Indian languages.

As practicing Muslims, Abid and Tahir, like my wife, Mariam—a former Muslim, but now, like me, a Catholic—and every one of her Muslim relatives, grew up with a sense of the sacredness of Arabic, even though they were not taught to speak it in conversation. Instead as children they learned to memorize all the standard Muslim prayers and greetings in Arabic and were instructed to sight-read the Qur'ān in the original at a *madrasa* (Islamic school) or by a teacher visiting their home. But for the most part, the words that they sounded out as they traced their finger across the page were not translated or understood. This limited grasp of Arabic is still typical of most of the Muslim world today.

My nephews will not allow their "Mariam Aunty" and "Bradley Uncle" to push our luggage carts. But as they take over they are immediately joined by five uniformed porters who have stepped out of the darkness and jostle each other for position. "Like bees to honey," remarks Abid with a grim smile. The porters, all of them small and thin, but of varying ages, do not earn much and must rely on the generosity of travelers to support their families. Abid pushes his cart across the parking lot as three porters "help" him by lightly laying a hand or even a single finger atop the luggage as they walk beside it. Tahir is "helped" by two more. When we arrive at the van, three additional porters appear out of nowhere to assist us in loading the luggage. Even though we wave them off, they, too, extend their upturned palms to us for payment. Karina looks on calmly. Two years earlier she had spent most of the summer in India with her mother and brother and has learned to take everything in stride. After the luggage is loaded and we have climbed into the van, Abid takes out his wallet and distributes ten rupee bills all around, before getting in himself.

The driver of our rented van is a young Muslim with a black curly beard and white skullcap (*kufi*). His appearance suggests conservative Islam. For many Americans back home his is the face of "the enemy," the "Muslim fanatic." Abid and Tahir know nothing about him, and he speaks only when spoken to. Like many hired drivers, he likes to go fast. We tear through the streets of Mumbai, weaving and bouncing, and less than an hour later enter the newly constructed Mumbai-Pune Highway, seven years in the making, with wide double lanes in both directions. The distance between the two cities is 170 kilometers (about 105 miles). The speed limit is eighty kilometers per hour (about 50 mph), but given the opportunity most drivers will go faster.

The air is cooler here in the mountains. Our driver, Khaled, needs a tea break to stay awake and finds a café where we stop. Even in the blackness of four o'clock in the morning, almost all the outdoor tables are taken, mostly by men. We enjoy fresh tea, bottled juice, and white bread rolls sprinkled with a mixture of chopped peanuts, red chili, and unidentifiable spices. Abid and Tahir have already provided us with large bottles of purified drinking water at the airport. Bottled water is readily available throughout India and safe and inexpensive for foreigners. More and more Indian families are consuming clean bottled water for health reasons, if they can afford it.

After a leisurely half hour, we head back into the night. Dawn is still a few hours away. Since India is not far north of the equator, the average length of daylight is twelve to twelve and a half hours year-round.

•　　•　　•

Traffic is sparse just before dawn when we arrive in Pune, but the first Puneites are already up and about, heading off to work. Men and women, even some visibly old, walk briskly along the side of the street under a row of broad-limbed trees. Stray dogs lie curled up on sidewalks in front of shuttered shops or stand motionless in the middle of the road. Waiting at a traffic light, we hear above us the harangue of crows in the overhanging green and orange canopy of a *gulmohar* tree. As we pass through the city I scarcely recognize old neighborhoods and must now learn new traffic patterns. The city's population has more than doubled since I was last here fourteen years ago; it is now four and a half million. In many places, stately bungalows and gardens have given way to crowded high-rise apartments and office buildings; two-lane streets have doubled in width and are now separated by uninterrupted traffic islands of planted flowers. Now and then we see half-built cement overpasses, called "flyovers," towering over houses at treetop level. Once they are complete they will relieve congestion by diverting traffic above the city. This is but one small feature of the new India that I must get to know.

Our driver, Khaled, unexpectedly pulls the van to the side of the road and climbs out. There is no tea stall here on this block, only drab apartment buildings, crumbling walls, and run-down homes and shops. I'm thinking he might be looking for a public urinal. But Abid explains, "He's paying his respects." What do you mean? I ask. "He's going to that mosque to pray," he says, pointing across the street. I see the small green building—in Islam, green represents the heavenly paradise—but the only one entering is our driver. It is time—predawn—for the first of the five formal daily prayers, called *ṣalāt* in Arabic, but here in India usually referred to by the Turko-Persian *namāz*. After ten minutes, his prayers completed, Khaled jogs back across the street to us, a grin on his face. He says nothing as he settles back into the driver's seat. Again we are off like a rocket. But what is the hurry?

A half hour more and we are in Wanowrie, one of the city's southern neighborhoods. The buildings are newer here than in central Pune, but they cannot compare with the gleaming stylish malls and expensive gated communities located in other parts of the city that have sprung up like air-conditioned oases during India's economic boom over the past three years. The landmark we are looking for is Kedari Garden, a two-story wedding hall with a spacious green lawn bordered by rows of stately palms. Across the street from the hall is the sixth-floor "flat" or apartment where Ābid and Tāhir live with their mother and little brother, Adil. This will be our home for the next four weeks.

After the luggage is unloaded, I signal to Khaled that I would like to take his picture before he leaves us. He smiles and shakes his head no. I insist. He pauses for a moment out of politeness, just long enough for me to snap his portrait. In it he is wide-eyed and wistful. I hold my digital camera at arm's length for him to see himself in the viewer. He wrestles with the idea briefly, then submits to the urge to take a brief look. He smiles. Later I learn that Khaled is the kind of strict Muslim who has been taught to be wary of having himself photographed. There is always the danger of giving too much attention to the creature and forgetting the Creator.

Inside the apartment, Tabassum, the mother of three sons, is waiting for us. She is a tiny woman in her early forties, fair complexioned, a real beauty in her younger years, according to Mariam. In India, lighter skin is preferred, and a dark-skinned man of wealth will normally select a bride who is lighter in appearance than himself. My wife calls Tabassum *bhabhi,* a Hindi word that means "brother's wife," for Tabassum is married to Razaak, one of Mariam's two brothers. All told Razaak has four wives, and Tabassum is his first. They were married when she was only sixteen and Razaak twenty-six. Standing beside Tabassum is her ten-year-old son, our other nephew, who everyone calls Adi, a shortened form of Adil. He is good-natured, but a bit spoiled, being more than ten years younger than his brothers, Abid and Tahir. Mariam and I embrace both mother and son. Karina and Adi immediately go into the next room to play, as if they had been separated for only a day instead of two years. Despite our protests, Tabassum insists that we take the formal bedroom for the duration of our visit.

A few hours after our arrival in Pune, the two children and I step out of the apartment building into the bright morning sun to explore the nearby woods, despite the danger of lurking snakes. Our spirits are high on this glorious morning, and we are in a joyful mood, eager for adventure. We follow the edge of the street, looking for a path into the shady forest, but are prevented, even in this upscale neighborhood, by mounds of garbage, broken glass, and human feces blocking our way. And so instead of entering the woods, we abandon our original plan and decide to take a casual stroll down a quiet avenue of recently constructed three- and four-story apartment buildings. Simple bungalows of wood and stone had once stood here, but with India's booming population the price of city property has skyrocketed, and so many of the local families have taken advantage of the opportunity to increase their wealth and have sold their houses and land for a tidy profit to real estate developers and then moved into one of the "flats" or apartments in the high-rise that has replaced their original homes. Yet even with these newly con-structed buildings towering all around us, the neighborhood somehow remains surprisingly lush and natural, replete with bright-colored trees and bushes that blossom yellow, orange, red, and blue.

At the end of a small lane a ditch of raw sewage and garbage pre-vents us from going farther; it is impassable to anyone but scavenging dogs and pigs. On the other side of the ditch stands a row of dilapidated tin shacks, before which children in tattered clothing play with sticks and dogs. These children will probably never go to school, and for some of them life will be spent as ragpickers and in other menial labor. They are separated from India's new wealth by invisible social barriers that stretch back thousands of years.[1] In all the country's teeming cities, poor children such as these—often Muslims and low-caste Hindus—will rarely benefit from their country's rising prosperity. Indeed, even our modern city of Pune, sometimes labeled the "Oxford of the East" with its thirty-nine colleges, and which has recently become one of India's premier centers for information technology, contains the third-highest percentage of poor people in all of India's cities, roughly 40 percent of the metropolitan population. Many of these poor have arrived from the villages of Bihar and Uttar Pradesh to the north and east, some of them having traveled across the country by camel or horse caravan, seeking work in the rapidly expanding construction industry that is now reshaping Pune and Mumbai.

The gaping gulf between rich and poor persists, both in the villages and the big cities. Rural villagers, mostly farmers who today comprise two-thirds of India's population, have remained largely unaffected by India's recent economic boom. In many cases the farmers have been driven to despair under the combined weight of international economic pressures, high-interest bank loans, extended drought, and falling water levels. Over 180,000 farmers committed suicide in India between 1997 and 2007.

By midmorning, as the sun continues its climb, the fierce heat presses down on us with greater force, and so the children and I are finally compelled to relent and take refuge indoors. By early afternoon we are reduced to sitting in a circle in the apartment, all of us, adults and children, waiting for cooler evening to arrive. The apartment is not furnished with air-conditioning. Colorful chiffon curtains, reaching almost to the floor, billow lightly toward us with the scorching breeze. On such afternoons, even in a modern apartment like this one, there is not much to do other than talk or nap or read, especially when the electricity has gone dead. The ceiling fan hangs motionless, and the television screen is dark. Outside, under a now molten sky, the sun beats down mercilessly upon the city in one-hundred-degree heat. From late March until early June, India's hot season, one moves more slowly to conserve energy. Most of the shops and stores will not reopen until late afternoon.

Inside the apartment we pass the time conversing about the usual topics: the children's schooling, impending weddings, household budgets threatened by rising inflation, the dismal prospects of landing a lucrative job in a telephone call center, complaints of petty injustices, ceaseless lamentations about widespread political corruption, somber reports on the illness and death of friends and neighbors, and juicy gossip about secret rendezvous and trysts. The conversation shifts effortlessly between English and Hindi.

Here on the sixth floor a waft of hot air carries up to us the mixed sounds of urban India: the hum and sputter of rickshaws and scooters from the street below, the startling variety of exotic bird calls and shrills, small bells clanging, the human cry of pushcart vendors, the bleating of goats, and the faint sound of hammers from nearby construction sites.

Just after midday, Tabassum, our sister-in-law, prepares a "breakfast" of chapati (unleavened flatbread) and vegetables, after which a knock on the door announces the arrival of a young man named Soyub, a Muslim cousin from an adjacent neighborhood. He is tall and clean-shaven and sports dark glasses, jeans, and a black Western-style shirt rolled up to his elbows. His girlfriend, Huma, is with him, completely covered from head to foot in the traditional black burqa, except for her round face, which is fair and serious. Together they symbolize an Islam in transition. In recent decades more and more young Muslims from around the world have been drawn to Western culture, entertainment, and dress, but at the same time many remain suspicious of its materialism and secularism. When I return to the living room some minutes later, I see that the two are sitting closely together on the couch. Soyub quickly removes his arm from around Huma's waist when he sees me, while she hastily covers her head with a veil. I am older than they, and they fear I might disapprove of even this little display of intimacy. They smile sheepishly when formally introduced and do not speak much, except to each other. Huma's eyes are directed at the floor. They met six years ago working at a local telephone call center and fell in love. Because Huma's parents oppose the relationship they have been forced to meet secretly for more than two years. Sometimes they come here to Tabassum's apartment, where they are accepted as a couple. Huma will remove her burqa and reveal a *salwar kameez,* a pajama-like outfit worn in public by women of all religions. Huma and Soyub are determined to marry. I ask if I may photograph them. He says yes, but she says no. She is very shy. Perhaps another time.

Adi, the youngest of my three nephews, has playmates in the apartment building who are both Hindu and Muslim. Though they have their occasional quarrels like all children, they look forward each day to playing cricket in the street below or games unfamiliar to me like "shake and shampoo," a variation of tag. It is generally true that in India, people of different religions tend to coexist peaceably, if not always harmoniously, with occasional outbreaks of violence. Pune has been relatively free of such interreligious clashes. Yet often enough an unspoken undercurrent of distrust and prejudice between religious communities remains, and it affects all religions, especially Hindu-Muslim relations.

India's neighbors have been accused of manipulating these interreligious tensions. During the past few years a series of well-coordinated bombs have detonated in railway stations, marketplaces, restaurants, bazaars, and even hospitals in major cities across India, such as Mumbai, Hyderabad, Varanasi, Gorakhpur, Jaipur, Bangalore, Ahmedabad, and, most recently, our city of Pune.[2] It was a year and a half after our visit that the famous terrorist attack on Mumbai occurred, which for several days captured the world's attention. The attack, as is now well known, was orchestrated by hard-line Muslims from Pakistan. The general consensus in the Indian press is that Pakistanis and Bangladeshis are trying to destabilize the emerging superpower that is India by exploiting age-old tensions; their goal is to trigger violence and counterviolence between Hindus and Muslims. It is a tribute to the Mumbai population that after the terrorist attacks in November 2008, there were no Hindu-Muslim clashes and no Hindu backlash against the Muslim minority. For their part, the Muslim leaders of Mumbai urged the faithful to celebrate their annual 'Īd feast day in a more restrained and less festive mood than normal.[3]

Islam, then, is not the same the world over in its attitude toward people of other religions. Indian Islam, often enough exercising reason and restraint even under threats from other religious groups, is in some ways situated at the opposite end of the Muslim political and social spectrum from, say, Wahabism in Saudi Arabia (the brand of Islam to which Osama bin Laden subscribed), with its strict adherence to law, its hostility toward other religions, and its successful banishment of mystical Islam, especially Sufism, from its land.

The Islam with which I am familiar in India is very different from the kind of Islam we often hear about in the media. It is truly a religion of peace. There are obviously various kinds of Muslims and Muslim attitudes in India, some of them narrow-minded, rigid, and intolerant, to be sure (as with members of all religious communities, including at times people from within my own Catholic community; we should not therefore compare what is best in our tradition with what is worst in theirs), but my experience for the most part has been edifying and even inspiring. I am thinking in particular of my many interactions and conversations with Indian Muslims in their homes and my frequent visits to various Muslim shrines (*dargahs*), sacred sites where men and women saints are interred and venerated. In short, Islam in India has been a pleasant surprise for me over the years.

Though we are exhausted from our long flight from America, we remain talking deep into the night to catch up on all the news about family and friends. It is enough to be here, sharing this conversation. India feels like home.

2

A First Conversation About Jesus

The next day our conversation takes an unexpected turn. As we are eating, Abid says to me, "Uncle, if you don't mind, I'd like to ask you some questions about Christianity." Up until then we had not ventured into a discussion of those topics that divide our two religions. There are no doctrinal debates about how the one creator God can logically be a Trinity or how the man Jesus can be simultaneously divine. These are the two Christian teachings that Muslims the world over most vehemently oppose, as they seem to contradict the oneness and transcendence of the Creator. It is because of Trinity and Incarnation that Muslims sometimes mock Christianity as a "mystery religion." To them, Christianity professes "mysteries" that seem to defy all logic and common sense.

I know that Abid is a devout Muslim. He prays *namāz* five times a day,[1] and he goes to the mosque on Fridays for the communal prayer and sermon. He has no bad habits, as far as I can tell, and he doesn't drink or smoke. He works six, sometimes seven days a week as the foreman for a building contractor. I wonder what questions he has about Christianity. Will it be about the Trinity or perhaps about Jesus's divinity? "Go ahead," I say to him. "I'll do my best to answer your questions."

But the question Abid poses comes as a surprise; it is one that has nothing to do with the Trinity or with Christianity's relation to the standard teachings of traditional Islam. "Some time ago," he says, "I was reading a book that says Jesus traveled to India. Uncle, I wonder what you think about that. The book gives evidence. Do you believe Jesus came to India?" I am certain that Abid is not trying to lure me into a debate. His question is genuine.

I ask him the name of the book and author, but he can't remember. It was a while ago when he read it, he says.

I answer that I do not believe Jesus ever traveled to India. There is no hard evidence that he did, as far as I can tell. But I acknowledge that I have heard the story a number of times over the years, sometimes from Westerners who have turned away from institutional Christianity but have not rejected Jesus, a man they continue to regard as a holy teacher of divine love and wisdom, a wisdom they claim he learned from Hindus and Buddhists. As for me, the account of Jesus's life I know best and the one I accept as true is the standard one based on the four Gospels of the New Testament.

There are no references to Jesus traveling to India anywhere in the Qur'ān or Bible. So where does the story come from, and, more important, what is its significance today?

The person who first propagated the story of Jesus traveling to India was a Russian journalist named Nicholas Notovitch. He claimed to have seen two Tibetan scrolls in 1887 in the library of the Hemis monastery in Ladakh, high up in the Himalayas, while he was recuperating from a broken leg. The library scrolls, he claimed, were in effect an unknown gospel describing Jesus's missing years in India and Tibet, the two places where he absorbed the wisdom of Buddhism, Hinduism, and Jainism before returning home to Galilee. The original title of this gospel was "Life of Saint Issa, Best of the Sons of Men." Notovitch published the book in French in 1894 under the title *La vie inconnue de Jesus-Christ (The Hidden Life of Jesus Christ)*. It was subsequently translated into English, Italian, German, and Spanish. The book was an instant sensation in Europe and went through eight printings in France its first year.

Notovitch's claims were immediately received with skepticism by scholars who set out to check their authenticity. Foremost among these was the famous German indologist Max Mueller, who wrote to the chief lama at Hemis monastery about Notovitch and received the reply that, despite Notovitch's claim, no Westerner had visited there in the past fifteen years nor was the monastery in possession of any documents having anything to do with the story Notovitch had made public in his famous book. At around the same time, also in response to Notovitch, a British professor teaching in Agra named J. Archibald Douglas took it upon himself to make the arduous journey to the Hemis monastery to conduct a personal interview with the same head monk with whom Mueller had corresponded. What Douglas learned there completely concurred with what Mueller had learned: Notovitch had never been there, and there were no documents in the monastery about any Issa (Jesus).[2]

Despite the successful investigative work done by Mueller and Douglas to debunk the Notovitch hoax, the story that Jesus visited India has, in the intervening decades, taken on a life of its own, even spawning a number of competing versions to the original narrative. One finds many of them on the Internet today.

The claim that Jesus left Palestine and traveled to India would provide an explanation for the age-old mystery of where he was during his "missing years," that is, from the time he was a boy of twelve to the time he was thirty, when he began his public preaching and mission. The New Testament is strangely silent about those missing years.

The Jesus-in-India stories are not unified, however. I will give three versions here. The first and most popular version states that during his absent years Jesus traveled to India and Tibet to learn wisdom at the feet of Hindu and Buddhist masters. He is supposed to have learned especially the high philosophies of Hinduism, in particular Vedānta, and was also trained in the practice of yoga and meditation. The implication is that it was in India that Jesus was first indoctrinated into teachings about the nonduality of God and our inner Self. He then returns to Palestine with a radical new teaching about the Kingdom of God being "within" us. Christians, it is often said by advocates of this story, have never truly understood that Jesus's proclamation of the Kingdom of God was an essentially mystical message, addressed to helping us uncover our inner divine identity. To truly understand Jesus, then, according to this story, it is necessary to see that the source of his wisdom lies in the religions of India.

Yet another Hindu account states that Jesus traveled to India not once but twice, the first time during his missing years (more or less as described above), and the second time after he miraculously survived his crucifixion through the use of special yogic powers that helped him mimic and evade death. He did not really die; he only appeared to die. After escaping death, he returns to India, where he lives out his life as a teacher of wisdom and then dies an old man.

A purely Muslim version of the story, most often propagated by the Ahmadiyya movement, states that Jesus traveled to India not in search of the wisdom of the East, but rather to search for and minister to the lost tribes of Israel. Accordingly, 'Īsā (Jesus) did not in fact die on the cross as Christians believe—here the Hindu and Muslim versions are in agreement—but, instead, another man took his place. God, after all, in Muslim understanding, does not allow His prophets to suffer death at the hands of people. And so after his persecution had begun, 'Īsā some-how managed to escape his crucifixion, leaving Palestine once and for all to travel to Tibet and India. According to the Muslims who tell this story, 'Īsā lived out his final days in Kashmir. There is even a shrine of Jesus in Kashmir that is visited by Hindus and Muslims today. It is here that he allegedly passed away. The Jesus linked to the Kashmir story is called Yuz Asaf, "son of Joseph."

In none of these accounts, starting with Notovitch, whether they are propagated by Hindus or promulgated by Muslims, do we find, of course, anything like standard Christian teaching that Jesus actually did die on the cross or that his death was some kind of sacrifice for humanity or that he was afterward raised from the dead by God and transformed into a glorious transcendent state that Christians call the resurrection.

Even though Jesus is not regarded in the Hindu and Muslim narra-tives as the unique incarnation of God or the savior of humanity, he is nevertheless held in high esteem in Hinduism and Islam. Hindus usually regard him as a genuine incarnation, though only one of many. He is also seen as a sage, a social reformer, a mystic, and a miracle worker. For Muslims he is a genuine prophet sent by God, but only one of twenty-five prophets mentioned in the Qur'ān.

Jesus is many things to many religions, and the understandings of him diverge in almost countless ways from the way Christians see him. The Jesus who is the cornerstone of Christian faith also turns out to be the stumbling block to unity with other religions. Hindus, Buddhists, and Muslims each have their own understanding of who Jesus is, and they inevitably interpret him through the lenses of their respective faiths. Indeed there is probably no human being in history who has been so variously interpreted and adopted by other religions as has Jesus. His life in service to others, his renunciation of family life for the sake of God, his radical teaching of divine love, his fellowship with the poor and marginalized of society, and his example of patient suffering have endeared him to many.[3]

After having been away from India for so long, it felt good to be back again in a world where discussions about faith were so easy and natural, unlike in the secular West, where the very existence of a transcendent realm was often questioned. Here, in the give-and-take of dialogue, I found myself coming away with an appreciation of the serious challenge of other ways of understanding God and the world. After that discussion with Abid, many memories came flooding back to me from those early years in India: first encounters with people of other faith traditions, studying among Hindus, meeting and marrying a woman who had been raised a Muslim. I realized that so much of my thinking now was formed by those first years in India. It is to those first years that I now turn.

3

First Arrival in Asia

The plane's wheels had barely touched down on the tarmac, and despite repeated admonitions by the crew to remain seated, the passengers were already rising from their seats and reaching into the overhead compartments. I was puzzled by this disregard for normal travel etiquette and resigned myself to accepting that I had now entered a world of unfamiliar customs. As the plane taxied down the runway, brown-skinned men and women stood milling in the aisle, shoulder to shoulder, speaking softly in unknown languages. I felt keenly my place as the only person on board of Caucasian origin and as the sole outsider from the West. And yet no one took notice of me, no one stared.

The plane gradually came to a full halt. I remained in my seat, in no hurry to rise, and apprehensive. I had not made plans about what I would do once I stepped outside the plane into a world that would be totally unfamiliar to me. I observed intently the native men and women as they slowly made their way down the aisle and disappeared out the exit door. After some time, I took a deep breath and rose to my feet. I shuffled my way to the exit, beside which a young Sinhalese stewardess stood draped in the airline's signature red sari. With hands reverently clasped before her she bowed her head to the few remaining passengers ahead of me, thanking them one by one for their patronage and simultaneously welcoming them to the little green island nation of Sri Lanka. I returned her gesture with a slight bow of my own and stepped past her outdoors into a monsoon-drenched world, into what seemed like a painting that had come alive with various swirling hues of green and gray.

Pausing for a moment atop the metal staircase leading down to the runway, I looked upward at dark and swollen clouds. A fierce storm had lashed the area only minutes before, leaving behind shining pools of water on the blacktop. As I stood there, immobile and uncertain, a gust of warm moist air washed over my face and hands, reminding me that I was now no longer a spectator. I was now a living participant in a world I had imagined in so many different ways during a long period of waiting in Germany.

Below me, at the bottom of the stairs, passengers hurried across the glistening tarmac toward the terminal under a light rain. Uniformed workers on the runway barked instructions to each other in words I could not comprehend. Across the landing strip a row of stately palm trees curved upward into the sky, as graceful and slender as the long-necked Sinhalese women who had served coffee on the airplane. The clouds above swirled silver and black. Tiny streams of water coursed downward over the hard shell of the airplane. But now the time had come to begin moving, to descend the stairs and step onto Asian soil for the first time.

And it was also time to figure out what to do next. I had not reserved a hotel room in advance of my arrival. I had not given much thought to such practicalities. I only knew that I was on my way to India and that Sri Lanka was a necessary twenty-four-hour way station en route to my final destination.

A sense of disorientation and trepidation swept over me. As I descended the stairs I observed my feet stepping down onto the metal steps one by one as if they belonged to someone else. I found myself asking, quite unexpectedly, who this person was who was now so anxious and disoriented. My nationality—American—and my experiences of having lived in Europe for several years were of no help in answering this question of selfhood. All past identity seemed of little value now as I sought to establish new bearings. Everything was new and unfamiliar. How had I gotten here?

· · ·

The path that eventually led me to India began when I was just fourteen, long before I had ever even heard of India, on the day when I first became aware of my mortality. I remember very clearly that it was an afternoon in the early spring. I had been sitting on the front steps outside my family home in upstate New York, basking in the return of the sun's warmth after what had seemed like an endless winter of dreary overcast skies and brutal cold and snow. Sparrows and starlings were now chirping melodiously above me, the sky was a bright shining blue, and the first green leaves were in bud. There was not the slightest stir of a breeze. It was in every way a perfect day, and I was happy that the world was again so full of beauty and harmony and peace. And then without warning the reality of life's impermanence hit me full force, from out of nowhere. *One day I will die,* I thought to myself, *but the world will go on without me.* And then: *Why am I here?*

I have no idea where this idea came from or why it struck me so forcefully, but it opened my eyes to see my life in a new light. Everything changed for me from that day onward, starting in middle school and continuing all through high school and beyond. Time and again the truth about life's transience would rise up unexpectedly in the back of my mind, whispering to me, mocking me, reminding me that everything we do is ultimately pointless, since everything ends in death. This realization led to some radical changes in my life. I began critically examining the relevance of all my school activities, the classes I would take, the sports in which I might participate, and I realized that what I had been doing so far in my life, my little fourteen-year-old life, was simply following blindly what everyone else was doing.

And so I began dropping out. If something did not seem pertinent to the question about life's meaning, I did not see the point of continuing with it. The usual academic goals leading to college were now all distractions to me, limited and unfulfilling, as far as I could tell, nothing more than diversions from more important issues that first needed to be addressed. By the time I reached my senior year, I had dropped all math and science courses and was spending half my school day in study halls randomly reading whatever happened to capture my interest. It was rumored that I had turned to drugs, because I was now withdrawn and had let my hair grow long. At home I had not been provided with the existential and metaphysical awareness offered by religion or philosophy, and so I was completely unaware that my inner hunger for a final meaning and transcendent fulfillment was a completely natural human desire, echoed in virtually all cultures across time.

W hen my older brother and I were quite small, our mother spent a few months reading Bible stories to us, but the stories were incomprehensible, and we were bored. Today I don't recall what any of the stories were about except the one about Noah and the animals getting onto the ark two by two before God unleashed the Great Flood. I don't recall any stories about Jesus or a God of love, though it is likely I must have heard a few of them. I think the reason my mother tried to give us a little religion was because all her siblings were evangelical Christians, and she felt that it was her responsibility as a good mother to give us at least some information about there being a God, which was better than no information at all. But her heart wasn't in it, because she felt most Christians were hypocrites, going to church on Sunday and then sinning the rest of the week. So we never went to church, we kids weren't baptized, and as a family we never talked about God, who seemed like a curious abstraction. The religion thing disappeared out of our lives as suddenly as it had entered. The good thing about being raised this way was that we didn't have religion forced down our throats, we weren't raised with a morbid fear of hell, and we didn't have any religion-based neuroses to work through in adulthood.

My father, moreover, was an atheist. He said he believed the scientists, who said there was no God. On my father's side, my grandparents were former Christians, who had left one of the Protestant churches years before. They said all the churches wanted was your money.

All this lack of formal religion in my own upbringing notwithstanding, my mother gave me an important lesson on my very first day of school that helped prepare me for a healthy sense of God. I remember how when I was five years old she knelt down before me, straightened my collar, placed her hands on my shoulders, looked me straight in the eyes, and said, "Now when you're in school I want you to *love everybody*." She didn't say that I should just behave myself; she said I should *love everybody*. What better advice could one receive at any stage of one's life?

I shared my inner distress with no one. It was not until my final month of high school, more than four years after the onset of my questioning, that a teacher, perhaps sensing my anguish during the many study halls I attended, handed me a book that was almost eight hundred pages long, with the recommendation that I finish it before graduation and return it to the library on time. That was all she said. To this day I know nothing about the teacher, what it was she taught, or even what her name was. The book she gave me was a biography of Leo Tolstoy, the great Russian novelist.[1] In that book I learned of Tolstoy's sudden confrontation with his own mortality and the meaning of life, a crisis that was one of the great turning points in his life. I was naively surprised to learn from Tolstoy that others before me had wrestled with the issue of life's ultimate purpose. And I learned that for Tolstoy the question of mortality was connected to the existence of God. But I did not know what to think about God, a topic about which I knew next to nothing.

Because of my frustration with high school—other than having read the Tolstoy biography—I was convinced that classrooms had very little to teach me about life. I therefore reasoned that after high school graduation I should renounce formal schooling forever and instead go to life directly, to venture out into the world and learn firsthand what it had to teach. I felt impelled to get away and explore the world on my own. But where should I go?

One day after graduating from high school I opened up a map of the United States, looking for a place to spend the winter that would be far from snow and cold. I settled on Arizona, probably for no other reason than that it was so far away. My plan was to spend the winter there and then return home in the spring. I did not know at the time that my journey to Arizona would turn my life upside down and eventually lead me to other parts of the world. If I had chosen some other place on the map than Arizona to spend that first winter after high school, my life might well have gone in a completely different direction. I am sometimes awed by the fact that one brief impulsive decision I made at eighteen would determine my whole future, how one thing would lead to another, leading me to discover Christ, eventually taking me to India, and there discover the value of other religions, and finally enable me to meet the woman I was destined to marry. I believe all this had to be, and I also believe that my free will is real. How the two go together I'll never understand. Divine providence is a mysterious and marvelous thing.

After high school I saved up money to buy a car by working for a poultry farmer up the road from where I lived. That long summer and into the fall I painted his barn and silo and drove his truck into town to deliver eggs at local restaurants. By late November, after an unusually beautiful and colorful autumn had come and gone, it was time to go. I left home just as winter was descending. I said good-bye to my parents on a cold damp morning and told them I would return in the spring. I remember the silence of that morning, the few words spoken, and my mother's worried face.

It took me five days to cross America by car. When I arrived in Phoenix, I checked into the cheapest motel I could find. I had with me only enough money to live on for one week. I had obviously not planned my trip well. But two days later I landed a job in a restaurant washing dishes. I worked twelve hours a day, seven days a week. This went on for several months. I was up early every morning, washed dishes all day long at the restaurant, returned to the motel late at night, and read books until I fell asleep. All in all I lived two years in the Phoenix area working various jobs. After starting off as a dishwasher, I became a short-order cook, and after that a warehouse worker unpacking merchandise for a large department store. I lived alone on the second floor of a dilapidated house in a crime-ridden neighborhood in central Phoenix, without friends and community, yet I was happy with my life. After having read Tolstoy, I continued reading literature that dealt with ultimate questions. I read as much as time allowed: initially more of Tolstoy, then Dostoevsky, Camus, Hermann Hesse, and Simone Weil. During those first months away from home, when I wasn't working or sleeping I settled contentedly into a world of silence and solitude with my books. I had no television or radio, and, of course, back then there were no computers, no iPods, MP3s, cell phones, or any of the electronic tools that we have today and whose mesmerizing effect very often delays our spiritual turn inward, at least perhaps until the day some calamitous event intrudes upon our life and causes us to question our previous assumptions about the world, our accepted social conditioning, and what until then had counted as important, even indispensable knowledge. I was not yet aware of the valuable distinction between lower worldly knowledge (*apara vidyā*) and the liberating higher inner wisdom (*para vidyā*), so central to Hinduism and Buddhism.

It was also at this time that the Vietnam War was still going on, and race relations in the United States were so strained. Dr. Martin Luther King Jr. had been assassinated just a few years earlier. I started reading protest works such as Eldrige Cleaver's *Soul on Ice* and books by the Berrigan brothers, Catholic priests who were at the center of the antiwar movement. The book by Cleaver was especially important, because in it I discovered the monk Thomas Merton, who was the greatest Catholic spiritual writer of the twentieth century. I was startled that an African American social critic like Cleaver could write with such appreciation about the insights of a white man hidden from the world in a monastery in Kentucky.

About a year after I left home, I was baptized into the Catholic Church. While working in the restaurant I mentioned my interest in Catholicism, and some of the other young people I worked with invited me to come with them to a "folk mass" on Sunday evening. I received Communion that first visit to Mass, thinking it was available to anyone who got in line. When the priest, Father Doug Nohava, found out I wasn't Catholic, he gently informed me that Communion was for later, not yet for someone just finding out about the Catholic faith. He was a compassionate man with a good sense of humor. He did not scold me, and he seemed to take a real interest in me as a person trying to find himself. I began going to Mass regularly. Father Doug talked a lot about unconditional love, about God loving us completely and from all eternity even before we were born. I was very attracted to such a beautiful teaching.

The priest and I met regularly for almost a year in preparation for my baptism. Instead of giving me formal catechism, he would simply say, "Just keep reading." I was reading Merton and other spiritual literature, and in that context we discussed church teaching and praxis. Through my reading I was strongly attracted to the church's mystical tradition and to its sense of social responsibility.[2] Merton's writings were especially influential in opening up to me the world of prayer and in conveying a sense not only of God's mystery and transcendence, but also of God's unconditional mercy, love, and forgiveness, particularly as revealed in Christ. Merton's joy and freedom in God were infectious. Perhaps no modern Catholic writer has spoken so meaningfully to a searching secular audience as he. My conversion to Catholicism, then, was not the result of a years-long tormented inner struggle, as it was for so many others. Joining a community that helped nurture a vibrant love of God and neighbor made completely good sense.

I had expected that my baptism day would be full of joy, but it turned out to be one of the longest and hardest days I had ever experienced. The whole day leading up to the evening Mass and baptism was overcast and cold, very unlike the weather one normally experiences in the Arizona desert. I spent the day in silence with my godfather, Celestine Chinn, on a Native American reservation outside Phoenix. Father Celestine was an old Franciscan missionary priest who lived on the reservation. He was half Chinese; his father had been a Buddhist. Although he never mentioned it to me, I think he must have wanted me to experience the silence and struggle that come with waiting and preparation. I felt empty and lifeless all day long as the hours ticked by. I wondered what was wrong with me that I wasn't feeling joy. But in retrospect I believe that the Spirit was already leading me into an interior desert, one that was unfamiliar and bewildering, detaching me from emotional excitement, working quietly at the very center of my being. The aridity we experience in solitude helps detach us from earthly things and aids us in dying to the old self. The cold wind, the overcast sky, the waiting in silence—all these things drove my mind inward. In the ritual of baptism, I learned later, we are to die to our old self and awaken to new life. "You were buried with him in baptism," says St. Paul, "in which you were also raised with him through faith in the power of God, who raised him from the dead" (Col. 2:12). In the years since my baptism I have experienced this inner aridity in particular on Holy Saturday, the day before the celebration of Christ's resurrection at Easter, when he is still buried in the tomb. The Spirit can lead us through an inner death even before our physical death. In one way or another we all have to die a spiritual death, a death of the ego. Otherwise we will never be free. If it doesn't happen before our physical death, it certainly will occur after death, through the power of God's purifying love. It is something we should welcome, as difficult as it is. The inner death purifies our heart, humbles us, makes us grateful for all the little gifts of life, and deepens our capacity to love with God's love.

As a new Catholic I did not yet have much knowledge of the Trinity nor did I understand much about what the Incarnation was about. The instruction I had received from the priest had not touched much on those things, even though they were central mysteries of the Christian faith. Father Doug did not focus so much on doctrine as he did on following Jesus, living the Christian life, preparing for the sacraments, living the call of love.

While living in Phoenix, at the urging of the priest, I volunteered to work at a Catholic soup kitchen, first in my spare time, and then full time. I did not know how I would support myself after I quit my job at the warehouse and ran out of money, but I felt called, nonetheless, to work at the soup kitchen and serve the poor. I also visited various high schools and raised money to help keep a Catholic day care in existence. I do not report this out of a sense of accomplishment, but rather because I learned an important lesson about myself. Although I was doing useful and meaningful work for others at the soup kitchen and day care, I still did not have a strong enough sense of my own identity in God as to put my mind at rest. In helping others I still did not know who I was. I had a community of faith, but I was in some ways still a question to myself. Putting it in Hindu terminology, I had begun to travel the path of *karma-mārga* (the way of selfless service to others), the path of *bhakti-mārga* (the way of loving devotion to a God of love and mercy), but I had barely begun the path of *jñāna-mārga* (the way of higher inner knowledge of one's true self, usually aided by the practice of meditation). I still felt at times frustrated. I was troubled by a nagging and perplexing sense of the impermanence and unreality of what we normally regard as our everyday self and of the world as a whole. In retrospect, though, I think that if I had in fact chosen to follow the paths of prayer and service alone, as most Christians do, without exposure to *jñāna-mārga*, I would still have developed a deeper sense of self, since all three paths lead to an emptying of the lower false self. And, too, I was still only at the beginning of the Christian spiritual life. I did not yet have a strong sense of myself as a creature loved into existence by the Creator, destined to find my fulfillment in loving union with the Divine.

During the time I worked at the soup kitchen in Phoenix, I met a Catholic monk who was traveling from a monastery in New York State to another in New Mexico. I confided in him that I was looking for a place to make a short spiritual retreat. He invited me to visit the Monastery of Christ in the Desert in the mountains of New Mexico. And so I went, leaving behind the soup kitchen for what I thought would be about ten days. The transition from the noise, crime, and tension of big city life to a serene monastic setting in the semiarid mountain wilderness could not have been more appealing to me at the time. The Benedictine monastery, only ten years old, was situated along the Chama River in a remote canyon many miles away from the nearest highway, at over six thousand feet altitude in the Sangre de Cristo Mountains. The monastery at the time was officially described as a "primitive foundation," since it was without electricity and many other modern conveniences. The private rooms or "cells" in which the monks lived were unheated, and the dining area was warmed only by a wood fire. Water was pumped directly from the river every few days by a gas-operated generator. The glow of kerosene lamps was the only source of light within the buildings. Stone cliffs towering hundreds of feet above the adobe buildings reminded me of Chinese landscape paintings I had seen showing the tininess of the human form in the vastness and beauty of nature. Thomas Merton visited the monastery twice in 1968, the year of his death, and he spent a good part of his time there trekking and climbing along the cliffs. Only five monks lived in the community when I was there, though numerous visitors came in the summer to share the silence of monastic life.

Monastic life agreed with me; I loved its silence and rhythms, the attention given to the great questions of life and death and God, and I gradually learned to appreciate all the spiritual advice and correction I received from the monks on a daily basis, whether I initially wanted to hear it or not. I learned from them that as much as I valued external silence, I also needed to learn to keep an eye on my emotions, to keep them in check, so as not to be eaten up by them. At least that was the theory. Keeping one's mind centered and composed, unruffled by gain or loss, achievements and disappointments, is a challenging lifelong task.

I found monastic life so agreeable that, despite my original plans, ten days at the monastery did not seem long enough. And so the monks allowed me to remain a few months longer, until the end of the summer, and finally I was given permission to stay on the whole winter and into the following spring. I had no plans or goals at that time that might have prevented me from staying longer at the monastery. I was entirely free to go where I wanted in the world and to stay as long as I pleased. I had no social obligations and no financial debt.

I fully participated in the life and work of the community. We gathered for prayer several times a day,[3] starting at four o'clock in the morning, when we left our rooms or "cells" to walk to the chapel in darkness. I was given the task of taking care of the farm animals and sharing the cooking. I remember one winter morning also being asked to chop wood farther up the canyon, away from the main building and the other monks. It had snowed heavily the night before. I was standing alone in knee-deep snow, the massive canyon walls rising hundreds of feet above me and snowflakes falling gently to the ground. There was not a sound anywhere, no rustling of wind, no movement, no human voice. I took a metal wedge and placed the point downward onto the surface of the log and gave it a tap with my sledgehammer—a tink—to hold it in place. Then, gripping the hammer with both my hands, I swung the weighted end into the air until it came down full force onto the wedge. It took several blows to split the wood in two. Each strike of the mallet against the wedge caused the sound of metal against metal to ring out through the canyon and echo against the canyon walls until the sound was swallowed up by silence. I spent the morning doing this, going through the same motions, fully concentrating on every stroke. I remember gradually losing myself in the activity, no longer aware of myself as a person separate from my work, and thereby experiencing a self-forgetful harmony and oneness with the world, as if all that mattered was the activity itself.

Though I was not officially a monk, I moved into a monk's cell as a long-term guest, not as a postulant or one who would eventually seek permanent admission to the monastic life. I felt God had led me to the monastery, but I didn't have a sign yet that God intended to keep me there.

In this wilderness isolated from normal human society there were also dangers, mostly in the form of wildlife: rattlesnakes lived in the hayfields and cliffs; bears and mountain lions roamed the canyon, and black widow spiders hid in the laundry room. Sitting outside my cell at dusk, after all the monks had fallen asleep, I could sometimes hear the snarl of a mountain lion from deep in the canyon.

As a fresh convert to Catholicism I knew very little Christian theology and absolutely nothing about other religions. I was therefore uneasy and very reluctant to participate in the study program on world religions that the monks had devised the winter I spent with them. I suppose one reason I feared the unfamiliar was because it might force me to revise my way of looking at life; I would have to leave my comfort zone of interpreting the world. *If Christianity provides the answers to all my questions,* I thought to myself, *why should I bother with other religions?* But the monks decided that we would listen to tape recordings of spiritual talks given by teachers of different religions. I was a reluctant listener, to say the least. The recordings were of presentations from a conference that had convened a year earlier at Mount Savior Monastery in upstate New York. Mount Savior was the mother house of Christ in the Desert. The conference was called "Word Out of Silence," and it had brought together important figures from various religions, some of them spiritual masters, to discuss spiritual practice and various understandings of the Divine. The participants included Raimon Panikkar, Swami Satchidananda, Alan Watts, David Steindl-Rast, Baba Ram Dass, Pir Vilayat Khan, and many others. While listening to the tapes it was not long before my head was swimming. I was bewildered by references to Zen, Sufism, Russian Orthodoxy, Hinduism, and Native American wisdom and spirituality. The speakers spoke with confidence and authority about the wisdom and experience of their traditions. But nobody attempted to interpret the meaning of the other religions and spiritualities from a Christian perspective, neither the speakers on tape nor the monks listening with me. That was perhaps a good thing, I think now, to be exposed to the challenge of other religions so nakedly without first being able to force them into convenient categories that would lessen their value and impact. As I listened to the tapes, all kinds of questions rose up within me: How could these people be so spiritual if they weren't Christian? How could they have such different understandings of God? Was one religion better than another? Was one more right than another? And how did Jesus fit in?

After we were done listening to the tapes, I decided to write Panikkar, who I knew was a Catholic scholar of Hinduism teaching in California. Originally from Spain of an Indian Hindu father and Spanish Catholic mother, he would go on to earn doctorates in chemistry, philosophy, and theology. He was also a pioneer in Hindu-Christian studies. I began my letter with an introductory sentence stating that I was a person temporarily living at this monastery in New Mexico. And then I launched into a long list of burning questions that I posed as directly and frankly as I could, questions totally lacking in philosophical or theological nuance:

What is truth? Who is God? How do you understand Jesus? What is the meaning of the other religions? What is enlightenment? How does meditation relate to prayer? I can't remember all the questions I asked, but I know that my handwritten questions went on for a full two pages. The whole letter was nothing but questions. Then I signed it "Sincerely" with my name, and I smuggled it out of the monastery and into a mailbox the next time the monks and I drove to Santa Fe on business. I knew I should have asked permission from the monastery prior, Father Gregory, to write Panikkar, but I was afraid he would say no, and I could not wait to have my questions answered. Two weeks later a package from Panikkar arrived addressed to me. Inside was one of his books, *The Trinity and the Religious Experience of Man,* in which many of my questions were answered. Father Gregory asked why Panikkar had sent the book to me, of all people; had I written him? I shrugged my shoulders and lied that I was as surprised as anyone. I think the old monk saw right through me pretty easily, but he was merciful and did not scold me. Some time later I received a letter from Panikkar's assistant, Maria, who informed me that the mystic-professor was inviting me to enter into further correspondence with him. But I never wrote back; I felt that I was not up to corresponding with such a great and learned man. I was only twenty.

One day in the monastery library I happened on an autobiography called *The Golden String* by a British monk named Bede Griffiths. The book had first appeared in 1954 and gained the author some fame as a Catholic intellectual and spiritual writer. I was especially interested in it, because it told the story of a man who had converted to Catholicism after a long spiritual and intellectual search. Griffiths had returned to the Christianity of his youth with his Oxford teacher, C. S. Lewis. This book was my first exposure to a viewpoint espousing a common spiritual wisdom in the world's religions, a wisdom that, until recent decades, had been largely lost in the modern West for various reasons connected to the rise of science, secularism, and an understanding of truth that had been reduced to empirical investigation. Part of my attraction to Father Bede was his eloquent and spiritual prose, so clear and illuminating that the Divine seemed almost to shine forth through the pages in my hand. He communicated well a sense that various religions had experienced, each in its own way, something of the one unfathomable Mystery that Christians call God, and which is known elsewhere as Tao, Brahman, Allah, and so on. I told myself I would one day like to meet this wise man, who was now living far away in India in a Catholic ashram or monastery.

Another time while living in the monastery I was sent by the monks to Santa Fe to have a vehicle repaired. I would not return for two days. I entered a bookstore and purchased a little volume by a Hindu sage named Ramana Maharshi. The book was called *Who Am I?* Sri Ramana had not authored the book himself; rather, one of his followers had copied down some of the spiritual conversations that had taken place between the sage and visitors to his ashram in India during the first half of the twentieth century. I was immediately drawn to what the Maharshi was saying, even though I didn't understand him well. The focus was continually on the Self, the true Self that we are, as opposed to the everyday understanding of self that we normally think we are. This was no abstract theory. As a boy of sixteen Ramana (not then his name) unexpectedly awakened to the Self, and that experience changed him and liberated him forever, centering his attention on an inner spiritual reality that was more him than his own body and mind. The saint spoke with a quiet unshakable authority, rooted in a profound inner experience. Later I learned that Ramana Maharshi was regarded as one of the greatest of modern Hindu mystics, something of a living embodiment of ancient Upaniṣadic wisdom. But I had no idea how Maharshi's spirituality of the Self could be reconciled with the notion of God as loving Person and gracious Lord, as was taught in Christianity. It was a question that remained with me for years to come, each time that I returned to Maharshi's published conversations. Why was it that both spiritualities spoke so powerfully to me, even though I could not reconcile them conceptually?

After almost eleven months in the monastery of what was to have originally been a ten-day visit, it was time to move on. One reason the monks urged me to go to college was that I had gotten into the habit of sometimes breaking the silence that was supposed to be observed from evening prayer until the next morning. I had many questions about truth and God and religion, and I couldn't keep them all in.

With the help of a letter of support from the monks in New Mexico I enrolled at Saint John's University in Minnesota. Both places belonged to the same Benedictine order, which made it possible to be admitted without having taken any college entrance exams. I declared philosophy and German as my two majors, not theology. I had grown wary of theology by then, because it seemed to me at the time to be nothing more than the study of religious doctrine through a blind faith in the authority of the church and Bible. But I was not well informed. Theology is ideally reasonable speech about God, though it differs from philosophy in that it considers divine revelation to be a valid—indeed the primary—source of information in addition to reason and experience. Having blind faith in God is all right when you're a child; you have no choice but to trust the authority of your parents. But in Catholic thought, when you are an adult, blind faith is actually not a virtue; such faith is finally an irresponsible act if it is made without supporting evidence and contrary to the faculty of reason given to us by the Creator. We are not called to believe in God or God's revelation in the absence of any evidence and in contradiction to all reason.

I studied two years at Saint John's until I ran out of money. Along the way, and certainly one of the most important things I learned in college, was the practice of hatha yoga. The yoga course I took on campus eventually led me to weekend visits at a Hindu community in Minneapolis. There I practiced mostly *āsanas* (postures) and a bit of meditation. I learned that yoga as a path of spirituality governed your whole life, including your diet and your relation to others. This was also my first real exposure to the practice of learning to understand and control my own mind, to calm it and bring it to a state of receptive silence, which turns out to be harder to do than taming a wild animal. I saw for the first time how any spiritual journey needs to pay close attention to the mind and its habits. The purpose of the whole path of yoga, starting with moral injunctions, continuing through postures, controlled breathing, and meditation, was to learn to control our own mind, to open it to the freedom of the spirit within, and thereby to free it from the cravings and fears that so often threaten to enslave it. On such a path, in which divine grace is not normally accepted as integral, it is helpful to have a virtuous and compassionate teacher to inspire and guide one on the way to inner transformation and wisdom. For me that man was Usharbudh Arya, a Sanskrit pandit who had renounced his position at the University of Minnesota, where he had been an award-winning professor, to offer full-time instruction in meditation and Hindu thought. He was a man of great spiritual depth, kindness, and virtue. He was tangible evidence of Hinduism's greatness. In the intervening years he has embraced formal renunciation and is now known as Swami Veda Bharati.

I was now twenty-three years old, five years out of high school, broke, and about to drop out of college. One of my German professors, a saintly elderly nun named Margretta Nathe, suggested I spend a semester abroad in Germany with her student group before I left college. That way I could at least see a bit more of the world before I discontinued my studies. She gave me some money, and my mother gave the rest. Without the help of these two I never would have traveled to Europe and beyond, and I never would have continued my studies. And I might never have reached India.

We American students lived for a semester in a small city in central Germany called Königstein, not far from Frankfurt. While living in Königstein I discovered a small Catholic theological college, the smallest one in all Germany, which was housed in a single three-story building. The college had been founded after World War II for the training of seminarians displaced from their homeland by the war and its aftermath, especially those from the German-speaking region of Czechoslovakia. My fellow students, all of them preparing for the priesthood, were not only from Germany, but also from Croatia, Poland, Zaire, and India. I was the only American at the college and the only student not preparing to become a priest. Listening to stories from students from other countries, I learned to appreciate what it meant to be a member of a worldwide Catholic community, each local church having its own history, customs, culture, interreligious encounter, and even experience of persecution. The other foreign students had all been sent to Germany by their bishops for theological training. At the time, Germany still enjoyed the reputation of being one of the premier centers in the world for the study of Catholic theology, if not *the* premier center. That reputation has waned somewhat in the meantime, I believe, because of German theology's continued Eurocentrism and its disproportionate attention to the historical development of doctrine—at which the Germans are still without rival—over new developing theological trends in Asia, Africa, and the Americas. German theology has traditionally been very good at looking to the past to discover how we got to where we are now, but we must look elsewhere these days to discover where we are heading.[4]

I found that if I were to enroll at the little college in Königstein I would have to begin my studies all over again. Money would fortunately not be a problem now, as most of the tuition for university education was underwritten by the state, and at the time the German government allowed foreign students to work, so between semesters I would be able to earn enough to pay for my room and board. I jumped at the chance to continue my education.

At this stage of my education I was ready for theology, having now recognized not only the value, but also the limitations of philosophy when it came to knowledge of God. Reason alone might logically deduce that there must be a God who created the world, but it could not tell me that the Creator was a God of love or that God had incarnated as a Palestinian Jew two thousand years ago, had suffered, died, was buried, and had been raised from the dead. This was the free self-unveiling of the Creator, the supreme Person, who gives us knowledge of the divine will and of divine love that we could never arrive at through reason alone. I cannot know the truth and character and intent of even another human being, not even of a child, unless those individuals freely choose to reveal themselves in their actions and their words. How much more difficult it is to penetrate the mystery of the divine Person. Persons must act, in order to reveal themselves. Biblical revelation is the history of God's activities, starting with Israel and culminating in Christ, the Divine Word made flesh. In those activities the love of God for humanity is unveiled as well as the promise of the resurrection, our future life in God.

And so instead of visiting Germany for one semester as I had originally planned, I ended up living there eight years, the first seven years studying theology in three different cities: Königstein, Fulda, and Tübingen. My final year in Germany, while waiting for my visa to India, I translated documents for a Catholic relief agency. To support myself during my student days I worked between semesters in two auto parts factories, working punch-press and drill-press machines. I loved working alongside men and women from other countries. Since the 1960s German factories had been filled with "guest workers" (*Gastarbeiter*) from all along the Mediterranean: from Spain, Italy, Portugal, Yugoslavia, and Turkey. Some of the foreign workers lived in Germany with their families, while others sent money home every month and returned only for annual visits. All the Turks I worked with had been raised Muslim. They were hardworking and mostly kept to themselves. The younger Turks, because they spoke good German, were more outgoing and sociable. A small number of the younger ones had also become secularized by having lived in Europe since childhood. Some no longer considered themselves members of any particular religion, while others did not believe in God at all. But the great majority of Turks were eager to maintain their Muslim heritage in an alien land, though they rarely tried to propagate their faith among others. Working in factories alongside these Turks was my first direct exposure to Islam.

The people with whom I worked in the factory were, as a whole, less interested in my being an American than in my being a Catholic theology student. The Italians, the Spaniards, and the Portuguese were all Catholic, as were many of the Germans. During lunch breaks in the canteen they would ask me such questions as: If God is so good and so powerful, why is there so much suffering in the world? That always seems to be the most frequently asked question about God. And they would sometimes ask about the new practices of the Catholic Church that had emerged with Vatican II. It wasn't just about replacing the Latin Mass with the vernacular or local language; it was also about new relations with other churches. I remember the confusion of my German foreman, who once said to me, "I don't get it. When I was a kid growing up Catholic, we were always taught never to set foot inside a Protestant church. But now they're telling us it's all right. What's going on?" What he did not know was that the theologians and bishops of the Second Vatican Council had articulated a new vision of the church, one that sought unity among all Christians and that now reached out in dialogue toward a greater fraternity with all the people of the world.

Occasionally questions would even be posed on the factory floor, with the machines nearly drowning out our conversation. You had to shout to make yourself heard. One day Gaspar, an old Spaniard and normally the joker in our bunch, approached me while I was working a punch-press machine. He was very agitated, almost tormented, it seemed, and he began shouting above the din about his problems with the sacrament of Reconciliation: "Why should we even bother to go to confession?" he yelled. "The priest forgives your sins, and then, boom, boom, boom, you go out and sin all over again. What's the point of even going?" Their questioning was often intense, but never impolite or disrespectful. This was in marked contrast to my experience at the University of Tübingen a few years later. There I would frequently meet students who would ridicule me for believing in God and for choosing theology as my major. They were often sarcastic and scornful. But many of them were clearly searching.

After a year and a half in Königstein, the theological college was closed by the bishops, because it had grown too small, and so most of us students transferred to another small theological school in the city of Fulda, a few hours to the north, near the East German border. Fulda represented Germany's earliest age of Catholicism. It was originally established as a Benedictine monastery by St. Sturmius in 744, at the behest of St. Boniface, whose relics are buried in the famous cathedral, which for hundreds of years was the largest church north of the Alps. Fulda is still important today as the location of the annual German bishops' conference. I studied there for one year and then transferred to the University of Tübingen in southern Germany, only a few hours' drive from France and Switzerland. This is where I did most of my theology.

Tübingen was a real university city, with a distinguished academic reputation stretching back to its founding in 1477. Kepler, the astronomer, had studied there, as had Hölderlin the poet, and the philosophers Schelling and Hegel. Hermann Hesse, as a young man, had worked in one of the city's bookstores. More recently, from 1966 to 1969 Joseph Ratzinger, now Pope Benedict XVI, had taught and chaired the faculty of Catholic Theology. At the time he enjoyed the reputation of being at the cutting edge of new and innovative Catholic thought. But in 1969 he left for the University of Regensburg, because of political tumult in Tübingen that had infected the classroom and made it increasingly difficult to teach.

When I arrived in Tübingen, an idyllic university town with cobblestone streets located on the Neckar River, it was still one of the great centers of Catholic and Protestant theology in the world. One out of every ten students in a university population of twenty-two thousand studied theology. Among my teachers were Walter Kasper and Hans Küng in Catholic systematics, Jürgen Moltmann and Eberhard Jüngel in Protestant thought, and Gerhard Lohfink in New Testament exegesis. All these and other professors drew hundreds of students to their classes, very often a mixture of Catholics and Protestants.

After I had studied theology at Königstein and Fulda for five semesters, this was my first real exposure to self-critical Catholic thought, one that was open to the cultural and social movements and challenges of the day. Before my arrival in Tübingen, the approach to the contemporary world and modern culture offered by my professors had been mostly confrontational, and the political orientation was at times strongly rightwing. There was sometimes overt hostility toward Protestantism. Such a theology, with its narrow and defensive posture, seemed out of date and out of touch with the world, in light of the developments of the Second Vatican Council (1962–65).

By contrast, I found the courses in Catholic theology in Tübingen enthralling. Kasper, Küng, and Lohfink were all ecumenical minded, seeking common ground with Protestant scholarship in their lectures and writing. Kasper, for many years now a cardinal in Rome and president of the Pontifical Council for Promoting Christian Unity,[5] emphasized the importance of a Christ-centered theology, of returning to the basics of Christian faith by focusing on the life and work of Jesus Christ. He, like Küng, also taught the indispensable link of systematic thought to developments in biblical scholarship.

From Kasper, with whom I was fortunate to have worked for two years as a research assistant, and from Lohfink, I learned to rethink the meaning of biblical revelation. Revelation, I came to learn, is the unveiling or manifestation of God's presence and activity in the world. In the biblical understanding, it is simultaneously the disclosure of the human person. In light of God's love and mercy, the meaning, value, and destiny of the human person are revealed. Revelation is not, therefore, information about divine mysteries in heaven sent down to earth, divorced from all human experience and having nothing to do with the meaning of our life in this world. It is rather the knowledge that emerges in the transformative and liberating encounter that people have with God. The operative word here is *transformation*. The purpose of biblical revelation is not to pluck the soul out of the body and out of the material world in order to lead it to its true heavenly home above and beyond the drama of earthly life, as if life in this world were merely a spiritual testing ground or a waiting room for heaven. The goal is not the separation of the spiritual from the physical, as if only the interior dimension of the human person—the soul—would alone constitute its identity. Revelation, manifested in God's liberating activity in our world, is oriented to the transformation of everything human, starting with the human heart and then moving outward to human society and to peace between nations. Our life in the body and our life in the world are part of the totality of our life in God. Revelation is intended to bring about God's rule of love, justice, and peace into the world; as such it is as much a social or interhuman reality as it is an interior experience. It is not a mere interior transformation of consciousness. When Jesus famously declares that "the Kingdom of God is within you" (Lk. 17:21), the translation could just as well be rendered as "the Kingdom of God is among you" or "in your midst." The latter meaning is actually closer to the original Greek preposition *entos*.

This biblical understanding of revelation and the Kingdom is still too little understood by many Catholics today, who are often unfamiliar with the original teaching of their Christian faith. When asked what is the purpose and goal of the Christian life, many of my students will answer that it is to get our soul to heaven. The answer is not entirely wrong; it is just very incomplete. It leaves out the body, human relationships, and the value of our life here on Earth. God's involvement with the world gives a dignity and meaning and final purpose to all dimensions of human life.

During my time in Tübingen I began hearing about a new social and theological movement, originating in Latin America, called "liberation theology," with phrases like "God's preferential option for the poor." There are many kinds of liberation theology, some of them more in harmony with the Catholic theological tradition than others, but they all take as their starting point God's involvement in the lives of the powerless and the destitute, God's special identification with those in society who are most vulnerable and unprotected. This does not mean that God does not love all people; it's just that divine action is especially oriented to remedying the plight of those who are most urgently in need of God's mercy and help. And so God not only sends prophets to Israel to command justice and mercy for the oppressed; God finally becomes incarnate in Jesus as a poor man in solidarity with all the poor and oppressed of the world. What distinguishes liberation theology from other kinds of theology is its emphasis on combating the social institutionalization of sin in oppressive regimes and unjust societal structures, and not just ridding the human heart of sin in a private, individualistic manner. Both are connected, of course. Without individual sin there would be no corporate sin. Liberation theology doesn't want to simply give alms to the poor but to reform the social institutions that are the direct cause of the impoverishment, marginalization, and exploitation of the poor.

As a result of this more earthly orientation of biblical revelation, I was now compelled to rethink my understanding of God and God's activity and to give even greater attention to the dignity of the human person. I started to understand God's relation to the world in a new way, keeping my eyes fixed on social injustice and oppression as the place where God is most actively engaged in the world. The God who is the hidden Ground and inner Mystery dwelling in the hearts of all beings is also the one who emerges from His hiddenness to actively engage the world in combating sin and evil. And God, finally, is the one who leads us into full union with Him in the mystery of the resurrection.

But in Tübingen I learned only a little about other religions when I studied theology. The whole focus was on the Christian theological tradition, on relations between the Christian churches, and on the modern encounter with atheism and secularism. Not even Islam seemed a worthy dialogue partner, even though millions of Muslims from Turkey had flooded German factories since the 1960s.

After my theology days in Tübingen had come to an end, I hoped to travel to India within a few months to do research on a dissertation,[6] but my visa was delayed for a year without explanation. In the meantime a conference for Hindu-Christian dialogue on the theme of revelation was being held in a Catholic monastery outside Vienna, and so I decided to attend. Some of the biggest scholars from both religions would be there, among them Karl Rahner[7] and Walter Kasper from the Catholic side, and R. N. Dandekar and V. A. Devasenapathi from Hinduism. I didn't have much money, so I hitchhiked. I left central Germany in the morning, and I arrived at the monastery in Austria well after dark. It was almost a four-hundred-mile journey.

At the conference two things happened that opened the door to India for me. The first was that Professor Kasper asked Professor Dandekar to write a letter of recommendation to the University of Poona (now the University of Pune) to admit me as a student, even though he didn't know me. Professor Dandekar graciously obliged, as a favor to Kasper, who knew me as his student and research aide.

The second thing was my meeting a graduate student from India named Paul Roche. Paul was a Catholic from a little village in Tamil

Nadu. He was doing a doctorate in anthropology at the University of Vienna. Through him I eventually met my wife in India.

When I left for India, I had only enough money with me to stay a few months. I had applied for a grant to live one year there, but I had not yet received word as to its outcome. And so I left, unsure what I would do if the grant did not come through.

A nd now I found myself in Sri Lanka, in a crowded airport, feeling that I had become a stranger to myself, scarcely able to remember—or reassemble—that other me, that self, who had only weeks before confidently ordered the ticket in Germany that would take me here, to a land where I did not know a single person and where no one would be awaiting me. Tomorrow I would be flying on to India, but for now I needed a place to spend the night.

My mind reeled as I allowed myself to be led by instinct, walking zombielike behind strangers into the terminal. My legs and feet seemed to move of their own accord.

After a brief interrogation by dour-faced customs officials, I found myself outside the main terminal building in a state of acute mental confusion, overwhelmed by the noise and clamor of honking taxis, rickshaws, shouting porters and passengers, all heading in different directions. The sound of languages I did not recognize rang in my ears.

I was without a plan. Should I look for a hotel in Colombo, the capital, twenty miles away or would it be better to remain close to the airport? How did one begin to find a room with reasonable rates in a foreign country in South Asia? What would be a fair price? Would people take advantage of me? In this throng of brown faces I found myself again conscious of being an ignorant Caucasian and outsider. I thought I must be looking like some kind of exotic animal that had just escaped from the zoo and was wandering around outside the airport terminal. I did not know the customs here nor did I speak Sinhalese or Tamil. And I had brought very little money.

Suddenly I spotted a middle-aged man in a white suit I had noticed on the plane. He looked different from the others. Perhaps he was Chinese. Though I did not know him, my instincts told me he might be of help. Since he appeared to be a foreigner, he might recommend a hotel. I hurried to him with great hope. "Sir," I asked, "where can I find a room?"

"Just get into a cab and ask," he said sharply, then disappeared into the crowd.

I raised my hand to signal a taxi. Within seconds I was leaning into the passenger window. "I'm looking for a hotel," I said to the driver, "not too expensive."

The driver nodded without expression for me to get in. After ten minutes, we pulled up to a plain single-story building bordered by a few half-grown palm trees. We were on a highway still very close to the airport. My original idea of exploring the big city of Colombo would perhaps not be such a good idea after all, I thought, since I would be catching a plane the next day to India, and I was in no mood for exploring. It was now late afternoon.

A glum-looking man at the hotel front desk took my money and passport. In answer to my question about meals, he pointed behind me to a plain room of bare tables and wooden chairs, entirely devoid of customers or decoration, save a few potted plants. Though I had not eaten for some time, I went directly to my room, too exhausted and too much in culture shock to take food.

I locked the door behind me and lay down on the bed. The room was clammy, dimly lit, and utterly lacking in charm, in a run-down hotel at the edge of a small highway in an unfamiliar land. Shabby hotels were familiar to me, though, and in a new and unfamiliar environment like this one, anything that would awaken a sense of the familiar helped restore a sense of self.

I felt the weight of my body pressing down upon the mattress. Lying on a mattress, too, was a familiar experience. From the ceiling hung a motionless wooden fan. The hotel was without power, probably due to the earlier storm. The room smelled of mildew, the bedsheets were torn, the bathroom faucet and shower leaked. A small worn-out towel hung at the sink. As I lay there my mind whirled with questions about what on earth I was doing here at all. I wondered what India would be like. I calculated how long I might stay there. I tried imagining what the people would be like. I wondered whether I would fit in. I considered with some uneasiness what might happen after my money ran out in a few months. My funding request was still in limbo, but I had decided to fly to India, anyway, unwilling to wait any longer.

It struck me years later how appropriate it was that this experience of alienation, fear, and loss of the old sense of self, perceptions that began on the airplane and continued on in the hotel, had taken place in a predominantly Buddhist country. It is a fundamental Buddhist teaching that the conventional socialized self that is full of anxiety and desire has no permanence or final validity.

As I was now close to the equator it would soon be night. After some time I gave in to drowsiness, let my eyes close, and drifted off to sleep.

I spent most of that night in Sri Lanka in fitful sleep as storms raged outside my hotel room with crashing thunder and driving wind and rain. In the early afternoon the next day, when the sun returned, I boarded a plane to Trichy, India, for what I thought would be a one-year visit, completely unaware of what lay in store for me.

4

An Indian Village

When I arrived in Trichy, in southern India, I was met by Paul Roche's brother, Adaikalam, a smiling young seminarian who would be with me nearly every waking minute during the next three days, to make sure that all my needs would be immediately met.

We climbed into a motor rickshaw and headed off to Trichy proper. Within minutes after our departure from the airport we passed an old man with a long white beard and wooden staff walking down the road. He was wearing saffron-colored robes. "A Hindu monk?" I asked my companion. "Yes, a *sannyāsi*," he replied.[1]

In Trichy we boarded a bus, and two hours later, at dusk, we arrived in the town of Perambalur. While waiting for the bus to the village, I was immediately surrounded by smiling boys and girls of various ages, each of them staring inquisitively into my face. Apparently they had never seen a person like me before. One boy, bolder than the rest, touched the skin on my forearm and rubbed it. Adaikalam shooed him away.

After a short trip by bus, we alighted at the entrance to the village of Palayam. It was now almost pitch black. I followed Adaikalam past barely perceptible silhouettes of trees and thatched huts under an overcast night sky. We walked together in almost complete silence. I was now more than ever aware that I was in a place very unlike the world from which I had come. I wondered what kind of village daylight would reveal. We met no one as we walked in darkness. Our destination was the Roche home, the largest dwelling in the village, built of brick and cement. The grown children of the house, some of whom drew good incomes outside the village, had paid to construct the house for their parents, complete with electricity and indoor toilet, unlike most everyone else in the village.

All the family members in the house were awaiting us. Adaikalam's father, white haired and dignified, was a local teacher, now retired. The mother, gray haired but considerably younger than her husband, beamed at me the whole evening and asked questions, through her children, about my life and my family. With a twinkle in her eye she suggested that I might want to marry an Indian girl one day. But I told her that marriage was the last thing on my mind.

Neither father nor mother spoke English, but the children spoke it fluently. The father had impressed on all his children the importance of a good education. Instead of farming the land like the other villagers, the eldest son had become a teacher in Perambalur. Victor, another brother, was a mission priest in Papua New Guinea. Adaikalam was in training to be a priest in a north Indian diocese. Paul was doing a doctorate in Europe. And there were two other brothers and a sister.

Soon after my arrival, the family gathered in the main room to pray the formal evening prayer of the Catholic Church, sitting cross-legged on the floor. Prayers were recited in Tamil, some from memory, others out of a book. The little family liturgy lasted half an hour. After the prayers were complete, I was offered both Indian food and white bread with jam, since I was from the West. These people had gone to the trouble of buying food that they themselves would have never eaten. As we ate I could not help but notice the faces of village children pressed against the bars of the house windows, all of them fixing their eyes on me, the strange-looking and unexpected visitor. Gradually their number increased, as did their desire to see me. The children began pushing and jostling one another to get a better view, and eventually they were emboldened to shout questions about me to the family members inside. Mr. Roche kept warning them to stay back and give me some peace, but they would not listen. It was clear that my arrival in the village was the big news of the day.

After some time, a very frail-looking old man stepped into the house, dressed only in a *lunghi*.[2] His brown bony chest was bare, and his arms were thin as sticks. When he entered the house, everyone became silent. I looked at Adaikalam, my eyes questioning him. "This is the village elder," he said. "He is the oldest man in the village."

The old man stepped up to me and with his thumb marked my forehead with the sign of the cross. "You are the first foreigner to visit this village in eighty years," he said, as Adaikalam translated. "A young man like yourself came here back then, but he was very ill, and he did not speak our language. We nursed him back to health. We don't know where he came from, and we don't know where he went after he left us. You are the next foreigner to come here."

I awoke the next morning on the house balcony and gazed upon a world that seemed to exist in some earlier century were it not for the few power lines leading into the village. There were no cars, and only a few scooters. Almost all the people were involved in farming, and the tilling was done with bullocks. The villagers rose before dawn, left their huts, and headed out to the fields to spend the day. The women cooked meals over wood fires, drew water from the well in buckets, and washed their clothes by hand. My drinking water was boiled in a metal pot atop a fire. As is true almost everywhere in India, cows roamed aimlessly through the village with brightly painted horns.[3] Coconut and banyan trees, rich with Hindu symbolism, offered welcome shade to villagers and pilgrims. Beyond the lush green fields blue-colored mountains rose up and touched white cumulus clouds. It was a serene and idyllic setting. More than anything else, what struck me was the silence. The loud cawing of crows did not so much disturb the tranquility as accentuate it.

At midday Adaikalam and I sat outside the house, answering questions from a throng of children. In the course of our conversation I noticed an old woman down the lane who had been watching me. When I looked in her direction, she drew back and hid behind a hut. After some time I saw her again looking in our direction. I waved to her, but she hid again. I asked Adaikalam to invite her to join our conversation. After a few minutes, he returned smiling.

"Where is she?" I asked.

"She doesn't want to come," he said.

"Why is that?"

Adaikalam paused. "She says you're terrifying to look at. She's never seen anyone like you. She's afraid to come closer."

The village was half Catholic and half Hindu. It was also divided by caste. There were both high-caste and low-caste Hindus and Catholics. Discrimination against the low castes in both groups continued as it had for thousands of years. Even after Hindu families convert to Christianity, caste consciousness often lives on, perpetuated by those with an originally higher rank in society. This is especially true in the state of Tamil Nadu, in which Palayam is located. When I attended Mass the following year with the same family, I asked why some people entered the church through the side door. Father Victor, who had briefly returned from the missions abroad, told me, "It's because they're lower caste. They're not allowed to enter through the main doors. And they can't receive Communion until the high castes have received first."[4]

Once I was approached by another old man of the village, also a Catholic. He looked to be in his seventies. He asked me why I had come to India. I told him I was going to study Sanskrit and Hindu thought. "You'll never convert Hindus that way," he said. He thought I was studying Hinduism as a strategy to win Hindus to the Christian faith. "Dialogue doesn't lead anywhere. It's just a lot of talking," he continued. "I have converted some Hindus in this village. But I didn't do it through dialogue. I did it through healing. One time a Hindu lady came to me who was very ill. She asked if I could heal her. I said yes, but only in Jesus's name. She said all right, she would let me try. So I waited three days. For three days I fasted. I didn't eat anything; I only drank water from time to time. And I prayed the whole three days in preparation for the healing. And then I put my hands on her and prayed that Jesus would heal her. She was healed immediately. She asked to become a Christian, even though she didn't know any Christian teaching. After a time she was baptized. And I have healed others here, too."

Two out of every three people in India today still live in villages. People often remark that it is in the villages that the ancient soul of India can be found. I did in fact observe much innocence and purity in Palayam in the faces of the people, and I know that this is typical of most Indian villages. But there is at times also brutal lawlessness, cruelty, and violence in the villages, especially in the north, and the powerful crush the weak. The women are controlled more in the villages than in the cities, too. In some parts of northern India, in places like Haryana, Hindu married women are forced to wear the veil, as do the Muslim women. Traditions are strong in the villages for both good and evil. Caste, too, is even more entrenched there than in the cities.

And yet many Indians who were brought up in villages but have since left behind the old way of life to pursue a career in the city or are now living abroad will speak wistfully of village life, contrasting the hectic pace of modern city life with the rural traditions. They remember the simplicity of life, the closeness to nature, the spirit-nurturing silence.

5

A Crossroads of the Spirit

After a few weeks in southern India, I took a train north to the city of Pune. I did not know where I would be living long term in Pune once I arrived, but during my first week there I stayed at a Catholic seminary connected with the local theological college, the Pontifical Institute of Philosophy and Theology, called in Sanskrit *Jnana-Deepa Vidyapeeth* (JDV).[1] This was perhaps Catholicism's most important center of theological learning in India, in large part because of its comparative study of Christianity and other religions, such as Hinduism, Buddhism, and Islam. What immediately struck me about the way Catholic theology was done there, in contrast to my experience of studying theology in Germany, was its openness to exploring and incorporating the truth and wisdom of other religions while remaining committed to the foundational truths of Christian revelation and tradition. Some of the faculty even went so far as to stress the value of contemplative practices for theological study and urged their students to take up meditation and yoga as a supplement to Catholic prayer and liturgical celebration. They also felt that theology should prepare the students, most of whom would become priests, to better serve the poor and downtrodden of society. Done together, the attention to the inner presence of the Divine coupled with a keen awareness of the needs of the poor and disenfranchised of Indian society has prevented Catholic theology in India from drifting off into abstractions that only professional theologians can understand.

Aware of my desire to study Śaṅkara and Hindu thought, and knowing that I was looking for a more permanent place to live, some of the faculty members at the seminary recommended that I spend time at the C.P.S. or Christa Prema Seva ("Love and Service in Christ") Ashram, just a few miles from the University of Poona, where I would be enrolled in the Sanskrit department. At the ashram I would be able to pursue a scholarly and contemplative life under the influence and counsel of Sister Sara Grant, who was also a professor at JDV. Sister Sara, a Scotswoman who had many years before taken Indian citizenship, was an elderly member of the Sacred Heart Sisters, a Roman Catholic order. Her academic specialty was the metaphysics and spirituality of nonduality (*advaita*), especially as taught by Śaṅkara (ca. 700 CE), Hinduism's most well-known thinker. Having earned a doctorate in Bombay on Śaṅkara's understanding of nonduality, she had for many years been a leading figure in Indian Catholic theology and Christian dialogue with Hindus. In 1993 she would become the first recipient of the Ba-Bapu Puraskar Prize presented by Gandhians in Pune for a life exemplifying the precepts and ideals of the Mahatma. During the academic year, Sister Sara lectured at the Catholic faculty, mostly to seminarians. She recognized the potential impact on Christian theology and spirituality of Śaṅkara's teaching about the nondual nature of reality, and she tried to convey it in her classroom to those in training who would one day be ordained as Catholic priests.

The C.P.S. Ashram where she lived and where I would stay for seven months had been founded in 1927 by the Anglican priest Jack Winslow, for the purpose of living out the Christian life of prayer and renunciation in a manner more in tune—"inculturated" is the term used in recent decades—with the simplicity of traditional Hindu ashram life. It was at this ashram that Mahatma Gandhi sometimes spent the night when he visited Pune. Since Winslow's death the ashram had in the intervening years fallen into disuse but was resuscitated in 1971 by Sister Sara and Sister Vandana Mataji, a Parsi convert to Catholicism. The community was composed of mostly Catholic and Anglican sisters plus a small number of long-term guests, both male and female, Christian and Hindu. Sister Vandana herself eventually left Pune years before my arrival to begin a monastic foundation in the Himalayas, where she established herself as a well-known spiritual author and dialogue partner with Hindu *sannyāsis* (monks). She lived in close proximity to a number of Hindu ashram communities and enjoyed deep spiritual bonds with the local monks. Her writings were given more to spirituality than to theology, and her major theme was that we Christians have much to learn from the deep wisdom and spiritual experience of Hindus. Sara Grant shared that vision, although she was more orthodox in her Christian theology than was Sister Vandana.

Since the C.P.S. Ashram in Pune was under the joint jurisdiction of the local Catholic and Protestant churches, its leadership was shared by two co-*ācāryas*, or spiritual heads, one of whom was Sister Sara, the other being Sister Brigitta von Loesch, an Anglican sister of German origin.

Another scholar living at the ashram was Sister Arati (originally Kathleen) Snow, also a member of the Sacred Heart order, who was originally from England. She was a tiny, snow-haired woman, close to eighty years old, frail, and hard of hearing. Though she suffered from constant back pain, she always greeted fellow ashramites and visiting guests with a kindly smile and welcoming presence. She revealed to me that the one thing Christ did not suffer from was the travails of old age and that she hoped to help "complete Christ's suffering" (Col. 1:24) in her own body. Sister Arati had been trained in Arabic studies in the United Kingdom, and although she was an expert in Islamic teaching and Sufi spirituality, she gave up a promising academic career in her homeland to work with the poor in Calcutta. Prior to living at the C.P.S. Ashram in Pune, she had spent many years there helping young women find their way out of prostitution. She spoke fluent Bengali. It was Sister Arati to whom one turned to find just the right Sufi text from Rumi or al-Hallaj or a passage from the Qur'ān to precede biblical readings at daily Mass. For prior to the first part of the Mass, called the Liturgy of the Word, where selections from the Old and New Testaments are read aloud, an additional reading would be selected from Hinduism,

Buddhism, or Islam to broaden the spiritual context of liturgy and to hear the biblical passages with new ears. This incorporation of readings from other religions into daily worship is typical of Catholic ashrams in India, though not of Catholic parishes, which for the most part continue to follow traditional Western forms of liturgy. Sister Arati's life ended abruptly one day when she dropped dead of old age while tending to her beloved parakeets. It was discovered that she was well prepared for death. When the other sisters entered her room, they discovered that the old sister had left all her possessions and papers and instructions in perfect order for anyone to dispose of. She also left behind marvelous poems about her love for Christ.

Sister Brigitta, the third intellectual figure at the ashram and co-*ācārya* with Sister Sara, was herself strongly drawn to the academic life and well read, but she did not consider herself a true scholar of religion, as were Sisters Sara and Arati, because of a lack of systematic training in Eastern religions. She was a tall, robust, white-haired German woman who had been educated in England. From extensive private reading she had become quite knowledgeable about certain aspects of Hindu spirituality, in particular the *Yoga-Sūtra* of Patañjali, and she occasionally offered lectures on the subject. But she was even better versed in Christian biblical exegesis, doctrine, and spirituality. Before we were married, Mariam received catechism for a year from Sister Brigitta in preparation for baptism into the Catholic Church. What Mariam learned that year was how the love of God was made manifest in the life and teachings of Christ. The local Catholic bishop knew of Sister Brigitta's qualities and readily gave his blessing to allow the Anglican sister to prepare the young Muslim woman to become a Christian of the Catholic Church. Such is religion in India; the boundaries are often fluid.

And so the ashram was the perfect place for me to be at this point of my life. It was a "crossroads of the Spirit," as Sister Sara liked to say. It was a meeting place of people from many religions and from no religion at all. Believers, atheists, agnostics—all had come to India through an inner prompting, and all were ready to share with others their perception and experience of truth. The sisters' openness to truth, while at the same time remaining firmly rooted in their own Christian tradition, was like a breath of fresh air. I had spent so many years in Germany studying the development of religious doctrine, but always within the framework of a single tradition—my own. It was now time to drink from the wells of other traditions of wisdom and experience.

I lived seven months at the C.P.S. Ashram. When my grant money from the West came in, I decided I could now afford to live more independently. I put an ad in *Sakāl*, the local Marathi newspaper: "American Sanskrit student seeks lodging with Indian family." Mr. Harshe at the ashram had told me I would get a good response from Hindu families, if the ad mentioned Sanskrit. Sure enough, within two weeks I received eighteen responses, all of them from Brahmin families. The Brahmins, Hinduism's highest caste, are the people most closely connected to the Sanskrit textual and ritual traditions.

After collecting all the responses, I visited a number of houses and apartments in different parts of the city and introduced myself to the people whose lives I might be sharing. Some of them hardly spoke English, while others were quite fluent. They were from quite different economic backgrounds. Some were upper-middle-class families in fine homes; others were old people living alone and poor, unfortunately in locations very distant from where I needed to be. I settled on a Brahmin home on a quiet lane in Deccan Gymkhana. It would be less than half an hour by bicycle to the university, and it was affordable. I was offered a large room inside the house proper, but I preferred to stay in the empty servants' quarters at the back of the house, where I would have more privacy. I had two small rooms, one with a bed, and the other for study and yoga practice. Outside my door was a banana tree and a tall mango tree that provided shade during the hot season. Sometimes I would hear a large thump on the ground outside my room, and I knew that another mango had dropped off the tree. Late at night I would stand outside my room and look up at the Milky Way and contemplate the mystery of creation and consider the many ways Hindu

thinkers have explained the relation of the world to its transcendent
Source. There were perhaps as many as twenty-two Vedāntic interpretations of creation. Our existence is quite mysterious and unfathomable.
Studying Hindu thought in such a beautiful and harmonious setting, I
could not have been happier.

6

Crossover Communion

Iused to spend afternoons in the library of my university's Sanskrit department, laboring over grammar and taking notes on Hindu texts. On one of my first days there, a little man in a worn gray uniform approached me as I was hunched over my work. He carried a silver tray covered with little pieces of coconut. He held the tray out before me and said simply, "*Prasād*."[1] The man's official occupational title was "peon," one of the lower-level support staff in the department. His main task was to carry papers back and forth between offices. This was back in the days before computers were used at Indian universities. On Fridays the peon was given the additional task of going to a nearby Hindu temple with chunks of coconut to have them blessed and brought back to the department as *prasād* or sacred food. He then offered the coconut to everyone he met in the building, to administrators, professors, fellow peons, and office staff, on down to the students. One might take and eat a piece of coconut on the spot or take it home and share it with a loved one. "Would you like *prasād*?" he asked, holding the tray out to me, a Christian.

Prasād is food that has been made sacred by God through the intermediary of a Hindu priest. The food offered by the worshipper could be one of any number of things, but it is usually fruits or sweets.[2] The temple priest recites the proper sacred words over the offering and then touches the main "idol,"[3] or physical abode of God, with the tray of food.

The whole ritual might take less than a minute. The long line of devo-tees one observes every day in Hindu temples needs to move quickly, if everyone is to be accommodated. The deity, it is believed, graciously[4] and freely accepts the food when it is properly offered through the prayers of the priest. This activity is not understood as magic, whereby divine power would be forced to yield to the force of mere human ritual. Rather God, the all-powerful, freely deigns to become part of the ritual action. It is understood that the Lord then consumes some of the food and leaves the rest for the devotee to eat as part of a meal fellowship. Such food is now sacred. Those who eat the blessed food are in fact communing with their Lord.[5]

When the Hindu man asked me if I wanted *prasād*, it was not because he mistook me for a fellow Hindu. Everyone in the Sanskrit department, whether professor, staff member, or student, automatically assumed that if I was from the West I was probably a Christian. It didn't matter that I was attending classes in Sanskrit and Hindu thought like everyone else; I was regarded as a Christian and not a Hindu. But being a Christian did not automatically exclude me from being offered *prasād*. It was understood that God's grace extended outward beyond the Hindu community even to members of other religions.

What was I to do? Should I accept and eat the *prasād*? I knew that many of my Christian fundamentalist relatives in the United States would have recoiled at the thought of accepting food offered to a "false god." But the God to whom the coconut was offered, according to this Hindu theology, was the supreme Lord and Creator of the universe, an infinite and eternal God of mercy and love, a God who, Hindus believe, periodically incarnates into the world to relieve humanity of its suf-fering and to guide it to the peace of liberation. This was not a minor deity, limited in power and bound by the law of karma. This was the ultimate reality. This God's name was "Viṣṇu," the "All-pervader," and He or It (Hindus know that God is, in some sense, both) had no trace of impurity or evil. Viṣṇu is a purely benevolent and merciful God who is worshipped by about three-quarters of all Hindus under various names. In many ways Viṣṇu was my God, the God of Jesus Christ. There are some very real and significant differences between the merciful Viṣṇu and the loving creator God of Christians, to be sure,[6] but the similarities far outweigh the differences. And *prasād,* after all, was not being offered to some kind of malevolent and destructive demon; it was food offered to and blessed by the gracious God of all creation. And so I took the coconut and ate it. I consumed it with reverence, treating it sacramentally as one more way in which the one God of creation was reaching out to transform my heart into a heart of love, to turn me into grace for others.

Now, the question can't help but be raised, what about the other way around? Can Hindus receive Holy Communion from Catholics? Is it the same thing as Christians receiving *prasād* from Hindus?

Years ago I was the best man in a Catholic wedding where I first stayed in the little village of Palayam in the state of Tamil Nadu. The family I stayed with, like other Catholic families in the village, regularly attended Mass and displayed a strong devotion to Mary, the mother of Jesus. Each evening, before darkness descended, many of the villagers left their fields and gathered together in the village church to pray the rosary. Praying to God and honoring the mother of Jesus was for them the most natural thing in the world.

A few days after the wedding, on August 15, the Feast of the Assumption of Mary,[7] we went on pilgrimage to the eastern seacoast, to the little town of Vailankanni.[8] Vailankanni is located on the Bay of Bengal, about 150 miles south of the great city of Chennai,[9] and it is there on the beach that a famous shrine for Mary is located. The intention of my Indian family in going on pilgrimage was to offer special prayers for the new bride and groom on one of the four major Marian feast days.[10]

Vailankanni is to India what Lourdes is to France and Europe. It is the location of the most famous Catholic shrine of Mary in all of India. It is the place where people go to receive blessings and be healed of physical ailments. The basilica is formally dedicated to "Our Lady of Good Health." I once met a man from Chennai named Joseph who took his dying daughter on a train to Vailankanni when the doctors could not save her, and she was healed. Many Catholics and non-Catholics in India have a strong faith in Mary and Jesus; they are confident that at shrines dedicated to her, Mary answers their prayers for every need. Countless miracles are said to have taken place at the Vailankanni basilica over the centuries, and those who are healed are from all religions.

When we arrived for Mass in Vailankanni, there were already thousands of people in attendance, most of them forced to gather outside a church that was too small to contain such a large throng of visitors and pilgrims.[11] We were fortunate to eventually find our way inside the basilica, where we could hear the words of the many priests who had gathered from various regions of India. They would speak to the crowd in most of the country's major indigenous languages and also in English. By far the overwhelming majority of people in attendance were Hindu. This is not surprising for two reasons. First, Hindus number more than 80 percent of India's population, while Christians make up only little more than 2 percent. Second, it is well known that many Hindus will visit the shrines of other religions to avail themselves of the power and blessing of the Divine made present there. They are not concerned that the shrines may be Christian or Muslim. The power of the Divine is there, which transcends all religions, and the blessing is for everyone.

It is perhaps because of the large Hindu presence at Vailankanni that so many Catholic priests from all over India were present that day. Each priest was there to speak to the crowd in a different language, in particular when it came time to receive Communion. Everyone in the church was to be made aware of the Catholic Church's official teaching about who can and cannot receive Communion. The priests knew from past experience that Hindus would come on this day to receive what they understood to be *prasād* from the hands of Catholic priests. That was the Hindu understanding of the Catholic ritual: Catholic priests were offering *prasād*. To prevent this from happening, that is, to prevent Hindus from receiving Catholic Holy Communion, one by one the Catholic priests stepped forward to deliver the same message to all those present in the church. The message was this: "We are now going to receive Holy Communion. Holy Communion is only for those Catholics who are in good standing with the Catholic Church and who have recently gone to confession. Communion is not for Catholics who are not in good standing with their church, nor is it available for Protestants, Hindus, Muslims, Buddhists, Parsis, or people of any other religion. Holy Communion is only for Catholics who are in good standing with their church. So everyone else please stay seated when it is time for Communion to be given." The message was first delivered in Tamil, the local language, then in English, Malayalam, Kannada, Telugu, Konkani, Marathi, Hindi, Punjabi, and many other major Indian languages. It took a long time to deliver the message in so many languages. There should be no mistake: Communion was only for Catholics of a special type and for no one else.

After all those present had been duly informed of the official Catholic restrictions about Communion, the anticipated moment at last arrived. A priest standing before the altar announced in Tamil and English that Communion could now begin. I expected that only a very small number of people would walk to the front of the church to receive Communion. But I did not know about the Hindu openness to the rituals of other religions. As soon as the priest completed his announcement, *everyone* rose to their feet and rushed to the front of the church to receive Communion. There was nothing the priests could do, then, but try to determine somehow—perhaps guess—which would-be communicants were Catholic and which were not. Non-Catholics, mostly Hindus, would be turned away. The easiest way to determine who was Hindu was by the way they attempted to receive Communion. Communion in the hand was forbidden; only tongue Communion was allowed. So if individuals seemed unsure how to receive the wafer on their tongues, especially if they closed their eyes while attempting to receive it, they were sent back empty. "The Body of Christ," said the priest as he held aloft the wafer before the face of the communicant. And more often than not he lowered his hand when he deduced that this was probably a Hindu who was standing before him. Perhaps the Hindu had not responded with the customary "Amen," when the priest said, "Body of

Christ." If so, the priest would move on to the next person and again hold aloft the small piece of bread. In most cases the wafer would not be given. Nonetheless, it is likely that a good number of Hindus received First Communion that day.

I am sure that many Hindus were surprised, probably dismayed, that day when Catholic *prasād* was denied them and they were sent back from the Communion rail empty-handed. If Catholics can receive *prasād*, why shouldn't Hindus be allowed to receive Communion? One way of understanding the official Catholic position is this: receiving Communion from a priest means, among other things, accepting Jesus as your sole Lord and master and being totally committed to being his disciple, not someone else's disciple. It also means that you accept Catholic doctrine in its totality.[12] That is the ideal, anyway, though many Catholics around the world surely go to Communion with less certainty about official Catholic teaching than did Catholics of previous generations. But they go, nonetheless, and no one checks to see how orthodox are their beliefs.

Sometimes when Catholic Communion is not offered to Hindus, something else is given instead. One of the most common venues where Hindus might expect to receive Communion is at wedding ceremonies between a Catholic and a Hindu. Anticipating this, the Catholic priest might say to the Hindus, "We do not want to force our beliefs on you." The Hindu visitors are then informed that Communion is connected to certain Catholic doctrines that are different from Hindu teaching and unacceptable to them. So instead of being offered Holy Communion, each Hindu visitor is offered a flower taken from the church altar, a gesture that is said to resonate with them, because of its resemblance to the distribution of sacred flowers in Hindu temples. Still, I wonder how many Hindus must be disappointed at not being allowed to receive Catholic Communion.

In rare instances, Hindus in India are sometimes officially allowed to receive Communion. I know a Christian ashram where a Hindu couple lived for several months. The husband and wife, Raju and Swati, were both expert yoga instructors, highly intelligent and well educated, and so open-minded about religion that they freely chose to participate in all the daily Christian liturgical activities that were not required of visitors, such as attending the daily Eucharistic celebration. Communion was not offered to them, however, since they were Hindu. Each day the Christians and the two Hindus gathered together in a half circle around the altar as one ashram community. And each day the consecrated bread and wine passed by Raju and Swati as they were handed from Christian to Christian. The Hindu couple was disturbed by this, but said nothing. After a few weeks, they could take it no more. Out of exasperation they approached the head of the ashram, requesting that they, too, be allowed to receive Communion. "We believe that Jesus is specially present in the bread and wine," they said. "Why can't we receive Communion?" The ashram head sympathized with them and decided to talk things over with the local Catholic bishop. The bishop basically instructed her to follow her conscience in this matter. He did not say that henceforth all Hindus at this ashram may go to Communion. He just said that in this particular case, with this particular Hindu couple, Communion might be offered.

One question that might be asked here is why the Hindu couple did not simply request to be baptized and become full members of the Christian community. I am not sure of their personal reasons not to seek baptism, but a few things come to mind. First, they saw themselves as *Hindu* followers of Christ. This is not unusual in India. There are many Hindus who see themselves as disciples of Christ, which means that they strive to abide by his Gospel values of compassion to all and by the recognition that all people have equality and dignity before God. And so, while they are followers of Christ and live his *values* they cannot identify with all Christian *doctrine*.[13]

The little village of Palayam, as noted earlier, is divided by caste.[14] When I first visited the village, Father Victor told me a story about an event from his boyhood involving the local parish priest. The priest had grown frustrated by the old caste divisions within the parish and decided to put an end to them once and for all. He chose Palm Sunday as the day to begin making changes. Up until then the high-caste Catholics had kept their distance from the low-caste parishioners and had even insisted on receiving Communion first. And so, on Palm Sunday, as everyone stood outside the church in two separate groups, palm branches in hand, ready to process around the church, the priest made the announcement that on this particular Sunday he was introducing a new practice. He began by quoting scripture. Since in Christ, according to St. Paul (Gal. 3:28), there is no longer Jew or Greek, slave or free man, male or female, there would henceforth no longer be high caste or low caste in this parish. In Christ everyone was made equal before God. As a living sign of their unity before God, he urged the two castes that had been standing apart to now merge together for the first time as children of the one Father and process as one united people around the church before entering it to celebrate the Eucharist. The result was that the priest was immediately set upon by the high-caste parishioners and beaten so badly that he had to be committed to a hospital. There was no Mass that day, and the bishop transferred the priest to a different parish for his own safety.

It is clear that the parishioners who attacked their priest did not see any social implications for participating in the Eucharistic celebration. In their mind, to attend Mass meant that one gained access to the mystery of Christ's Real Presence in the bread and wine. That was what Mass was finally all about, but nothing more than that. The high-caste Christians did not see the Eucharist as also celebrating the equality of all people before God. They did not understand the sacramental meal as strengthening the bonds of love between themselves and other parishioners, a movement of love that should then flow out of the church and into the world.[15]

Catholics are taught that when they receive Communion they are supposed to have the proper inner disposition. They are to be free of serious sin before they head to the altar. Sin, in the Christian understanding, is behavior that harms one's relationship with God. And that relationship with God is measured in large part by the relationship one has with other people. We need to be in a right relationship with both

God and other people if we are Jesus's disciples and intend to sit at his table. Jesus says that we are to be reconciled with our brother before going to the altar (Matt. 18:15). But we see in the Palayam example that receiving Holy Communion had not overcome the old sinful distinctions of higher and lower, clean and unclean. This was a problem that St. Peter had overcome in the earliest days of Christianity. According to Acts 10:28, Peter says to Cornelius, a non-Jew, "You are well aware that it is against our law for a Jew to associate with a Gentile or visit him. But God has shown me that I should not call any man impure or unclean." Peter means that God had revealed to him the equality of all people through the example of Christ's life and teaching.

Fortunately, there are also more inclusivistic attitudes in Catholic India than what took place in Palayam. As a Muslim girl, my wife, Mariam, attended Catholic school in Pune. "In school I used to sometimes go to Communion," she says. "Even though I was a Muslim, my Catholic friends would show me what to do. I'd get in line with them. I think the priest knew I wasn't Catholic, but he'd smile at me and give me Communion anyway. That's what I like about Catholicism in India. If the priest thinks you're a kid with a pure heart, he might let you go to Communion. It's one of the things that attracted me to Catholicism."

7

The Healing

The expected monsoon rains arrived not long after I had first settled into ashram life in Pune, causing unclean runoff to leak into the city's porous underground water system. In the rainy season, which runs roughly from early June into September or October, the consumption of public water can be hazardous; leaky underground pipes carry bacteria throughout the city, and if one is not careful, the tainted water enters one's intestines. That is what happened to me. The result for me and countless others in the city was inflammation of the intestines and severe dysentery. The physician across the street prescribed antibiotics, and that helped for a while, but just as suddenly the old illness reared up again. I was now allowed one boiled egg per day in addition to the regular vegetarian food, since, as one of the sisters remarked, I was visibly "wasting away." During my first two months in India I lost thirty pounds, and I am a small person to begin with.

Though still ill, I boarded the Dadar Express for a twenty-four-hour train trip south to the city of Madras (now called Chennai), after which I traveled by bus to the village of Palayam, where I had spent my first three days in India. I had returned to be the best man in the wedding of my friend Paul, and the wedding was now only a week away.

I had met Paul a year earlier outside Vienna at a Hindu-Christian dialogue conference. He was doing a doctorate in anthropology at the University of Vienna. He was a man at home in very different worlds:

in his simple village in southern India and at one of the premier centers of learning in Europe. He was fluent in Tamil, Hindi, English, and German.

Paul and his fiancée, Patsy, were Indian Catholics of very different social backgrounds. While he was from a village surrounded by rice fields, she was from Bangalore, a large modern city that would eventually be at the center of India's booming IT industry. Paul was a pure Tamil, while Patsy's family was Anglo-Indian. "Anglo-Indian" signifies any mixture of Indian and Western blood. Anglo-Indians often regard themselves as more Western than Indian, and they sometimes seek to reinforce their Western identity by adopting Western tastes, not only in clothing, but also in music and entertainment. On my first visit I was surprised to hear American country music played in Patsy's home. They thought I would be pleased. But I preferred Ravi Shankar.

From Vienna, Paul had sent a letter to Patsy in Bangalore, asking her to become his wife. She readily accepted. The wedding was to take place in the Catholic church in Palayam, only a short distance from a Hindu temple. The reception would be at the house of Paul's parents. Because of the many guests that were expected, the reception would be held outdoors under a large cloth awning joining together two houses across a narrow lane.

Patsy's parents were at first very much opposed to the idea of their daughter's wedding and reception taking place in a simple country village. They were accustomed to the comfort of their large bungalow in metropolitan Bangalore. Most of India's population still lives in villages today, tilling ancient fields passed on from one generation to the next, but city people have little reason to go there, unless they are called back by some event involving the gathering of relatives. Patsy remarked before the wedding that "It took all the butter in the market," that is, tenacious pleading, to get her parents to agree to a village wedding. But they finally agreed under the condition that there would be a second reception at their bungalow in the big city.

The priest officiating at the wedding ceremony was Paul's older brother Victor, a member of the SVD (Society of the Divine Word) missionary order. Every three years he returned from the Catholic missions in Papua New Guinea to visit his family and friends in India. Father Victor had received his theological and priestly training in Pune, far from his home in Tamil Nadu. He would one day introduce me to various people in Pune, including a Muslim family, one of whose daughters would become my wife.

In the days leading up to the wedding, Father Victor and I were both very ill, suffering from the same gastrointestinal ailments. I could tell by his haggard face, usually joyful, that he was suffering considerably, but he did not complain. He had already endured many illnesses in Papua New Guinea, including malaria. He tried to remain upbeat.

I remember clearly the wedding ceremony and reception, which took place on a steaming hot day. Many memories of that day remain vividly in my mind: Paul and Patsy wearing their finest clothing, she, as an Anglo-Indian, in the traditional white Western wedding gown, he in a dark suit with tie, both of them beaming before the cameras; the car, rented from a neighboring town, carrying the newlyweds through the village to Paul's home, repeatedly stopped along the way by well-wishing Hindu neighbors who, by peering through the car windows, hoped to catch a glimpse of the bride in her unusual white dress; the young Tamil poetess who at the reception recited a poem extolling the newlyweds; the large and joyful gathering of relatives and friends.

But what I recall the most is trying to get through the ceremony with my stomach in turmoil. The day after the wedding Father Victor and I were even more ill. I had been up all night with diarrhea and vomiting. By morning I was no longer able to keep even water down and had become so weak that for the first time it crossed my mind that I might actually die in this little village. Thousands of people die in India every year from dysentery, and so there was no reason for me to think that I might be spared. There was no doctor available in the village, and I was weak and demoralized.

Father Victor and I had formally committed to attending the second reception at Patsy's house in Bangalore. But this was obviously out of the question now. It was clear to me that under no circumstances would we be departing anytime soon. We would have to pay our respects at a later time. But Father Victor saw things differently; instead of calling off the trip, which seemed to me to be the only sensible thing to do, he announced to me at midmorning that we would not only be traveling to Bangalore, but that we would be departing *within the hour*. We were among the "honored guests" at the second reception, he said, and so we could not disappoint those who would be awaiting our arrival. We had to board the train in Trichy that would take us to Bangalore.

I could hardly believe what I had just heard. "You go if you want," I said incredulously, "but I'm staying here. There's no way I'm going on any trip."

Victor was nevertheless calmly adamant that we would go. In fact, his brother Dominic was at this very moment getting a *motorcycle* ready for us. *A motorcycle?* I thought. How could either of us, as ill as we were, travel anywhere by motorcycle? Victor's plan was that we would go by motorcycle to the little town of Perambalur, about twenty minutes away, and from there catch a bus to the city of Trichy and after that take an overnight train to Bangalore.

Before I had time to argue about the absurdity of this plan, Father Victor said to me, "We need to pray. Get down on your knees, and I'm going to pray over you." He placed his two hands on my head as I obediently knelt before him with my hands clasped together in prayer. He crossed himself in the name of the Trinity and prayed roughly as follows: "Heavenly Father, you know all things before we even ask them of you, but we know it is your will that we should pray for all things that promote love and bring people together in your name. Please help Bradley be well enough to make the trip to Bangalore, so he might be part of this important celebration. Take away his sickness. We thank you for all you have given us, for the love and peace you put into our heart through faith in your Son, Jesus Christ. Please send your Spirit upon Bradley to make this trip possible. All this we pray through Jesus Christ, our Lord. Amen."

I must confess that although my head was bowed in prayer, in my heart of hearts I was skeptical and full of doubt. I had been seriously ill for days, and the dysentery was only growing worse. And no one had ever prayed over me before. As a Catholic I had prayed at Mass for world peace and justice for the oppressed and for the "souls of the departed," but never for a speedy and immediate healing of the sick. That was a bit much for me to hope for. Of course, I knew Jesus's teaching that if we wanted our prayers answered, the key ingredient was to have faith in God's power and mercy, and that this faith need not be great. It need only be the size of a tiny mustard seed; otherwise our prayers amounted to nothing but empty words. Yet I did not even have the faith of a mustard seed as Father Victor prayed over me. In fact, I had no faith at all in that prayer. But I kept my doubts to myself.

"OK, let's go," I said to Victor.

"No, now you have to pray over me," the priest said, and he went down on his knees before me. So now it was my turn. I had never laid hands in prayer on anyone before, let alone a priest, and so I felt awkward. But since I was praying to God, the supreme and all-powerful reality, the creator of heaven and earth, I felt I should at least muster up as much good intention as possible. And so I crossed myself, as Father Victor had done, invoked the Trinity, and then prayed for the return of the priest's health. The key sentence was, "Help Father Victor become well enough to make the trip to Bangalore." The prayer ended in the name of Jesus. While I was praying I was concentrating on the words I was saying, but I was doubtful that God would answer them.

We packed our bags, and a few minutes later Victor's brother Dominic came roaring up on a motorcycle in a cloud of dust. I watched as Victor climbed aboard behind his brother. I waited for the two of them to drive off, wondering how long it would take Dominic to return for me. Instead the two men looked at me puzzled while I stood alongside the motorcycle. "Come on, hop on!" Victor shouted. "We don't have much time!" He pulled himself up closer behind Dominic, and I climbed on behind him, amazed that we were three men riding a motorcycle with our luggage. On the way to Perambalur, as we wove our way through the countryside under the hot sun, I focused my attention on my stomach, waiting for the telltale churning sign that was sure to come.

At Perambalur we boarded a dilapidated bus that was missing its front windshield. It did not take long for the bus to fill up with towns-people and villagers heading to the big city of Trichy. The midday heat was made worse by the men and women packed body to body inside the bus. The trip would take two hours, and there would be no opportunity for a toilet stop. I felt doomed.

The bus revved up its engine, the driver blared his horn, and we were off. What I then experienced as reckless and nightmarish driving I would have regarded in healthier times as a fine and thrilling adventure. In India there is an unwritten rule that larger vehicles such as trucks and buses have the right of way, and that pedestrians and smaller, slower-moving vehicles must clear the way, even scatter before the larger vehicles, if necessary, especially on narrow country roads. Yet buses and trucks barreling down the road do not always wait for the traffic to clear ahead of them, and so they often weave left and right, sounding their piercing horns as they go. If, as sometimes happens, a truck driver loses control and causes a crash that involves the loss of life, especially of schoolchildren, he immediately abandons his vehicle and runs for his life. Otherwise the enraged villagers might kill him on the spot, as is occasionally reported in newspapers across India. Add to this the additional experience of hot air blasting in my face, because of our missing windshield, and life that day could not have been more miserable.

Two hours later we arrived in Trichy. At the train station Father Victor asked me how I was feeling. "Thirsty," I said, "and I'm starving." I was surprised at my own words.

"Me, too," he smiled. "Let's get something to eat." We bought some chicken sandwiches on the platform and washed them down with Thumbs Up and Gold Spot, two of India's popular soft drinks. This was my first real appetite in over a week. We ordered two more bottles and drained them. Then we boarded the train for an all-night trip.

•   •   •

The next morning on the train Father Victor asked me how I had slept. "Like a baby," I said. "I slept all night and didn't get up once." Victor grinned. "I slept great, too."

It never occurred to me at the time that the long trip by motorcycle, bus, and train, in which all traces of my illness had completely vanished, had anything to do with the previous day's prayers. Though I was grateful that I now felt inexplicably well, I did not attempt to understand why.

What happened next took me completely by surprise. After arriving in Bangalore, Father Victor and I took a taxi across the city to the bungalow where Patsy's parents lived. But within a few hours we were both suddenly assailed by the same stomach ailments as before. The illness was just as strong as it had been the morning of the previous day, just before we had prayed. I was as baffled by its return as I had been by its sudden disappearance.

The next day Patsy's mother took me to a clinic, where I received a week's supply of antibiotics. That did the trick. I recovered my health for quite some time, though the stomach ailments did eventually return.

It only occurred to me afterward why our illness had mysteriously disappeared for almost twenty-four hours, why our appetites had returned, and why we had been able to sleep soundly on the train the whole night through. Father Victor and I had prayed that we might be healthy enough to *make the trip from the village of Palayam to the city of Bangalore*. Our prayers had been answered, but only for what we had asked, but no more than that. We had not prayed to stay healthy after our arrival in Bangalore.

To this day, I am not quite sure what to make of all this. I do believe that God healed me that day, but I don't know why God had answered a prayer uttered without hope or faith. Was the healing given so that my faith might increase?

8

A Hospital for the Poor

The monsoon had returned in full force, unleashing torrents of rain upon the city, and for several weeks I had been consigned to lying on a cot in my clammy room at the Pune ashram, suffering again from stomach ailments. After my episode in the village, the old illness had once again returned. Though I was often enough hungry, the mere smell of cooked food caused me to turn away in nausea and disgust. I nibbled what little I could, but week by week I continued to lose weight and grow weaker.

It was about this time that old Mr. Harshe suggested that I have myself admitted to Wadia Hospital on the other side of the city. At nearly eighty Mr. Harshe was one of the oldest members of the ashram community. No one living at the ashram ever thought of addressing Mr. Harshe by his first name, so revered was he by one and all, including the Catholic and Anglican sisters. He was a man of unusual gentleness and simplicity; I never once detected in him the slightest trace of irritation or annoyance. In appearance Mr. Harshe was of average height, with a broad smiling face, neatly combed silver hair, trousers too short, and thick eyeglasses through which intelligent owlish eyes peered childlike into the world. He was a compassionate and deeply spiritual person, an incarnation of humility, innocence, kindness, and joy, a man who struck me as representing all that is good and virtuous in Hinduism and Christianity, the two religions with which he was most familiar.

Mr. Harshe had been raised Hindu, and in his younger days as a Hindu he had been employed in Pune by an American missionary society to translate the New Testament into Marathi, and as a result of his painstaking translation of the Gospels he had converted from his Brahmin caste to Protestant Christianity. He had a strong devotion to Christ as his "savior and guru," as he put it, but I also noticed his continued Hindu belief in reincarnation and multiple incarnations (avatars) of the Divine. Mr. Harshe was thus a living example of the sometimes permeable doctrinal boundaries that connect Hindus and Christians in India.

Despite old age, poor eyesight, and a stiff lower back, Mr. Harshe's unfailing cheerfulness was infectious. We wanted to be like him. He never attempted to force his personal convictions on others. He never said one religion was better than another or that some people are good and others bad. He was completely nonjudgmental, and he treated everyone with kindness and respect. His aged wife, who was known only as "Mrs. Harshe," had been initially very reluctant to convert to Christianity, to follow her husband, and she agonized for years what to do until finally one night—as she narrated her story to me—Christ appeared to her in a dream, gently urging her to enter through a door.

Mr. Harshe assured me that it would not cost much money to be admitted to Wadia Hospital, and the chances for a full recovery were good. By that time, in addition to the stomach ailments I had known for weeks, I was also beginning to experience excruciating headaches, unlike anything I had ever known before. And so I consented to have myself admitted to the hospital. But I was physically incapable of traveling alone. It required the help of the old man for me to climb into a motor rickshaw and make the trip to the hospital the following day. We passed through the rainy neighborhoods of Shivaji Nagar and Deccan Gymkhana on the way to the other side of the city. Every bump was agony for my head, and I tried to cushion the jarring of the rickshaw by raising myself a bit off the seat with my hands.

Since no private or semiprivate rooms were available when I checked in at Wadia Hospital, I soon found myself in a general ward with about thirty beds in two parallel rows. The room was long and simple, with bare white walls, and open windows through which the warm moist monsoon air poured in. My bed was clean and tidy and identical to all the others. All the bedridden in the ward were men or boys. In the bed to my left, propped up against a pillow, was a large middle-aged Hindu policeman with a thick black mustache that extended even wider than his broad smile. He spoke very little English, but he was able nonetheless to communicate his amusement that an American would travel all the way to India to study something as impractical as Sanskrit.

In the bed to my right lay a small wiry teenage boy, dark skinned and clean-shaven, who spoke no word of English and who showed no interest whatever in communicating with me. He was rarely alone except at night, for every minute of the hospital's visiting hours he was attended to by half a dozen poorly dressed men of varying ages who sat on the floor around his bed cross-legged, in silence. Occasionally one would lean to the other and whisper something softly, followed by an interval of more silence. Their faces showed no expression. They seemed unfamiliar with hospitals and were reluctant to converse with people outside their own group. They wore the simple khadi cloth of the poor. Each also wore a purple turban and a purple thread around his wrist, which I took for some kind of amulet. I had seen this caste before. They herded sheep and goats through the streets of the city and allowed their flocks to eat on the C.P.S. Ashram land without first asking permission. Such men swarmed effortlessly up into the ashram's giant banyan trees with machetes and knives and hacked down branches and leaves to feed their herds. The sisters at the ashram had warned me not to go near these men or attempt to take their picture, for they distrusted cameras, fearful that a photo of them might unleash the power of the evil eye.

During my first afternoon in the hospital I made eye contact with one of these men sitting on the floor and offered a friendly smile, a feeble attempt at a greeting. My smile was answered with an icy glare that fixed directly upon me until I turned away.

·   ·   ·

Within minutes after I lay in my bed in the general ward, I was approached by two small young nurses dressed in white uniforms, both of whom had their hair tied back in a bun. They were pushing an upright metal stand attached to which was a large water bottle and a drip.

"What's that for?" I asked warily, already knowing the answer.

"We're going to give you glucose water and see if that makes your headache go away," said one of the two.

"That's fine," I said, "but I can just drink it from a glass."

"I'm sorry," she replied, "but we have orders to give it to you intravenously."

"But I'd be happy to take it in a glass. I can drink lots of it. It's really no trouble."

"Please give me your arm," said the first nurse. She took my right wrist in her tiny hand and turned my forearm upward. Already the large needle was on its way. She aimed for a vein in my forearm—and missed. The needle went into my flesh with a deep searing pain. I winced and tried to stifle a groan.

"Sorry, sorry, sorry" the nurse said rapidly, with evident sympathy and sounding a bit flustered, and then, "Let me try another place."

While that nurse, with her head lowered, closely studied my forearm, the other nurse examined my wrist. As she traced her forefinger across it she suddenly exclaimed with excitement, "Oh, look, *here's* a vein!"

Here's a vein? I thought to myself. *Here's a vein?* Were these nurses only in training? I felt dark panic well up.

The first nurse tried again to administer the tube, this time plunging the needle directly into my wrist, where there is very little flesh but plenty of bone and nerves. I shouted and watched as my hand and forearm, as if activated by an invisible switch, began to violently shake. The nurse quickly extracted the needle. "Sorry, sorry," she said. "I'm very sorry."

A third nurse, middle-aged and heavyset, shuffled slowly across the room over to my bed with a look of disgust, which I assumed was directed at me, because of my evident lack of bravery. But I was mistaken. "You two don't know anything," she said to the young nurses with unconcealed derision. "Let me show you how to do it."

Upon hearing that another attempt with a needle was imminent, I was about to swing my legs out of bed and make for the door, but the older nurse was already standing on the other side of my bed near my good arm. And with the skill of someone who knows exactly what they're doing, she slipped the needle effortlessly into my vein with barely a pinch. "That's how you do it," she said, and turned around and walked away.

For two hours the glucose water slowly entered my body. And little by little the visitors to the ward began leaving, so that by dusk only a few remained. The room was now quiet. For the first time since morning I found myself alone with my thoughts. I had time to think and daydream. I thought about the needle that had just gone into my wrist. I wondered how badly it must hurt if, instead of a needle, someone were to drive a thick nail all the way through it or maybe through the palm of one's hand.

Time dragged on. The room was silent except for an occasional cough and the soft murmur of voices in conversation. Nightfall gradually descended, and through the open window I could see a streetlight's halo in the mist. The street noise had subsided. The other patients lay quietly, some snoring.

After some time a new nurse strode into the ward and announced in Marathi and English that visiting hours had come to an end. Men and women visitors slowly said their good-byes to loved ones and began to leave. But one group of a half-dozen visitors, mostly women, remained gathered around a bed at the far corner of the room. On the bed lay an old man tethered by tubes to a dialysis machine. The nurse repeated more loudly this time that visiting hours were over. Yet the people around the bed did not react. The nurse walked the length of the ward and approached the group. "Visiting hours are over; you can come back tomorrow." The group still refused to leave. I concluded that the old man in bed must be seriously ill, and that his relatives did not want to leave him alone. The nurse insisted that they must leave, and they must leave now. A woman in the group near the sick man raised her voice in reply and spoke rapidly and plaintively. I could sense her urgency, even though I did not understand her language. The nurse soon realized she could not win this argument, so she turned around and quickly exited the ward.

A few minutes later she returned, accompanied by a burly middle-aged security officer in uniform, sporting a black mustache and beret, and armed with a club. Once more she commanded the group to leave. The old man's relatives pleaded their case, first with the officer, then with the nurse, but to no avail. Their pleading eventually gave way to crying and shouting. The officer and nurse answered with a rising indignation. The quarrel continued with mounting intensity and finger-pointing. Suddenly and without warning the exasperated officer raised his club high into the air and brought it crashing down on the shoulder of one of the women, who staggered backward, almost falling. He then began beating the other women on their arms and shoulders, driving them backward as one. The victims howled in pain and anger and raised their forearms over their heads to ward off the blows that rained down upon them. The officer did not let up; he beat them the entire length of the ward until they were out the door. After a few minutes I did not hear them anymore.

Time passed. I had no appetite, but my headache was beginning to subside. After another hour of silence, a nurse approached the bed and notified me that a doctor would visit me in the morning. Not long after, in the deep quiet that followed upon this day of anxiety and turmoil, I fell into exhausted sleep.

I awoke to the first light of dawn. In its half-light I surveyed the long quiet room. Because it was still too early for visitors, I could easily see across the room and make out clearly the more distant beds. I thought about last evening's confrontation between the policeman and the sick man's relatives. I looked for the old man on the other side of the room. I could see his reclining figure covered with a blanket, indistinguishable in appearance from all the others. Shortly thereafter a new and different nurse entered the room and walked directly to the old man's bed and began unhooking him from the machine. This struck me as odd. Why would she unhook him? Then a second nurse arrived and joined the first. Together they wheeled the bedridden man away from the corner of the room and down the aisle between the two rows of beds that led out of the ward. As they passed by me I noticed that the old man's blanket had been pulled up over his head. I was jolted by the realization that sometime in the night he had died. Had no one noticed until now? I said a prayer for this man about whom I knew nothing and who had died unnoticed and unattended.

Around midmorning a tall and distinguished-looking physician of about forty entered the ward making his rounds. In his conversations he alternated between Marathi, Hindi, and English, depending on the language of his patient. His average time per patient was less than a minute. He approached each person one by one and asked him the same general questions: "How are you doing today? Are you feeling any better than yesterday?" It made no difference whether the patient replied with a short answer or a long one; one minute was all each was given. And then the doctor would move on to the next bed, even if the last patient was still speaking. "How are you doing today? Are you feeling any better than yesterday?" He worked his way down the row of beds across from mine, then crossed over to my row and methodically approached where I lay. When he came to my bed, the tall doctor looked down at me, then at his paperwork, then back again to me. "An American?" he asked with raised eyebrows. I nodded. "What brings you here? You're having headaches?"

"Yes," I replied, "and stomach problems."

He asked me for more information about my stomach and head. He was especially interested in my headaches. And though he did not bother to examine me, he drew a very quick conclusion. "I'm fairly certain that you're suffering from spinal meningitis. This is very serious." And then he paused. "It could kill you."

I had no idea what spinal meningitis was, and though I was familiar with death at this hospital, I felt certain I was not dying. I also seriously doubted that I had spinal meningitis, since the glucose water had greatly reduced my headache. But the physician thought otherwise. "Sometime today or tomorrow," he said, "we're going to perform a spinal tap on you."

"What do you mean?" I asked.

"We're going to put a needle in your spine and draw some fluid out to see if you have meningitis."

"Look," I said, "I'm already feeling much better than yesterday. I think we should just wait."

"We're going to keep a watch on you," he said, "and if we need a spinal tap, we'll have to do it. Spinal meningitis is very dangerous."

I was prepared to tell any kind of lie about how great I was feeling to keep that needle out of my spine.

But in the course of two more days in the hospital, my headache gradually disappeared, and the physician mercifully did not bring up the issue of the spinal tap again.

I was prepared to be released on day five. Yet since the previous day I had noticed a new development in my physical condition that I did not dare report to the physician. The dysentery was flaring up again, and my stomach was churning worse than ever. At the end of day four I confided in a young medical student who had befriended me and who regularly came to chat with me at my bedside in the evening.

"How are you feeling now?" he asked. "Tomorrow you'll be leaving."

"My headache is completely gone," I said, "but I have another problem now."

"What's that?" he asked.

"My stomach is all messed up and I have to keep going to the bathroom."

"Let me ask you a question," he said seriously, studying my face. "Are you having someone bring you your meals from outside, or are you eating the hospital food?"

"The hospital food," I reassured him.

"*That's* the problem," he said. "Someone should have told you. You *never* eat the food prepared at this hospital. *Never*. I *never* eat the food here. It's not clean; it isn't prepared carefully. That's why you're so sick again. If I were you, I'd leave tomorrow and go see a doctor in the city. Just get out of this place as fast as you can. This is a hospital for *poor people*, so you have to be really careful."

When I checked out the next morning, I needed to pay the equivalent of only about four dollars for my stay. There were other hospitals, too, in the city for those even more destitute than I, but fortunately I never had myself admitted to any of them.

9

In the Hands of a Skilled Hindu Physician

I awoke one day in the ashram with such abdominal pain that I could not stand up. Sister Brigitta, who had been observing my physical decline for a number of weeks, said to me dryly, "Well, Bradley, you've suffered enough. It's time to go to Dr. Nanal. He will heal you."

"Who is Dr. Nanal?" I asked.

I detected a trace of a smile. "You'll see." She said nothing more.

Because the ashram had no telephone, Mr. Harshe, though advanced in years, volunteered to hobble down to the post office to make the appointment for me by phone. A short while later he returned to my room in his typical childlike excitability. "You have an appointment exactly at seven o'clock tomorrow morning with Dr. Nanal when his office opens! I've been instructed to tell you not to take any food or liquid for the last twelve hours before you arrive! Not even water!" He was plainly enthused that I would see the great physician.

"Thank you, Mr. Harshe," I replied weakly from my bed.

The following sunny morning the old man helped me into the rickshaw. We traveled ten minutes down Ferguson College Road in and out of the shade of banyan trees until we reached Deccan Gymkhana, a verdant neighborhood with a high population of Brahmin families living in stately bungalows. We turned up Prabhat Road and halted at precisely seven o'clock in front of a two-story gray stone building with a bright blue roofed wooden balcony. A sign on the house read GANESH

SADAN after the elephant-headed god. "1861" recorded the year of the building's construction. Mr. Harshe and I climbed the narrow stairs to the balcony, which served as the waiting area for Dr. Nanal's patients. When we reached the top, I noticed a closed door at the far end of the balcony, behind which, I imagined, the doctor was perhaps already sitting, awaiting me, the fortunate first patient.

But I was wrong. One patient had already been beckoned inside the doctor's office before I arrived. Not only that, three other people were already sitting on the balcony awaiting their turn. I reasonably concluded that I would be next, but to my surprise I learned that each of the others would see Dr. Nanal ahead of me. For it was the doctor's policy to tell *all* his patients to arrive at seven in the morning. He would then see them according to the order in which they arrived. No one complained about this; Dr. Nanal was a very famous and skillful Hindu physician, and he gave each patient as much time as was needed. In fact, new patients regularly spent more than an hour at the first consultation.

Four hours later, at eleven o'clock, I was the sole person left in the balcony waiting room. Mr. Harshe had departed a few hours earlier after my many assurances that I could make the rickshaw trip back to the ashram without his assistance. An hour later, at around noon, the doctor's door swung open. A woman quickly swept past me and headed down the stairs. I was next.

When I stepped through the doorway into the doctor's office, I took a quick inventory of what was before me. To my left was a small worn couch. At the opposite end of a nearly empty room was a plain broad wooden desk, behind which sat a large bald-headed, round-faced man nearing sixty. His fleshy arms were resting folded atop the desk. Running horizontal across his forehead were three broad parallel lines of what looked like ash or sandalwood paste, an indication of his devotion to Lord Śiva.[1] His face was expressionless. To his left, sitting on a wooden bench, was another man, slender and mustached, perhaps in his thirties, bent over a large open book that balanced precariously across his folded legs. In his right hand was a pen. This man, Dr. Ghatnekar, was the assistant physician and the recorder of the medical observations Dr. Nanal would make about me.

I greeted the two men, but received no answer. I found this strange.

What I did not know was that Dr. Nanal was already beginning his medical examination from across the room. By observing my demeanor, the way I carried myself as I stepped into his office, even the way I formulated my greeting, he was gathering information about the kind of person I was.

I learned later that Dr. Nanal was a professor at the local Āyurvedic college in Pune, a man so renowned and learned in his profession that he had been invited to set up Āyurvedic institutes in both Germany and Australia with their governments' funding.

Neither the expert physician nor his assistant spoke. Dr. Nanal studied me with great attention and, after a time, rose to his feet and walked barefoot across the room toward me, gliding lightly, it seemed, despite his heavy frame. He motioned for me to lie down on the shabby couch to my left. He then took my wrist in his broad hand and began to take my pulse. This, it turns out, is the reason why one is instructed to abstain from liquids beforehand; a completely empty stomach helps to determine a more accurate reading of the pulse. By taking the patient's pulse, the physician is able to establish the kind of physiological category to which the sick person belongs. But I think it also takes a certain gift to read the subtle signs given out by the pulse, something like palm reading, only more difficult. The doctor's face was all the time blank, and since he did not speak to me I remained silent. After taking my pulse at my wrist, he took it again at my neck and above one of my ankles. He shone a small flashlight into my eyes, checked my throat and tongue, pushed and prodded my belly in a circular motion with his large hand. The wordless physical investigation took a good fifteen minutes. When he had finished the examination, he finally said his first words to me, which were "You've come here because you have a stomach ailment."

"Yes," I said.

"Why is that?"

"Well, that's what *I'd* like to know," I replied.

"Have you had this kind of illness before?" he asked.

"I get stomach problems about once or twice a year that cause me to stay in bed a week."

"Why is that?" the doctor asked.

"I don't know," I said.

"You *should* know," he said abruptly. "You should be observing your body and all the habits that might contribute to your illness. Your illness now has to do with your illness from before. You need to be more aware of what's going on with you."

I was willing to accept that this might be true, but more than anything else I wanted the good doctor to do something to heal me immediately, like give me the right medicine, perhaps give me some kind of pill that would make me well. But for the next forty-five minutes, Dr. Nanal did not talk of medicine; instead he asked me every imaginable question about myself, questions that for the most part seemed to have nothing to do with my ailments, as for example: How did I see myself? How did I think others regarded me? What kind of friends did I have? What were my parents like? Did I get along with them? What kind of things in life did I like and dislike? What kind of food did I prefer? Spicy? Salty? Sweet? What kind of weather did I like best? Did I have a girlfriend? Was I having sex with her?

And, finally, he asked, "What brings you to India?"

"I'm studying Sanskrit," I said. "But I'm just a beginner."

The doctor's eyes seemed a bit brighter. "Studying Sanskrit? What kind of texts are you studying?"

"Along with grammar my teacher and I are going over some of the Upaniṣads."

"Very good," he said. "Have you memorized any verses in Sanskrit?"

"A few," I said. I was very much hoping he would not ask me to recite them. I was embarrassed about my American accent.

"Recite something," he said.

And so I began reciting the first verse of the Īśā Upaniṣad: *īśā vāsyam idaṁ sarvaṁ yat kiñca jagatyāṁ jagat,* which means "All this, whatever moves in this moving world, is enveloped by the Lord."

Dr. Nanal continued with the remainder of the verse: *tena tyaktena bhuñjīthā mā gṛdhaḥ kasyasviddhanam:* "Therefore find your enjoyment in renunciation; do not covet what belongs to others."

He continued for many more verses before halting. To become an Āyurvedic physician, one must be prepared to study the medical texts in their original Sanskrit. Though the Upaniṣads (800–200 BCE), sacred texts proclaiming the supreme reality, *brahman,* are not part of the canon of Āyurvedic texts one studies in medical training, they are likewise composed in Sanskrit. I have heard from others that Dr. Nanal had memorized all of the major Upaniṣads, texts that run hundreds of pages. His own father had been a highly regarded Sanskrit scholar and Āyurvedic physician, and so it was perhaps not surprising that the son would benefit from his father's learning.

In tradition-minded Brahmin families, the preservation of the Sanskrit language from generation to generation is important, even a holy duty. The most authoritative Hindu scriptures, whether they be the Vedic hymns to the gods, the Upaniṣadic treatises on the divine indwelling of the Absolute, or the Bhagavad-Gītā's teaching of divine love, were written—or rather revealed at first orally and subsequently written—in Sanskrit. *Pūjā*s, too, that is, religious ceremonies invoking divine blessing and favor, are also normally performed in Sanskrit as are cremation rites for the deceased. And the epic literature—the Mahābhārata and the Rāmāyaṇa—together with the ancient caste lawbooks, *sūtra* literature, and their *bhāṣya*s or commentaries, plus the most famous devotional hymns, erotic and spiritual poetry, plays, and philosophical treatises were for the most part composed in Sanskrit. Sanskrit is regarded as sacred for two reasons: both because its words are bearers of sacred content, meaning, and truth, and also because its very sound is holy and transformative to the chanter. Each individual Sanskrit word or sound is a particular finite expression in the form of a vibration of the eternal changeless

Divine. The only exception here is the syllable "Oṃ," which is not simply a partial manifestation of divine energy-sound, but rather encapsulates and summarizes the totality of divine creativity and vibration.

The lasting influence of Sanskrit over several millennia notwithstanding, its place in contemporary India has waned. One already notices this change in individual families when one compares members of different generations. It is not unusual for the grandfather to know and to be able to recite at length hundreds of Sanskrit passages from scripture, devotional hymnody, and poetry. His son, substantially less versed in the Sanskrit tradition, will be able to recite only a very limited number of *slokas* or verses from the past, not unlike the way the educated Westerner might be able to quote a line or two from Shakespeare's sonnets, though this is, of course, much easier for one already speaking modern English. The middle-aged Hindu will also be unable to translate from Sanskrit all but the simplest texts. The youngest generation, even when college educated, will not only be devoid of Sanskrit knowledge, never having been forced at home or school to learn it, but in most cases will show no interest in it whatever. Studying Sanskrit is not regarded as a practical pursuit in today's India, when so much attention and energy has been turned to international trade, industry, and the increase of wealth.

So Dr. Nanal represented in some ways a fading world, one that will be reawakened—according to some Hindu revivalists—when India rediscovers the limitations of a materialist orientation to life and returns again to embrace its ancient spiritual vision, one that is able to distinguish between temporal, fleeting, and material happiness and the deeper and more fulfilling experience of spiritual joy and peace. There must be room for both rather than the exclusion of one or the other.

Āyurveda, the system represented by Dr. Nanal, is an ancient holistic medical practice that is intimately connected to the practice of yoga. It derives from the compound *āyus,* meaning "life," and *veda,* meaning "knowledge." *Āyurveda* thus means the "(comprehensive) knowledge of life," life in all its dimensions: physical, mental, and spiritual. Good health is maintained when every sphere of our being is in harmony with itself and with all the other spheres. That is why it is called a holistic form of medicine; it does not look for the cause of illness only in the body. Dr. Nanal, then, in treating the patient both physically, mentally, and spiritually, is ideally not only a physician, but also something of a psychiatrist and spiritual guide. If necessary, he will recommend, along with the prescription of medicine, certain yoga postures (*āsanas*) and other spiritual practices to treat the imbalances.

Āyurvedic physicians do not fanatically insist that their medical approach is the only valid one. In certain circumstances they will recommend that a patient make use of an allopathic or more Western medical system. In very extreme cases, too, very little can be done to remedy an illness by Āyurvedic methods or any other means, and that is because of an altogether different reason, Dr. Ghatnekar informed me. What is that reason? "We Hindus believe in reincarnation," he said. "Sometimes illness is the result of your karma or actions from a previous lifetime, and nothing can be done."

D^{r. Nanal continued his interview with me. "Do you meditate?"}
   "Yes," I said.
   "What kind of meditation?"
   "Breath awareness."
   "Who's teaching you?"
   "The sisters at the ashram," I replied, "and others."
   "That is good," he said. "It is very important that you meditate."
   And then he asked, "Do you have a good memory?"
   "Pretty good, I guess," I answered.
   "Well, then, here's what I want you to do. First, I want you to be sure to continue meditating, every day and without fail."
   "All right," I said. That seemed easy enough.
   "Second, I want you to memorize the entire Bhagavad-Gītā in Sanskrit." I was taken aback by this. The Gītā is seven hundred verses long. I agreed that I would at least try, but I was well aware of how much time I needed just to continue my study of Sanskrit grammar and the Upaniṣads.

"Third," Dr. Nanal said, "tell me what you feel like eating. What is your body saying to you?"

I paused to sense what that might be. After a few moments, I replied, "I feel like grains and also something sweet."

"When you go back to the ashram, then, tell the cook that you'd like a bowl of *lapsi*."

"What's that?" I asked.

"Broken wheat porridge. Put a spoonful of honey in it, two if you'd like. And one more thing. Do you know what ghee is?"

"Yes, I've heard it called 'clarified butter.' You keep it in a jar and use it for cooking."

"That's right," he said. "Be sure to add a big spoonful of ghee to the *lapsi*, along with the honey, a large spoonful. Whatever you do, don't forget the ghee."

"Why ghee?" I asked.

"Never mind," he answered.

I wondered why he wouldn't tell me.

"All right," I said, "*lapsi* for lunch today with honey and ghee. What about dinner this evening?"

"*Lapsi* again, with honey and ghee. And when you're thirsty, drink warm water. Your digestive fire is very weak. We need to stoke it with cooked food and warm water."

"What can I eat tomorrow?" I asked.

"Tomorrow," replied Dr. Nanal calmly, "you will eat *lapsi* morning, noon, and night. Nothing else. And you'll do this seventeen consecutive days."

"I'll die," I said.

"No, you won't," he answered dryly.

"Should I at least take vitamins?" I asked.

"Throw your vitamins away; you don't need them." He went on. "And here are two things to remember about eating in general. First, never eat until you're completely full. Always end your meal still a bit hungry. Second, take your largest meal of the day before the sun has reached its zenith. That will aid your digestion."

"Another thing," the doctor went on to ask, "are you doing yoga?"

"Yes," I answered. "Every day."

"Which *āsanas?*"

"Different ones: standing, sitting, inverted."

"Stop immediately," said Dr. Nanal. "You are too weak to be practicing yoga. And the worst *āsanas* for you to be doing are the standing ones. When you start to feel your strength returning, you may go back to yoga. But for now you have to give it up."

"And this evening," he continued, "I want you to go to my clinic in Sadashiv Peth and pick up the medicine I'm going to prescribe. And I'll see you here again in seventeen days."

And with that the conversation abruptly ended. No small talk or chitchat. I quietly left Dr. Nanal's office and returned to the ashram. I asked Devikabai, the cook, for a bowl of *lapsi* and some honey and ghee. In broken English she asked, "Why doctor say eat ghee?"

"I don't know," I replied.

In the early evening I traveled down the narrow and chaotic Laxmi Road, one of Pune's busiest shopping arteries, badly congested with traffic and pedestrians, until I arrived at Dr. Nanal's clinic at Kunte Chowk. The clinic was located on the second floor of a cavernous and decrepit stone building that amply provided both office and apartment space. The clinic was packed with what seemed to be wearied people of all ages who were prepared to wait hours, if necessary, to meet the famous doctor for at most a few minutes and then pick up their medicine.

Inside the clinic was a small dispensary, out of which an unsmiling tiny aged woman emerged. She handed me three small paper pouches with instructions. Two of the pouches contained tiny light brown and dark brown pills. They seemed to be made of dried earth, rolled by hand into little balls upon which fingerprints could still be seen. They were to be taken three times a day with water. The other pouch contained a light brown powder. In halting English the woman explained that the powder should be mixed with honey and consumed with warm water. And do not forget to put some ghee in the *lapsi*, she added.

By the next day I was delighted to discover that my abdominal pain had entirely disappeared, though I was still weak. For the next seventeen days I followed instructions exactly as the doctor had given them: a bowl of *lapsi* three times a day with honey and ghee, earth pills three times a day, and warm water as my only liquid. Surprisingly, I did not crave anything else, and day by day I could feel my strength return.

After seventeen days, I visited Dr. Nanal again at his home. As before, there was no wasted time with small talk. "How are you feeling now?" he asked.

"Much better," I said. "I've been doing exactly what you told me, eating only *lapsi* with honey and ghee, and I've been taking my medicine regularly, and only drinking water. And I've not been doing yoga."

"That is good," replied the doctor, and for the first time he smiled, apparently pleased with my growing recovery. "But you still can't go back to regular food yet; your stomach is still too weak. Continue to eat *lapsi* three times a day. But you can add one thing to your diet. Do the sisters at the ashram have a toaster?"

"Yes," I said, "and it works fine."

"Good," he replied. "You may now have toast with your *lapsi*. And spread lots of ghee on the toast."

"Why ghee?" I asked.

"Never mind. And remember, never eat until you're completely full. Hold back a little."

"OK," I said.

"I'll see you in a week," said the doctor. "And no yoga practice."

A week later I made my third visit to Dr. Nanal. His first question was, "What did you have for breakfast this morning?"

"Two bowls of *lapsi*," I replied, "and twelve slices of toast covered with ghee."

"*Twelve slices of toast?*" he asked in amazement. "I told you never to eat until you're full!"

"I'm not anywhere near being full," I said. "I now have an enormous appetite."

"Very good," said the doctor. "You may now instruct the cook to start making you boiled vegetables. In a week you can start taking fruit juices. But stay away from meat. And remember to keep taking ghee every day."

"Why ghee?" I asked.

"Never mind," he said.

A few weeks later a friend of mine, an Australian yoga teacher living at the ashram, was referred to Dr. Nanal. Lee had exactly the same symptoms as I: nausea, dysentery, the inability to digest food. Like me her first visit with the doctor involved a fifteen-minute physical examination followed by a lengthy question-and-answer period about her likes and dislikes. Lee was not surprised by this, having received from me a thorough account of my own first encounter with the famous Āyurvedic physician. But when it came time to prescribe medicine and food, Dr. Nanal surprised Lee by telling her that she must take pains to avoid taking any ghee in her diet.

"But Dr. Nanal," she said, "wasn't one of your recent patients a man from America named Bradley?"

"Yes," he replied.

"And didn't you heal him of his illness?"

"No, I did not," replied the doctor. "I merely helped restore a balance his body needed to heal itself."

"All right," she continued, "but he had all the same symptoms as I. Isn't that true?"

"Yes," said Dr. Nanal.

"And isn't it true that you told him that he should take lots of ghee with his food?"

"Yes," replied the doctor.

"But you're telling me *not* to take any ghee, even though I have *exactly* the same symptoms as Bradley?"

"Yes, that is true," said Dr. Nanal. "But you see, you and Bradley are very different people, and although your symptoms are the same, the imbalances and the personalities are different. Bradley, you know, is very high-strung. He tends to speak very fast, and he floats above the clouds. Taking ghee will help bring him down to earth. But you, you're down here"—he dropped his hand near the floor—"we need to bring you up. No ghee for you!"

10

Buddhist Vipassanā Meditation

Since I had come to India to study Hinduism, when I first arrived I knew very little about Siddhartha Gautama, the Buddha, and absolutely nothing about Buddhist meditation. But within days after my arrival, I started to hear about a kind of Buddhist meditation called vipassanā.[1]

I was living at Bede Griffiths's Saccidānanda Ashram, in a community made up not only of monks, but also of pilgrims and travelers from around the world who were continually passing in and out of the monastery. These seekers often discussed Hindu and Buddhist spirituality and compared notes on meditation practices they had learned in their travels. Sometimes they exchanged information about various spiritual sites in India and other Asian countries they had visited. They did most of the talking, while I, the newcomer to India, mostly listened.

One of the recurrent themes of those early conversations was a meditation method called "vipassanā." Though I had already practiced yoga and learned some meditation from Hindu teachers in America, Buddhist meditation was entirely new to me. I remember bluntly asking what vipassanā was, and I recall how a German man replied that it was a form of meditation taught in various parts of the Buddhist world, and that in India it was especially connected to a teacher named Goenka, who lived in Igatpuri in Maharashtra. "Vipassanā is very ancient, but very popular today," he added. "Goenkaji is sometimes there himself giving the retreats."

"I've never heard of him," I said. "I suppose he is well known?"

"Yes, he is very famous," answered a woman. "I'm surprised that you, with your spiritual interests, have never heard of him."

"Well, I'm trying to learn about Hinduism," I said, a bit stung. "I don't know much about Buddhism." That was my ego speaking, wrapping itself in excuses and defenses, even while engaged in spiritual conversation.

Someone added that vipassanā was a meditation tradition that went back all the way to the Buddha himself more than twenty-five hundred years ago. It thus made the claim, rightly or wrongly, of being the oldest form of Buddhist meditation practice in the world.

Since I would be traveling to the state of Maharashtra for my studies in Hindu thought, I was urged to look into vipassanā. "You should do a vipassanā course, no matter what," the German man said. "Igatpuri is not far from Pune."

"Well, maybe I will," I said, but I doubted I would find the time. I had come to India to study Hinduism, and I was already feeling lost by what seemed to be an almost impenetrable forest of doctrines, temple rituals, and spiritual practices. I would have no time to explore Buddhism—or so I thought.

At the C.P.S. Ashram in Pune I met yoga practitioners from Australia, Europe, and the Americas, some of them advanced teachers back in their homelands. They were enrolled at the Ramamani Iyengar Memorial Yoga Institute, located only a short walk from the ashram. The yoga students took rooms at the Christian ashram only because of its proximity to the Iyengar center and because it was an inexpensive place to live. Most of the practitioners had no interest whatsoever in Christianity, and the sisters did not try to convert them. Instead they witnessed to the love of Christ by patiently listening to the yoga students, offering counsel only when asked. From what I saw they were almost completely nonjudgmental.

One day Sister Brigitta remarked to me that a few of the yoga students were about to travel to Igatpuri to do a vipassanā retreat.[2] This was now the second time I had heard about vipassanā, the first time being at Father Bede's ashram a few weeks earlier. "You should go, too, Bradley," she said. "Almost all the sisters here have done a vipassanā retreat." And then she added after a pause, "It will change your life." I was surprised to hear her put it that way, and I couldn't help but wonder if she were exaggerating. How had vipassanā practice changed the lives of Christian nuns?

By then I had made friends at the ashram with a fellow guest named Anup, a Buddhist from Varanasi. Anup was a short muscular fellow of about thirty, clean-shaven and always neatly dressed. He and I were both afflicted at the time by stomach ailments, and so there was a bond between us brought about through a shared suffering. I jokingly called him my "amoeba brother."

Though Anup lived at the Christian ashram, he never visited the chapel except during the quiet meditation hour at dusk. As a Buddhist he was impatient with the whole idea of God, and he was straightforward with his opinion. "I don't get this," my friend would say to me and to the ashram sisters. "What is this reality that Christians call 'God,' and why should He be so important? If you want to be spiritual, you don't need God. You can do things by yourself." He paused. "You know what I think? I think God is just a big unnecessary distraction." He spoke with passion. He did not mean to offend, but he felt impelled by his experience as a Buddhist to challenge us who were his Christian friends.

One day when the conversation again turned to Buddhism and Christianity, Anup related to me his return to Buddhism some years earlier. He weighed his words thoughtfully. "You know," he said, "I've never told you this before, but I used to be bad. I mean I was *very* bad. People were afraid of me. I'm not that big, but I used to be very strong. I worked out all the time, lifting weights. Once I was so angry I put my hand around a man's neck and lifted him straight off the ground—*with one hand!*" He scrunched up his face to look as fierce as possible. "I could have killed him. And I was the leader of a gang. People were afraid of us, because we were always raising hell. And," he said softly, "I was bad with women."

I was disturbed to hear this, because the Anup I knew was soft-spoken, gentle, and kind. He continued. "But I was very unhappy inside; I couldn't control my rage. I was angry all the time. But then somebody got me to try meditation. I liked it, and it wasn't long before I started noticing that I wasn't so angry anymore. That was years ago, and I've been practicing ever since."

"What kind of meditation do you do?" I asked.

"Vipassanā," he said. "I've done a number of courses with Goenkaji at Igatpuri. He is a very great man. You should do a course, too."

I was starting to feel that divine providence was sending me so many signals to do a vipassanā course that I had no choice but to submit and discover for myself what this kind of meditation had to offer. So I sent a letter to the vipassanā center at Igatpuri requesting permission to enroll in my first meditation course. Not long thereafter I received a reply saying that I was officially registered for a course that would begin soon, in early December. The notification did not say whether Goenkaji himself would preside over the retreat or whether instead the meditation teacher would be one of his assistants.

During the weeks leading up to the vipassanā course, guests continued to come and go at the Christian ashram, and so my roommates were frequently changing. We were always three to a room, and for a bed each person was given a broad wooden plank a few inches high covered with a thin mattress, a pillow, and a mosquito net. There was no other furniture in the room. If you wanted to write a letter, you would do it sitting cross-legged on the mattress or else go to the ashram library where there were simple desks and chairs. Since the library was the largest room in the entire ashram, yoga students often practiced their *āsanas* or postures in whatever open spaces were available there. They were often observed by sparrows that regularly flew in through the open windows and perched atop the bookcases. The yoga students otherwise spent a good part of each day at the Iyengar Institute, learning advanced poses.

One of the most expert yoga practitioners and also my roommate for a few weeks was a tall dark-haired instructor from Paris in his early thirties, who I will call G. He had a brooding—almost melancholic—disposition and, though he was not unfriendly, he was not given to lighthearted conversation. We did not speak much. But one day he mentioned to me matter-of-factly that he was about to make a trip to Igatpuri. It was not his first vipassanā retreat, he said; he had already made two others. He asked if I'd like to come along. And so it was decided that we would travel together.

Before I left for Igatpuri, Sister Brigitta said, "I should tell you before you go that when you come back you're not going to want to read anything for a month, not even a newspaper."

The journey to Igatpuri was fairly simple. From Pune we took a public bus to the city of Kalyan and from there a little train that slowly climbed to Igatpuri, which was itself nothing more than a small town. After getting down from the train we hiked up a hill outside the town where the vipassanā center, Dhammagiri, itself was located.

By the time we finally arrived at the vipassanā center, it was late afternoon and near dark, and the temperature had noticeably dropped. Most of the people who had arrived for the course were already settled in. Only a few stragglers like ourselves waited in line to have their names checked off a list. The check-in process was quick. After showing my identification to a young Indian man and woman, both wearing shawls, I handed them almost everything I had with me, except what I absolutely needed for the next ten days. The things I didn't need were put in a bag and locked away in a safe. It was not for me to decide what was essential or nonessential, however; the rules were already in place. And so while I was permitted to keep toiletries and some medicine, in addition to my change of clothing, nothing more was allowed. Money, travel documents, books, pens, paper: all were collected, placed in a bag, and labeled with my name. They would be returned on the last day of the retreat. No money was demanded of us, though donations were welcome. During the next ten days there would be no talking, no reading, no note-taking, no journaling; not even eye contact with others was permitted. This was to be what the Chinese call a "fasting of the mind," not a fasting of the body. It was a deliberate restriction of thought, memory, and sensory stimulation. The sole orientation of the retreat was to give oneself completely to vipassanā meditation and to nothing else. The practice of yoga was forbidden, too, and even private prayer was discouraged. We were to give vipassanā a chance to see what it could do.

"Do you believe in God?" asked the young man who registered me.

"Yes," I answered.

"Do not pray for ten days here," he said.

"All right," I said. I thought to myself, *If God is Truth and God has led me here, then I should try to discover the truth that God wants me to learn through vipassanā practice.* And so for the next ten days I did not pray.

G. and I were separated, probably because he was advanced in meditation and I was not. I was given a thatched hut furnished with nothing but two simple cots. Others on retreat were placed in similar huts or in long dormitory-like buildings containing extensive rows of beds. I was glad to have the privacy of the little hut. I did not know the name of my hut-mate or where he was from or anything about him, because we were not allowed to speak. And since we were also forbidden to have eye contact with anyone but the meditation instructor, I did not know what my roommate's face looked like, though I was able to determine from his physical frame that he was probably a young man. Never did we try to bend the rules, not even the day a large rat scurried loudly between our beds, bringing us both to a sudden upright position. It was all I could do to not look into my roommate's face or to cry out in surprise.

For the duration of the ten-day course, all students are expected to take a vow of not killing, stealing, lying, engaging in sexual activity, or using intoxicants. These precepts were articulated by the

Buddha himself twenty-five centuries ago. Such a high ethical code of conduct is of great benefit not only to a world afflicted by violence and self-destructive behavior; it also purifies the mind of the practitioner and prepares it to experience enlightenment. One is to avoid every kind of self-seeking and uncharitable action. But as demanding as these precepts seem to us when we first hear about them, they represent only the first stage, the most foundational Buddhist morality, and are thus common to all Buddhist schools.

The violence that we renounce applies not just to external physical action, but also to our thoughts and inner disposition. We should not even entertain the thought of harm. Such a lofty morality seeks to instill within us a habit that will eventually become a natural gravitation to nonviolence, peace, and compassion. It is reminiscent of the *ahiṃsā*, or nonviolence, advocated by classical yoga. *Ahiṃsā* is the first of the five *yamas*, or vows of restraint, in Patañjali's *Yoga-Sūtra*, and it, too, is very comprehensive, applying to both our outer activities and our inner disposition.

In much of Buddhism one should even refrain from harming animals, whenever possible. But it is well known that not all Buddhists are vegetarians. The Buddha himself ate meat, except during his six years of strict renunciation on a search that would eventually lead him to enlightenment. In fact, the probable cause of his death was food poisoning from eating rancid boar meat at the home of a family where he was the honored guest.[3] The Tibetans likewise are not vegetarian. Since arable land is limited on the Tibetan plateau, yak meat has always been a substantial part of the people's diet. This applies even to the monks. Tenzin Gyatso, the present—and fourteenth—Dalai Lama, was himself not a vegetarian until later in life, after having been influenced by the example of Gandhi.[4] Gandhi, the Hindu, was himself influenced in his life of nonviolence not only by his own Hindu heritage, but also by the extreme nonviolence of Jain nuns and monks. The scope of Jain nonviolence is broader than any other religion or spiritual path. One refrains not only from taking human and animal life; ideally one does not even consume plant life. Hence the ideal of the Jain renunciate is to reach a spiritual level where even the taking of any kind of food, of any kind of life, is impossible. Self-imposed starvation is the result. This is obviously not attractive to the rest of us, but it does express an attitude of solidarity with all beings that is worthy of emulation in less extreme forms.

I was happy to learn upon my arrival at Igatpuri that Goenkaji himself would guide the course and lead our meditation practice. The first time I saw him walk into the meditation hall I was struck by the quite ordinary appearance of this famous teacher: he was of medium height, clean-shaven, with gray hair combed neatly to one side, bushy eyebrows, his face expressionless, almost sleepy, it seemed to me, dressed in a simple light-colored kurta and trousers. He sat at the front of the hall in a chair; his wife sat silently beside him in her own chair. She, too, was expressionless.

But when Goenkaji spoke, I was immediately affected by the extraordinary deep soothing calmness of his voice. He seemed to be speaking out of a deep center, and he spoke with the quiet authority of inner experience.

Satya Narayan Goenka's story is well known. Born in 1924 and raised in Burma as a Hindu in an affluent Indian family, he suffered from severe migraines from the age of thirty-one, after having established himself as a successful businessman. Visits to some of the world's best physicians, including those at the Mayo Clinic in the United States, did not help. It was only when he began the practice of vipassanā meditation in his homeland under the tutelage of Sayagyi U Ba Khin (1899–1971) that his headaches disappeared. But more important was the discovery that vipassanā practice brought insight into mental and spiritual suffering and led to a deep unshakable peace and happiness. Goenkaji, who began teaching vipassanā in 1969, would go on to become one of the world's most famous teachers of vipassanā in the twentieth century. Some of the most prominent vipassanā teachers in the United States have studied under him.

Vipassanā means "insight," a deep awareness of the true nature of reality, as opposed to how we normally understand ourselves and the world around us. In meditation we come to recognize the three marks of existence: that all things are subject to change and are passing away; the unsatisfactory nature of physical and mental phenomena, in that they are incapable of bringing happiness; and, finally, the absence of any soul or self. What is especially characteristic of Goenkaji's vipassanā method is its purity; he will not tamper with the meditation method as he received it, and which others had received from their teachers in a lineage going back all the way to the Buddha himself, over two millennia ago.[5] If the method was good enough for the Buddha, it should be good enough for us. Human nature, after all, or rather, the human mind, is universally the same; it everywhere faces the same problems, habits, cravings, addictions, fears, prejudices, self-deceptions, delusions, and ego-centeredness. And so for Goenkaji there is no experimenting with tradition, no grafting of new techniques on to traditional meditation practice.

The vipassanā method itself is remarkably simple and can be learned in just a few minutes. When Goenkaji taught it to us, he did not first provide any extensive metaphysical or psychological introduction. He simply taught the method; he just showed us what we had to do.[6] For the first three days we were to simply observe the breath passing in and out of our nostrils. This is called *ānāpānasati*, or "breath awareness."[7] If we lost our focus on breath, we were instructed to patiently and repeatedly bring our attention back to it. It was like falling off a bicycle and learning to pick oneself up again. We were to be patient: focus on the breath, be mindful of breath, stay with the breath, and if we lose the awareness of breath, then we should be aware of that and return again to the breath. We should not be discouraged by an initial lack of success and give in to the temptation of resignation. The attainment of sustained breath awareness was within our own power. Goenkaji's favorite phrase was "Just observe. Just observe the breath." He repeated the words very slowly all throughout the day. "Just observe. Just observe the breath." In fact, he repeated the phrase so often that I sometimes found myself becoming annoyed when I heard it.

If we found it difficult to return to breath awareness, we were instructed to hold our breath for a few seconds. The mind, impelled by the survival instinct, will then automatically race back to the breath. At that point our breath-meditation should resume.

After three days, we were instructed to refocus our attention from the breath to the skin, systematically investigating every area, starting with the scalp at the crown of our head. We were to remain fixed on that area until we detected any kind of sensation, whether it be an itch or a tingling; it made no difference. Thereafter we were directed to a new area, adjacent to the first, to repeat the exercise, working our way around our head, over our face, down the neck, over the shoulders and torso and arms to the hands, down the abdomen to the legs and feet, each time seeking to locate sensations as they arose on the skin. We were then led back to the top of the head again, this time guided to focus on smaller and smaller areas of our body as our minds grew capable of greater sensitivity, attention, and patience. So the entire method was to follow the skin sensations from our head to our feet—over and over again. We were not using our imagination here; we were simply learning to be more and more present and attentive to what is.

The vipassanā retreat for beginners, I am told, used to be forty days, but now it is limited to ten days, and one must complete several courses before being admitted to the longer and more grueling courses and extended immersion in silence. Apparently the modern mind, with its increased disposition to multitasking and assimilation of large quantities of information via electronic media, and with its exposure to the never-ending bombardment and diversion of consumerism, entertainment, news, and sports, has grown too weak, too restless, too scattered in its approach to everyday reality to begin meditation with a forty-day course in which the focus is deliberately reduced to one thing: the inhalation and exhalation of one's breath, followed after some days by attention to the sensations of one's skin. Silence, both external and internal, once the natural domain in the search for truth and self all across human culture and religion, has now become for many people in modern times unpleasant, difficult, and unnatural, something to be avoided, if possible.

I knew a middle-aged woman in the United States whose television broke down one day and could only transmit a snowy screen and a very disturbing crackling noise, not unlike the sound of uncooked rice being poured into an empty pot. Just after I arrived at her house, I asked her what was wrong with her TV and why it was on so loud. She replied that until the repairman arrived in a few days' time she'd rather hear something—anything, really—coming out of the TV than nothing at all. "Otherwise the house is too quiet," she said. She was able to endure a noise that grated on her ears, but she could not bear silence.

One of the assumptions of meditation practice is that external silence has great value for the spiritual quest. Without the distraction of noise we may more easily focus on our breath and skin. It allows us to more easily sink within to the center of our being in a place of awareness beyond thought. Silence can be a gateway to the true Self and to God. Should we, then, regard silence as sacramental? Jesus himself commanded his followers to go to their room and pray in secret. There is an old Christian monastic teaching, too, that says if we go to our room and persevere in silence, the very walls around us will teach us wisdom. When we surround ourselves with silence, we are more able to nurture an inner silence. Silence aids the mind in its attempt to turn away from the swirling world of multiplicity and change, from thought and projection, so that it might finally come to rest in a center of peace and pure awareness that is deeper than the thinking, desiring mind, and which is immensely more satisfying than what the world offers. Meditation is a practice that seeks to cultivate this inner silence. It demands a reorientation of our old habits and preoccupations with the world.

To reach that point where we are ready to renounce our old way of interacting with the world is not easy, but we are sometimes helped along by suffering. Suffering can awaken in us the desire for something greater than what the world offers and to begin taking to heart what the great spiritual traditions have always taught. Perhaps we have made the experience that the world is not enough to give us happiness. The things we once desired, whether wealth, the love of a certain person, the attainment of prestige or power, these all eventually reveal themselves as incapable of bringing a deep and lasting happiness. That is because we were made for the experience of something greater. But until then, unaware of the "lost paradise of stillness"[8] within, we remain in bondage to our restless mind. And so we begin again the pursuit of a new object of interest, only to find that the fulfillment it offers is short-lived, slipping through our fingers like sand. This cycle of longing, attainment, excitement, dissatisfaction, and exhaustion repeats itself over and over. Our natural human orientation to the external world of things and projects is normally reinforced through the education given to us by our culture; we are trained to learn a thousand things about the world around us and about human society, how to get ahead in life, but we are seldom, if ever, instructed to turn our attention inward. And because we are not made aware of our own inner depth, we are unable to learn the most important truth of all, and that is who we are. Spending time in silence and meditation gives us the opportunity to disentangle ourselves from the exhausting push and pull of worldly involvement, even if only for short periods of time. In Thailand it is still common for young men to temporarily withdraw into Buddhist monasteries before embarking on their career or profession. This experience of silence and meditation is designed to give them a deeper perspective on life, to help them arrange their values according to what is most important in the quest for happiness. They learn to distinguish between that which is subject to change and that which does not pass away. Likewise for Śaṅkara, the great early medieval Hindu monk and thinker, the ability to discriminate (*viveka*) between the eternal and the transient is an absolute necessity for the attainment of spiritual liberation.[9]

This turn within is very difficult at first, and it seems to run counter to our natural outward orientation to the world as we experience it through the portals of our five senses. But if we persevere in our meditation practice, we eventually learn something quite surprising, and that is that our unruly mind not only can be tamed, but that once it is made subject to the discipline of meditation it *naturally begins to gravitate within,* to the deep silent center of our being. Meditation enables us to transcend thinking and enter into a higher state of knowing, in the experience of an inner simplicity of consciousness that brings serenity and happiness.

W̶e meditated thirteen hours a day. I'd heard about this in advance, but no amount of imagination could prepare me for that much sitting.[10] The most difficult session was always in the afternoon, because it meant sitting without rising to our feet for an entire four-hour stretch. This was the time when the mental and physical challenges were at their maximum. It is impossible for one's ankles, knees, and hips not to ache when introduced for the first time to such long sessions of meditation. There is nothing one can do when sitting except to find the most comfortable position and hope for the best. But it isn't long before discomfort slowly creeps up one's legs to present a formidable distraction. That is one of the common obstacles to initial meditation practice: physical discomfort.

Scattered around the edge of the meditation hall were heaps of pillows, plenty enough for everyone. Most people settled for one pillow, but others took several. With a mixture of curiosity and sympathy I watched as a tall young German man I knew from the C.P.S. Ashram in Pune, apparently in great pain, arose several times from meditation practice to fetch one pillow after another, hoping that the right number and arrangement might lessen his discomfort. He built himself what looked like a throne of pillows, but to no avail. Every few minutes he shifted his position.

I suddenly became aware that by observing this man arranging his pillows I had given in to a distraction, and so I closed my eyes and returned to my meditation.

One particular hour of meditation practice was always the most difficult. At some time during the four-hour afternoon session Goenkaji would command us to sit completely motionless—not adjusting our posture—and with eyes closed for one hour. We were to be like Buddha statues, not moving, not fidgeting, not even opening our eyes. And we could never be sure when that hour would begin. Goenkaji would simply inform us that it begins now.

If Goenkaji hadn't told us to keep our eyes closed for an entire hour, it would have been a lot easier to do. But once he told you not to open your eyes it seemed like that was all you were thinking about—plus the passing of time. I remember sitting there one afternoon wondering to myself how long it had been since I last opened my eyes. How much more time would have to pass before the hour was up? I knew I wasn't supposed to be thinking about this; I was supposed to be meditating. What made it worse was my knowledge that a clock was mounted on a wall to my right in clear view, if I were to just open my eyes and look at it. And so I began wondering even more what time it was. That's all I could think about. I imagined the clock. I could see its white face and black numbers in my mind. After a while I rationalized that if I just opened my eyes for a quick peek, I could then forget about this distraction and get back to really meditating. But Goenkaji had said to keep our eyes closed, and so I resolved not to look at the clock and not to think about the passing of time. I went back to observing my breath.

And yet the craving to know what time it was would not go away.[11] I began wondering again how long I'd been sitting with my eyes closed. At last I decided it was better to actually take a look at the clock, admit defeat, get my answer, and then return to meditation with full attention. That would be better than half meditating and half thinking about the passing of time. I estimated that probably twenty to thirty minutes had now passed since the hour began. But when I opened my eyes, I discovered to my dismay that it had only been eight minutes. Not only that: everyone around me seemed to be sitting as still as Buddha statues with their eyes closed.

During the whole ten-day course I was unable to keep my eyes closed even one time for the whole hour, and yet after the course ended and I was back in my room at the ashram I found I could do it without a problem. I'm not sure what the lesson is here. Perhaps the additional pressure of being commanded to keep my eyes closed instead of making my own choice to do it was the problem. I don't know. I think of St. Paul who found that being commanded to do the law of God only awakened in him the desire to do the opposite, even though he knew the commandment was good for him.[12]

Some unexpected—even strange—things may occur in meditation practice. In my case it occurred on day seven of the vipassanā course. I was sitting with my eyes closed during the long afternoon meditation session when the image suddenly flashed in my mind of a tree trunk and a knife. *A tree trunk and a knife?* I thought. I was puzzled. Where did *that* come from? With my eyes still closed I now saw how the tree trunk began bizarrely *moving on its own toward me,* a dagger held aloft in one of its limbs. The scene made no sense. Tree trunks don't move on their own, and they don't carry knives.

And then it occurred to me: this was a memory from my early childhood. More than twenty-five years earlier, back in the United States, when I was only five years old, I had watched my first horror movie on television. It was broadcast in black and white on a Saturday afternoon. My mother sitting next to me on the couch was scarcely able to contain her laughter at ridiculous scenes that were supposed to instill dread in the viewer. This, like other films to come in the following weeks, was a low-budget scary movie. But for me, a small child, the movie succeeded in its goal; I was absolutely terrified by what I saw.

In that first movie there was one scene, I remember, showing a man who was about to be sacrificed on a Caribbean island. I can't remember what he looked like or the man who stood above him with his knife raised in the air or why there was to be a sacrifice at all. But I do remember how the victim being held down warned the man with the knife that after his death he would one day return to exact revenge. He promised that there would be no escape; the murderer would have nowhere to hide. And then the knife came down.

That was scary enough for me, but it was only the beginning. A few scenes later, at some undetermined time after the sacrifice had taken place, the killer was walking through the jungle when he sensed he was being followed. He turned around, but instead of seeing another human being, he saw a tree trunk with a knife slowly moving toward him. The man he had killed had apparently come back reincarnated as a tree trunk, in one of whose branches was a large knife. With the knife he would seek retribution. I don't know why the man came back as a tree trunk; in retrospect, it was obviously a poorly conceived movie script. But the important thing for me as a kid was that every time the bad guy turned around, there was the tree trunk right behind him with the knife. Even if he ran, and the tree trunk lumbered along slowly after him, the tree always seemed to be right behind him, always moving menacingly toward the camera. It was the most frightening thing I had ever seen.

I eventually forgot about the episode with the tree and the knife, and I never thought about it even once during all the intervening years. But now, twenty-five years later, sitting in a Buddhist meditation hall in western India on the other side of the world, the memory of it was as vivid and clear as the day I had watched it as a little boy. It seemed to have come out of nowhere as I practiced meditation.

The way I think vipassanā theory would explain what happened is this: the memories of everything we've ever done or felt or thought, especially memories involving desire and fear, get buried deep in our subconscious. All our mental and emotional reactions to life are retained in a storehouse of memories located in the subconscious. As we continue to live out our lives we make ever new experiences, and these new experiences with our reactions to them lead to the creation of new memories. These new memories do not simply evaporate into thin air, once they are made, but rather settle down into the subconscious, finally resting, as it were, upon older memories, just as the silt carried by a river is deposited as layer upon layer of sediment, so that the delta becomes gradually thicker and deeper.

But when we meditate in the vipassanā way, we are taught to no longer react to memories and skin sensations with desire or aversion; we just quietly observe them and let them dissolve. And so no new emotional reactions will arise that would, in turn, leave their memories in the subconscious. The old memories, buried deep within, are now free to rise to the surface of our mind and dissipate. On their way out they do not manifest themselves only in the conscious mind; they also come out through the skin everywhere on our body. At least, that is how it was explained to me by vipassanā meditators.

Sometimes in meditation the impurities within our mind threaten to overwhelm us, as do the painful memories that rise up from our past. Anup, my Buddhist friend, told me the story of a young man he had seen at a vipassanā course in Igatpuri who was forced to confront his buried memories in a very painful way. The man was a follower of a famous guru in Pune, who was notorious for his libertine teaching on sex. The guru's understanding of spiritual practice was very much the opposite of most Hindu and Buddhist spirituality, which teaches that the normal way to liberation is through the disciplines of renunciation, fasting, and chastity. But the Pune guru, instead of teaching his followers to discipline the body and harness their sexual drive, taught them the exact opposite. He said that bodily mortification was nothing more than a form of sexual repression. It only made people neurotic. It made them long for sex even more. If one wanted to free oneself of overpowering sexual urges, the thing to do was not try and bridle those passions, but rather to act in accord with one's human nature and give sexual craving full play and expression. One should have no inhibitions when it came to sex. In his ashram the guru taught that complete sexual freedom was integral to spirituality. For example, one might have as many sexual partners as one desired, as long as the activity was consensual. Sex was something to be celebrated, and so glow-in-the-dark condoms were distributed to the ashramites. The idea was that if a person practiced unbridled sex long enough, the sexual urge would no longer exert such a powerful and fascinating control over the mind. Sexual desire would naturally subside, and one could then more easily and naturally move on to a higher level of consciousness and freedom. At least that was the theory.

It was during one of the meditation sessions in the great hall at Igat-puri, Anup told me, a hall that was packed with rows of meditators—the men to the left, the women to the right—that the young man from the aforementioned ashram found himself. He was dutifully practicing his meditation, vigilantly observing his breath, striving to make his mind more and more tranquil. But then, without warning, with no prior indication that anything was amiss, the man began screaming at the top of his lungs, a piercing scream that was also a moan.

When you are deep in meditation and someone near you makes even a tiny cough or clears their throat, the sound seems magnified, and you are jolted out of your practice. I tried to imagine what it must have been like to be meditating next to a man who shatters the silence by scream-ing at the top of his lungs. The young man was obviously confronting something from his past that he could not deal with. All he could do was cry out in agony.

Now in vipassanā practice we are instructed not to be bothered by the sounds around us in the meditation hall or by the people sitting so near to us that when they shift position they almost touch us. We should just keep meditating and not allow ourselves to be distracted. But the case of the screaming young man was something entirely different; his behavior was so extreme, he was in such pain, his mental state was so fragile that an immediate response seemed to be demanded of those around him. And so many of the other meditators near him arose from their mats out of compassion and hurried to his aid. They surrounded him, spoke reassuringly to him, asked him what was the matter, tried to calm him down, some even holding him and caressing him tenderly like a mother her suffering child. To no avail. The young man continued wailing as before, his cries filling the meditation hall. He seemed not even to be aware of the others who were trying to help him.

Meanwhile Goenkaji had been observing all this from his chair in the front of the hall. He saw the ineffectiveness of those who would calm the young man. He arose slowly from his chair and began walking toward him. As he walked, the meditators in his path rose from their pillows and parted left and right before him like the waters of the Red

Sea. Goenkaji calmly approached the man but did not speak to him. Instead he took a seat on the floor directly in front of the troubled soul, who continued, as before, to scream and wail. Goenkaji then began chanting ancient Buddhist verses that seemed to rise from the center of his being, a mysterious and beautiful but also haunting sound that I once heard later during Goenkaji's early morning chant, when I made my own retreat.

"What happened next?" I asked Anup.

"You won't believe it," he answered. "The guy calmed down. He stopped screaming and became quiet. Goenkaji said nothing to him. And the man continued meditating until the end of the course, and he never made another sound, not even a whimper."

At the end of every year, so I have been told, Goenkaji makes a silent retreat with his wife that lasts up to three months. It is said that one of the reasons he does this is to rid himself of the impure energies he has absorbed from the people he has helped.

We meditators had only one opportunity each day to speak, and that was when Goenkaji called us up to the front of the hall in groups of four for a simple interview about our meditation practice. We would sit in a row at his feet, and then he would look down at us dispassionately and ask us one by one in English or Hindi the same basic question: "Do you have any questions about your meditation practice?" If you did, he would give a clear and simple answer, and if you didn't have a question, you just kept quiet. My response to his daily question was always a shake of the head that no, I had no questions. Things were pretty clear: you just had to do what the man said, focus on your breath or skin, not let your mind wander, and grind it out minute by minute. There were no shortcuts. The more effort you gave, the more you got back. It was like learning how to swim. It was that simple and that hard. The teacher provided the method; it was up to you how much effort you wanted to give to meditation. So every day you went up to the master, heard the same question from him, and a few minutes later you're back at your meditation seat picking up where you left off, doing what you know you absolutely have to do, if you want to make any headway. It was all a matter of effort. There did not seem to be a place for divine grace. Or maybe the whole thing is grace.

One day the question-and-answer session with Goenkaji went a bit differently. As usual, four of us sat before him. The same question was put to me as the day before, and again I shook my head that I had no questions about meditation. Goenkaji then looked into the face of the person beside me, a young willowy American with unkempt sandy-colored hair, who was slouching deeply as he sat cross-legged on the floor before our venerable teacher. Goenkaji asked the young man: "Do you have any questions about meditation?"

"Yeah, man," said the American. I turned suddenly to look at him, surprised by his almost disrespectful way of addressing Goenkaji. "I'm having some far-out experiences. I sit there with my eyes closed, and all of a sudden I see orange lights. They come from one side and whiz right past me," he said, his flat hand slicing through the air before him, "and then they come from the other side and whiz by me again. It's really far-out. What does it mean?"

I speculated that the young man was reliving some kind of drug experience from his past.

"And what do you do when this happens?" asked Goenkaji.

"I just keep following the lights, man," he said. "They're far-out."

"Then," replied Goenkaji simply, "you're not doing vipassanā. You need to keep observing your breath."

And that was the end of the conversation.

Sometimes I opened my eyes and looked around the large hall filled with hundreds of silent meditators. There were women to my right, strictly segregated from the men on the left. Those who had already made at least one retreat were placed at the front of the hall. Now and then I would look around in boredom to observe if anything new or different, however small, might be taking place in the hall; anything at all would do. My mind craved something new and interesting upon which to fasten.

It was a few days into the course before I located my Pune ashram roommate G., the one from France, sitting far from me at the front of the hall, wearing a long white kurta. Things seemed to be going well for him. He sat motionless, with his back straight. I could not see his face. I wondered how his meditation was going. Was he experiencing pain in his ankles and knees, like me? How did this course compare with earlier ones he had taken? And then I realized suddenly that I had again fallen into thinking and so returned to my breath.

Some days later, near the completion of the course, my gaze returned to G. I thought I perceived something different about him, but I could not be sure. Were his shoulders shaking ever so slightly? Was his head moving up and down? Was his hand moving to his face? G. was so far away that I could not be sure. I returned to my breath. But later that day I thought I saw it again. Was G. trembling? Was he crying?

It was only at the end of the retreat, two days later, when I met up with G., that I received an answer. "You'll have to go back to the ashram alone," he said calmly. "Tell the sisters I'm going to stay for another course. I really need this." I looked at him closely but did not dare to probe. G.'s face looked strained but at peace. "It's just like last time," he said. "When I do meditation, all this shit starts coming up inside of me, and I see so clearly all the bad things I've done, and I can't stop crying." He paused. "I really need to start treating women differently." He wished me well, asked me to greet the sisters, abruptly turned around, and walked off to the meditation hall. I never saw him again.

On the last full day before the course ended, Goenkaji announced that those who wanted to could now break the long silence, but they should first put some distance between themselves and the meditation hall, so as not to disturb others who wanted to remain in silence and continue meditating. The moment he completed his sentence the sound of many loud voices erupted in the back of the hall, coming from a number of middle-aged Indian men. They spoke uncontrollably, a torrent of words issuing forth from their mouths like waterfalls as they narrated to each other their experiences over the past ten days. Since I was sitting not far from them I could hear phrases like, "hated it," "don't see the point," "waste of time," and the like. It was as if all the words that had been bottled up inside them for ten days were now spewing out in a surge of anger, frustration, and scorn. These men had clearly gotten nothing out of the course, and they reassured each other that meditation had not delivered the peace it was supposed to. I, for my part, wondered how vipassanā could *not* have impacted them in a positive way, how it could *not* have purified their mind. The only conclusion I could arrive at was that, given the demands of long hours of sitting and meditating, these men had not persevered in their efforts. They must have given up on vipassanā before they had a chance to experience what it could do for them. They seemed relieved now to be able to speak again, to interact with each other verbally, but their loud words, punctuated with laughter and derision, were creating a disturbance for the rest of us, until Goenkaji politely but firmly instructed them to leave the hall. They continued speaking loudly as they walked out the main door of the meditation hall. It was their way, it seemed, of making a public statement about what they thought of vipassanā meditation.

After the retreat, as I took the long bus ride back from Igatpuri to Pune over the dusty roads of the Deccan plateau, I became aware of changes in myself. I now seemed to be more conscious of the people around me who were crowded shoulder to shoulder inside the bus, many of them dirt poor. I found myself wondering more about their lives and their sufferings. I think I felt compassion for them more than anything else. Though I did not speak Marathi, I felt a oneness with them. I also noticed something else. I now felt a spontaneous gratefulness and love for the Buddha. He had bequeathed upon humankind the great teaching of the *dhamma* and a meditation practice that brought transformation. I did not go so far as to pray to the Buddha as some Mahāyānists do, but I perceived nonetheless a quiet inner satisfaction and gratefulness to him. And I was at peace.

When I returned to the C.P.S. Ashram, my new awareness translated into a new quality of living, just as Sister Brigitta had predicted before I left for the vipassanā course. I did in fact lose interest in reading newspapers for a month, as she said I would. Turning to the sports page each day to read the latest on the Indian cricket team was now unthinkable. It is not that I had lost interest in the world as a whole, it was just that much of what passed for news now seemed not so newsworthy after all; some of it even appeared shallow and worthless. My mind seemed clearer now, more aware of the passing nature of things, and less inclined to being swayed by the announcements, arguments, and opinions served up by the world's news machines.

I did not entirely abstain from reading, however, and I turned to books on Buddhism in the ashram library. But I did not even read much of that. Most of the time I was content to simply observe what existed around me, to live in the moment, to be present to my environment in a new and heightened way. I remembered how the people in the vipassanā course, hundreds of them, had gathered each day on the hillside outside the meditation hall, just before the grueling four-hour session, standing together in total silence, draped in colorful shawls, now more attentive than ever to the birds soaring in the sky or the beauty of the flowers and grass at their feet, drinking in every detail of what was all around them. If the wind blew just right, we could detect the faint music of children's voices from the town below. Silence had deepened our awareness of the world around us.

While it was true that even prior to the vipassanā course I had been to some degree spiritually present to my surroundings, it seemed that I was now even more so. Flowers swaying in the breeze, tiny fish swimming to the surface of the ashram pond, the late afternoon sunlight streaming through the thick foliage of the ashram garden—all these I seemed to appreciate in a more intense way for their loveliness, harmony, and mystery. I was seeing the world out of a perspective of deep silence, emptiness, and receptivity. I was losing myself in my surroundings, and I was happy.

The day after my return to the ashram from the vipassanā course, I was approached by a teenage Indian boy from the neighboring boarding school. This was an unexpected encounter. Although the boarding school was adjacent to the ashram compound, and students were welcome to stroll around the ashram garden anytime they liked, none ever did so. Many of us at the ashram were much older than they, and there was nothing about the ashram setting that might interest them to make a visit. But on this particular day I was sitting alone on the veranda looking out onto the garden when a young man, a stranger, climbed the steps and sat down next to me. We had never met before. He did not introduce himself. He just said, "Hello."

"Hello," I said.

"I have a problem," said the boy. "I wonder if you can help me."

"You are in love with a girl," I replied, "but she doesn't love you back."

The boy's eyes grew wide. "Yes, that's it exactly. But how did you know?"

"I don't know how I know," I said. "I just know."

"What should I do?" he asked.

I recommended that he practice meditation to get a right perspective on things, but he seemed uncomprehending and dissatisfied with my answer. Within a few minutes he left. I had certainly not given him any help.

The only way I can explain my knowledge of the boy's problem was that I was still living and acting out of a deep meditative state. I was very attentive to him, listening carefully to his every word, studying his face as he spoke. Because of intensive meditation practice I had become more intuitive. In my mind there was absolutely nothing remarkable about this. It seemed to be the most natural thing in the world. But it is also true that this happened only once. During the month after my return from Igatpuri, I never looked for opportunities to read a person's situation, and no one else approached me for advice. Gradually, over the course of a month, my meditation practice lessened and I found myself returning to my old everyday awareness.

When I told this story years later in a university class, one of my students suggested that reading the boy's problem the way I had was not so remarkable. "A teenage boy with a problem?" she said. "Of course it will have to do with girls!" And everyone laughed. All right, then, I'm willing to admit there is probably some truth to what she said, but at the moment when the boy told me he had a problem, it was not like I had to think things through. I just *knew*.

So far this chapter has described one kind of Buddhist meditation practice and the considerable benefits that can emerge from it. But I have not talked about Buddhism in general nor have I attempted to locate the place of vipassanā in the broad spectrum of Buddhist meditation practices. Nor have I begun to map out some of the most central agreements and disagreements between Buddhist and Christian doctrine. And, finally, I have not addressed the question whether vipassanā meditation, stripped as it is—at least in Goenkaji's approach—of much Buddhist doctrine and all Buddhist ritual, can justifiably regard itself as authentically Buddhist. During the meditation course in Igatpuri I heard stories from the life of the Buddha, to be sure, but very little Buddhist doctrine, certainly much less than is presented in two very good books on Goenkaji's vipassanā method.[13] I recall no mention of the famous Buddhist no-self (*anatta, an-ātma*) teaching nor anything about *nirvāṇa*[14] nor reference to dependent coorigination (*pratītya-samutpāda*). We were for the most part simply given a method. The method brought results, but how authentically Buddhist was this spirituality and by what standards should we judge it? And, in the final analysis, do such questions even matter?

I was fortunate to have had such an effective teacher in Goenkaji, but I knew there were other great Buddhist teachers, as well, such as the Dalai Lama and Thich Nhat Hanh, who taught forms of Buddhism and Buddhist meditation that were very different from Goenkaji's vipassanā. The Buddhism I encountered was not Tibetan Buddhism or Pure Land Buddhism or Zen. It did not offer devotion to Kwan-Yin or Avalokiteśvara or Mi-Lo. It was just one limb of an enormous tree of wisdom and practice called Buddhism.

I learned some important lessons from vipassanā practice. I learned, first of all, that meditation can purify our mind and heighten our compassion, even independently of prayer. Its importance does not lie primarily in its ability to help us pray better; vipassanā is already valuable in its own right as a spiritual discipline, just as prayer is.[15]

Second, with meditation the results are directly proportional to the effort expended. The more we put into meditation, the more we get out of it. It is therefore understandable why there is no talk of grace in vipassanā teaching.

Third, vipassanā can be effective even when Buddhist doctrine is kept to a minimum. We don't need to subscribe to the doctrines of no-self and no-God to experience the value of vipassanā. Just how important is doctrine, then?[16]

Fourth, meditation can unlock the memories stored in our subconscious. And, finally, with vipassanā practice we should expect to gain insight into reality in a gradual process of deepening awareness. It is not therefore necessary to experience sudden bursts of insight, as happens in Rinzai Zen when a koan or riddle is solved. In vipassanā meditation, wisdom and understanding come gradually, arriving slowly and surely.

11

Yoga

Yoga was an important part of my experience in India. I practiced my postures every day at the C.P.S. Ashram in Pune, always early in the morning, fresh from sleep, when my mind was clear and calm. I performed them barefoot—the standard yoga way—on a mat spread over the stone floor of the veranda. When December arrived I was often very cold. I was not physically tough like those hardy Hindu *sādhus* (wandering renunciates) who do yoga outdoors year-round in extreme heat and cold, clothed, as they say, only with the sky.[1] I did about twenty-five basic poses each morning, including shoulder stands and head stands. I usually practiced alone and afterward joined the other ashramites for Mass and breakfast.

I had practiced yoga in the United States many years before, but I had neglected it during my theology studies in Germany. At the university all the learning we received, even the spiritual learning, was from lectures and books, and I gradually drifted away from any idea of emptying my mind of thought and desire. Now I was back doing yoga again, because I was in India, the traditional center of yoga practice in the world, and because I now had leisure. I remembered from previous experience that yoga would help center my mind, bringing it to a state of deep repose and greater awareness, and thus enable me to become more present to myself and to the world around me. Anyone can experience such benefits after even just a short period of yoga practice, as long as they really give themselves to it and understand that yoga is ideally a spiritual discipline and not just a physical workout.

It wasn't long before some of the more advanced yoga practitioners living at the ashram began correcting my mistakes and teaching me new poses. They were yoga teachers from all around the world, now enrolled in advanced classes at the world famous Ramamani Iyengar Memorial Yoga Institute, which was located within walking distance of our ashram. They convinced me to enroll in beginner's classes at the institute. And so I attended yoga class once a week for over three years while continuing to do yoga privately every day at the ashram and eventually in our apartment after Mariam and I married. Mariam joined me in doing yoga, even before we were married. She was the only Muslim at the yoga institute, but all the teachers there—every one of them Hindu—treated her well. The issue of her Muslim background never came up. In fact, Geeta Iyengar, the daughter of the famous teacher and herself a well-known yoga instructor,[2] guided Mariam through both her pregnancies by teaching her *āsanas* that would help her in giving birth to our two sons.

Nowadays there is a flood of literature on yoga, and it is impossible to keep up with it all. Some of it is scholarly, and some of it is polemical, often arguing against Christians practicing yoga. I think this is an important enough issue to discuss at some length in what follows.

Two objections are commonly raised against Christians doing yoga. The first, articulated by a number of Christian groups in the West, argues that Christianity is about God and grace, whereas yoga rejects the notion of God and places all its emphasis on saving ourselves through our own efforts. Hence yoga and Christian faith are seen to be incompatible. When you're performing yoga poses everything is about *you*, and you are not thinking about God or praying to God.

The second objection to Christians practicing yoga is that yoga often involves meditation. Yogic and other Asian forms of meditation, so say these opponents of yoga, far from leading their practitioners to spiritual liberation, open them to the influence of the demonic. They see no value in meditation, only its dangers. Meditation is said to lead us away from

God and make us more vulnerable to demonic powers. This is not an argument put forth only by Protestant evangelicals; I have heard it expressed numerous times by Catholics, as well.

I will return to these two objections later in this chapter, both of which I take seriously. For now I would like to state that I do affirm the value of yoga, both in its ancient and modern versions, for one's spiritual development, regardless of the religion to which one belongs, but only if one follows the entire yoga path from beginning to end, which means that one takes seriously its very demanding moral code. Yoga is not valuable, therefore, only insofar as it augments Christian spirituality. It is already valuable in itself. I consider yoga one of Hinduism's greatest gifts to the world. Perhaps the question about yoga's compatibility with Christianity will ultimately be answered by how well yoga contributes to the life of love and selflessness that is ideally at the heart of all Christian spirituality.

In what follows I will introduce the basic contours of yoga, focusing on the famous "yoga with the eight limbs" (*aṣṭāṅga yoga*), adding remarks from my own personal experience whenever pertinent. It will also be necessary to distinguish classical yoga teaching on God from modern yoga doctrine, because this distinction will help to answer the question about yoga's compatibility with Christianity. And, finally, I will return to the main point of this chapter, which is to show what is distinctive to both Christian and yogic spirituality, so that some light might be shed on the relation between the two.

In its broadest meaning the Sanskrit word *yoga*[3] denotes any kind of spiritual yoke or discipline we might lay upon ourselves. For example, the Bhagavad-Gītā (ca. 200 BCE), a Hindu text from outside the classical yoga tradition, refers to the three basic Hindu spiritualities or paths (*mārgas*), namely meditation, devotion to God, and service to one's neighbor, as *yogas*. In this broad sense the word *yoga* is a synonym for *mārga*. Hence *jñāna yoga*, *bhakti yoga*, *karma yoga*. We could even borrow the word from its original Hindu setting and apply it to traditional Christian spirituality and call this "Christian yoga," a discipline that involves the love of God and neighbor, prayer, and the practice of mercy and justice.[4] But this expansive understanding of yoga as referring to almost any kind of spiritual discipline or path is not the yoga I am presenting in this chapter.

The more particular and customarily understood meaning of yoga involves the pursuit of inner awakening through attention to morality, controlled breathing, bodily exercises, and meditation. That is the yoga I will be discussing here. In this restricted sense, classical yoga, sometimes called *rāja yoga* ("royal yoga"), like the Upaniṣads (ca. 800–200 BCE), represents a kind of enlightenment spirituality (*jñāna mārga/yoga*) rather than a devotional one. Here the goal is liberation from suffering through a profound spiritual awakening or Self-realization. You go deep within yourself and discover a freedom of pure consciousness that already exists, a place untouched by the external world of change and suffering. This place, your hidden identity, is more you than your everyday understanding of yourself. This emphasis on awakening to a state of pure liberated awareness stands in contrast to devotional or relational spiritualities oriented to a union of love with the Divine, such as found in Hindu *bhakti* movements, Sufism, and Christianity. In these religions we find our freedom in the act of loving, in the selfless giving of ourselves to God and neighbor. These two paths, the one of meditation and the other of prayer and service, are sometimes united, especially nowadays in the global merging of religions and spiritualities.

We do not know when or how classical yoga was first practiced, but on the basis of archaeological evidence, there is some reason to believe that its birthplace was the (now extinct) Indus Valley civilization,[5] going back perhaps well before 3000 BCE. Yoga is quite likely the oldest form of Hindu spirituality still in existence and possibly the oldest continually practiced spirituality to be found anywhere on earth.

The most authoritative and widely known text on classical or royal yoga is Patañjali's *Yoga-Sūtra*, a summary of yoga theory and practice that has been dated anywhere from 200 BCE to 500 CE.[6] Patañjali compiled information from various yoga traditions of his day and then organized it into his famous book. He edited and systematized the data, dividing the material into four chapters. We who are Christian might call the *Yoga-Sūtra* the "Bible" of yoga practice and theory.

The standard Sanskrit name given to the yoga path as presented in Patañjali's *Yoga-Sūtra* is *aṣṭāṅga yoga* or the "yoga with the eight limbs."[7] This path is made up of eight limbs or steps, some of which can be practiced simultaneously with others, some of which can only be practiced in sequence, the mastery of one leading to the practice of the next.

The eight limbs or *aṅgas* are:

1. *yamas*: vows of self-restraint toward others; moral commandments

2. *niyamas*: disciplines not pertaining to our relation with the outside world

3. *āsanas*: postures

4. *prāṇāyāma*: breath control

5. *pratyāhāra*: bringing the five senses under control

6. *dhāraṇā*: concentration of the mind on one point

7. *dhyāna*: uninterrupted concentration; absorption

8. *samādhi*: final elimination of the subject-object distinction

In his presentation of yoga as being composed of eight limbs (*Yoga-Sūtra* II.28-III.8) Patañjali was likely influenced by Buddhism, with obvious parallels to the Buddha's Noble Eightfold Path. In Patañjali's articulation of yoga theory and practice it is the third limb, postures, that is most familiar to Westerners, though the precise implementation of the *āsanas* may vary greatly, depending on one's teacher and tradition. So when we normally think of yoga in the West we tend to think about the postures and nothing more. But if we learn that yoga is a path geared to the uprooting of all self-centeredness for the sake of attaining enlightenment, then we need to know about all the eight limbs or steps.

Notice, on this path of eight limbs, the gradual movement of attention from the outer world to the inner world. The eight steps guide the practitioner on a spiritual journey, starting with attention to the external material world and the human body and proceeding inward to ever-deeper levels of interiority, self-awareness, and freedom. I shall return to those eight steps below.

The most famous passage in the *Yoga-Sūtra* is I.2, which tells us how the goal of the spiritual quest is to be attained: *yogas´ citta-vṛtti-nirodhaḥ*.

This may be translated as "Yoga (is) mind-fluctuations-cessation." Or: "Yoga (is) ending the movements of mind." Or a more simple para-phrase: "Yoga means bringing the mind to silence." Here yoga is defined in terms of the state of mind necessary for enlightenment to occur. The mind should be placed in a state of deep tranquility, making it as steady as "the non-flickering flame of a candle in a windless room."[8] This is made possible especially through the process of advanced meditation in the final stages of *aṣṭāṅga yoga*. It is a totally quiescent mind that makes possible the experience of *kaivalya* or "isolation." *Kaivalya* is the special term used in yoga teaching to designate spiritual liberation or liberation from suffering. The spirit within (*puruṣa*) is to isolate itself, extricate itself from its entanglement with mind (a special kind of subtle matter), body, and world. No longer under the apparent influence of matter, it rests in its own pristine nature, which is characterized by pure consciousness, peace, and bliss. Like all enlightenment spiritualities, then, Patañjali's *Yoga-Sūtra* gives special importance to the mind and its transformation. Bringing the mind under control, of course, is standard for meditation practice everywhere.

This goal of separating spirit from matter struck me early on, even before my theological studies, not only as being quite odd, but also as being very different from the Christian way of looking at things. *Why be so negative about the body?* I thought to myself. *And why should we try to separate our soul or spirit from matter?* The answer we are given in the yoga tradition is that our identity has nothing to do with our body and our mind. We are spirit alone. Our ultimate identity is not even human. We are called to transcend our humanness, not transform it into a higher form of human selfhood or unite it with God in love. And yet with all my doubts I could see that my first Hindu teacher in

America, Usharbudh Arya, was clearly a man of great spiritual attainment. He had peace and wisdom. But I did not know how to reconcile
his yoga view of the human person with that of Christianity. I ended
up just putting my questions on hold. I was more interested in yoga
practice, anyway, and its practical benefits than anything else. I was
not yet interested in yoga metaphysics or in comparing Hindu thought
with Christian doctrine.

Returning to the classical yoga path, the eight *aṅgas*, or limbs, of
yoga presented by Patañjali in *Yoga-Sūtra* II.28–III.8, which constitute the very heart of yoga practice, are the *yamas* (moral restraints),
niyamas (ascetical disciplines), *āsanas* (postures), *prāṇāyāma* (breath
control), *pratyāhāra* (withdrawal of the senses), *dhāraṇā* (concentration), *dhyāna* (meditation), and *samādhi* (absorption). The first five are
called the "outer limbs" (*bahiraṅga*), the last three are the "inner limbs"
(*antaraṅga*) of the yoga path. Since, as we saw in *Yoga-Sūtra* I.2, yoga
is defined in terms of a discipline leading to perfect mind-control, it is
clear that each of the eight steps of *aṣṭāṅga yoga* is oriented, each in its
own way, toward gradually bringing the mind under control. Let me
now say a few words about each of them.

The first limb of the yoga path is called the *yamas*, a collection of
five practices of self-restraint toward others. They are the yoga path's
ethical foundation, the moral commandments that regulate our behavior
with the people and things around us. The five *yamas* are nonviolence
(*ahiṃsā*), truthfulness (*satya*), nonstealing (*asteya*), sexual control (*brah-
macarya*), and nonacquisitiveness (*aparigraha*). The *yamas* teach us that
there can be no enlightenment or liberation from suffering without the
elimination of every trace of self-centered attachment and desire. The
yamas address not just our unruly thinking mind, but also our ego and
our ethical behavior. *Yamas* are evidence that a moral foundation must
be laid if spiritual liberation is to take place. There can be no inner liberation without freedom from selfishness and ego. It is not enough to
simply bring the mind to a state of no longer generating thoughts and

ideas. There can be not even the slightest trace or impulse toward self-ishness, whether conscious or subconscious.

The second yoga *anga*, or limb, is a set of five *niyamas*. These are practices that we can perform even when living apart from others: traditionally in a cave or on a riverbank, but for practitioners today it could be anywhere where we can be alone. When we practice *niyamas*, we are not interacting with people and things around us, as when we are observing the *yamas*. The five *niyamas* are purity (*sauca*) of body, mind, and food,[9] contentment (*santosa*), self-mortification or austerity (*tapas*), the study of ourselves and of sacred scripture (*svādhyāya*), and surrender/devotion/dedication to the Lord (*īsvara-praṇidhāna*).

It's important to look a little closer at this last *niyama* now, "surrender to the Lord," because it is so crucial for a comparison of yoga with Christianity. One of the questions we might ask today when comparing the concept of God in yoga with that of Christianity is exactly which God in yoga discourse we are talking about. Do we mean the Lord as *Patañjali* presented it or do we mean the Lord in its more contemporary yoga understanding?

When looking more closely at the history of yoga, we discover that one of the greatest differences between classical and modern yoga is indeed its conception of God. We might go so far as to assert that there is no God at all in Patañjali's *Yoga-Sūtra*, whereas modern schools of yoga for the most part do affirm the existence of God. The term *īsvara*, or Lord, has undergone a radical reinterpretation since the time of Patañjali. His conception of the Lord is very different from a supreme Person and creator God as it is understood in most of Hinduism and in Christianity.[10] *Patañjali's "Lord" is neither the world's creator, nor a giver of grace, nor present within us, nor the goal of the spiritual path.* It has none of the qualities of that we normally attribute to God nor is it personal and interactive. A strange "Lord," indeed! Who or what is this Lord, and why would Patañjali recommend surrender to *īsvara* if this Lord is neither our helper nor our goal?

To answer this question we must turn to Patañjali's metaphysics and anthropology. In his system each of us human beings is essentially a limited *puruṣa* or spirit trapped in a body. Having now entered into association with a human body and a human mind, the *puruṣa* suffers from the illusion of being a human being and thereby becomes subject to all the afflictions of human life,[11] for life in the body is inevitably and unavoidably painful. But in reality, our true identity should be pure spirit existing in isolation from the physical. The yoga path would return us to this *transhuman* or *prehuman* spiritual state uncontaminated by matter and suffering.

Now for Patañjali the Lord (*īśvara*) is ontologically a *puruṣa* or spirit just like us, differing only on one essential point. *Īśvara* is the only *puruṣa* that has never suffered, having never having been subjected to the five afflictions associated with bodily existence. The Lord is eternally free of matter and suffering. But why this is so, why this particular *puruṣa* or spirit called "Lord" (*īśvara*) has never been shackled by matter is far from clear.[12]

Also, *īśvara*, like the other *puruṣas* or spirits, is not an all-pervading reality. And this lack of omnipresence is one of the things that prevents it from being regarded as a true Absolute or God. *All puruṣas or spirits are in essence spiritual monads existing in eternal isolation from each other.* They will never be united, never commune with one another, not even in liberation. They will never be united in love. There are no omnipresent spiritual realities anywhere in Patañjali's yoga metaphysics. There is no God that pervades the world nor even a sovereign Creator ruling "above" it.

As to grace, there is only one instance in which the Lord is said to be a helper or giver of grace.[13] *Yoga-Sūtra* I.26 states that *īśvara* is the teacher (*guru*) of the ancient seers, though how this happened is not clarified. In any case, the yoga path is graciously revealed by *īśvara*. But after that initial action *īśvara* does nothing. Once we learn of the yoga path, we are on our own to apply it to our lives, relying on our own effort to attain liberation. We do not therefore pray to *īśvara*, and *īśvara* does not offer us help to overcome suffering, nor do we ever become united with the "Lord." We are to follow the yoga path on our own, with the help of a human teacher, but not with the help of *īśvara* or a God. Originally, then, Pātañjali yoga, like early Buddhism and Theravāda Buddhism today, was essentially a self-help discipline.

Since Patañjali's Lord was not conceived to be interactive it makes sense that Patañjali would place *īśvara-praṇidhāna* as part of the *niyamas* instead of with the *yamas*. The *yamas*, as we have seen, are a set of restraints that govern our *relation* and even *interaction* with other realities, whether they be persons or things. The *yamas*, in short, apply to us as socially interactive beings. By contrast, the *niyamas* guide us in our activities as individuals not interacting with our surroundings. And that is why, I believe, Patañjali includes *īśvara-praṇidhāna* with the *niyamas*. For Patañjali there is no real interaction between *īśvara* and us suffering *puruṣas*, certainly no dynamic interactive relation of Lord and devotee. Hence it makes perfectly good sense to place talk of *īśvara* in the category of *niyamas* rather than with the *yamas*.

What, then, does *īśvara-praṇidhāna*, "surrender to the Lord," finally mean for Patañjali, if it is not understood as an interaction with a divine Person? What kind of activity is it?

When Patañjali prescribes *īśvara-praṇidhāna*, what he is talking about is meditation practice, not prayer to a divine Person or the surrender of oneself to the power of another. Meditation is not an interpersonal spiritual discipline; it is the harnessing of one's unruly mind through the focus on one or another object, visible or invisible, whether it be the breath, the symbol "Oṃ," a visual image, or some mental representation. "Surrender to the Lord" for Patañjali simply means meditation on *īśvara* as Oṃ, the recitation (*japa*)—first aloud, then mentally—of the sacred symbol as representative of *īśvara* (I.27–29). Meditation here also means the surrender of our attention to the conceptual perfections of *īśvara* as a liberated *puruṣa*, in other words to meditate on the Lord's perfections.[14] *Īśvara* serves as a model or example for the rest of us *puruṣas* that the goal after which we strive is very real and attainable through our own effort. One day, when we have reached our goal, we will experience the same freedom from suffering that we observe *īśvara* enjoying now. But

we do not become united with the Lord, unlike in Hindu *bhakti* or devotional movements of love.

There is thus an important practical reason why the discipline of
īśvara-praṇidhāna is recommended by Patañjali: as with meditation in
general, repeated attention on a single object, on almost anything really,
leads to a calming of the mind and a greater readiness for awakening.
This is perhaps the greatest usefulness in practicing *īśvara-praṇidhāna*.
It calms our mind and brings us to the threshold of the highest awareness. In sum, *īśvara* is a help to us, but not because the Lord does anything for us, but rather because our choice of making *īśvara* the object of
our meditation is beneficial to our spiritual development. Meditation on
īśvara purifies and pacifies our mind.

For various reasons, in a process that slowly developed over several
centuries and is still not completely clear, *īśvara* in yoga discourse was
gradually given most of the attributes that we now typically ascribe to
God. Even the self of later yoga teaching now starts to resemble the Self
of the Upaniṣads and Vedānta, no longer a spiritual monad in isolation
from all other spiritual realities, but the Absolute (*brahman*) permeating all beings, dwelling within us as our deepest Center. To awaken to
one's innermost reality now in yoga discourse means to awaken to the
omnipresent Absolute. Thus the understanding of "Lord" in the *Yoga-
Sūtra* was expanded from a limited and disconnected spiritual monad to
become—in common with the understanding of "Lord" in Vedānta, the
bhakti movements, and Christianity—the world's omnipresent creator,
pervader, and goal. The Lord of later yoga metaphysics, then, having
borrowed from Vedānta and *bhakti* some of the attributes of God, ends
up in modern times resembling much more the Lord of Christianity
than it does the original Lord of Patañjali's *Yoga-Sūtra*. In both modern
yoga and in Christianity we are speaking about a world-transcending
Creator who also dwells within us. But that is about as far as the commonalities go. The Lord of even modern yoga understanding is not
actively engaged in the world calling humanity to a greater social justice
or to a union and final transformation in the resurrection. There is no
divine activity in history.

Nowadays, given the fact that *īśvara* has undergone such a profound conceptual transformation, it is not unusual to hear yoga teachers expound their teachings in terms of "God." The goal of yoga practice is now to "know God," to "experience God within," to "uncover one's hidden unity with God," to "commune with God."[15] Here we have an understanding of yoga that leads to "God awakening," of realizing experientially our natural hidden oneness with an immanent God. But it is never very clear what the exact relation of Self to God is in popular yoga discourse. And very often, even when the path to liberation is said to involve the help of divine grace, the concept and operation of grace, too, are not normally clarified.

To return to the eight limbs of yoga: the third one is the *āsanas*. There are hundreds of yoga postures, all designed to harness body and mind. When practiced properly, they can be regarded as a form of rudimentary meditation. When you do *āsanas* properly, you become totally present to every bodily movement and prolonged stretch. If you don't, especially with postures that require balance, you will topple like a tree. So great focus is required, much like one-pointed concentration in meditation practice.

It sometimes happens that yoga teachers are mentally stuck on the physical plane. They forget that the purpose of yoga is to develop our inner life. For them the *āsanas* are everything. That is all they are really interested in. I once had a yoga teacher in India who had previously been a bodybuilder. It was amazing to see how well he could stretch, even as muscular as he was. He was as big as a football lineman in the United States. He loved showing us what difficult postures he could perform. But he had little regard for yoga as a spirituality. He enjoyed the physical power he wielded over students, too. He was bigger and stronger than any of us, and his presence was imposing and at times menacing. He liked going around the room barking at us to push harder, to hold that stretch a little longer. Occasionally he would give students such a hard slap on their arm or leg that they would lose balance. Sometimes he would snarl at students to push their stretch a bit too far, almost to the point of injury. Teachers like this are fixated on the physical and do not recognize the centrality of mindfulness for traditional yoga practice. They are not interested in meditation or in spiritual development. They are drill sergeants masquerading as yoga teachers. They are practicing what should be called "military yoga." Such teachers should be avoided.

Another teacher at the same institute in India was fond of how young-looking yoga practice had kept him. He was another person obsessed with the physical. He was lithe and lean, a middle-aged man without an ounce of fat. If you looked at him only from the shoulders down, you would think you were looking at a twenty-five-year-old. He once placed third in a national *āsana* contest in India against practitioners thirty years younger than himself. We know this because he told us about it—repeatedly. There were times when we were lying on our back practicing some posture, and he would stand over us and say, "Look at this body. Can you believe I'm over fifty years old?" You had no choice but to look at his body, of course; you were lying on the floor, immobile and helpless.

Prāṇāyāma, the fourth limb, is breath control. The word *prāṇa* has been translated as both "breath" and "life force." In yoga, understanding the way we breathe influences the way energy or life force flows through our body.

In *prāṇāyāma* we aren't just observing the breath flowing in and out of our nose, as we do in meditation; we are actually *controlling* the breath, trying to lengthen our inhalation and exhalation, at the same time that we are fixing our attention on it. But it is very hard to learn to breathe the *prāṇāyāma* way. You absolutely need a teacher; you can't learn *prāṇāyāma* out of a book. And *prāṇāyāma* is even more dangerous than being pushed too hard with the *āsanas*. It is well known that if you learn *prāṇāyāma* incorrectly, you can seriously damage your health by disturbing the body's inner harmony. It is the most dangerous of all the eight *aṅgas*.

At the Iyengar institute in India I tried *prāṇāyāma* for a few days, but with no success. A long firm pillow was placed under my spine to open up my torso and diaphragm as I breathed. But I could not find the deep place from which I was supposed to breathe.

Ideally you're supposed to practice *prāṇāyāma* an hour in the morning and an hour in the evening. One of the benefits of practicing this art of breath control is something that many people will find difficult to believe, but which I accept as true: *prāṇāyāma* practice can actually take the place of physical nourishment. The more you master *prāṇāyāma*, the less food you need. Don't ask me how; I have no idea how it works. But it's due to *prāṇāyāma* that yogis living in the Himalayas can survive with little or no food. A middle-aged yoga teacher I knew in India reached the point where he was living on only four bananas a day, a liter of milk, water, and some tea. That was his entire diet. He was becoming a master of *prāṇāyāma*, and his goal was to one day survive on so little food that he could eventually leave society and head off to the mountains.

With *prāṇāyāma* some yogis train themselves to reach the point of taking only a few breaths of air per minute. It's because of *prāṇāyāma* that yoga masters can be buried in a coffin underground for hours at a time, and then later the coffin is dug up, the lid is pried off, and they pop up smiling and unscathed.

How does *prāṇāyāma* relate to mind control? There is a saying in yoga that "the breath is the spine of the mind." If you can steady your breath, lengthen it more and more, you can greatly control the fluctuations of your mind. We know that when children are excited, they are almost out of breath; the words just tumble out. Their breath is short and irregular, because of their state of mind. But long ago yoga masters discovered that the reverse is also true: the breath can impact the mind. By controlling and lengthening our breath we can learn to control our mind. *Prāṇāyāma* thus prepares the mind for the next stages of mind control.

Aṅga number five is *pratyāhāra*, withdrawal of the senses. Our mind is to turn its attention away from the constant bombardment of external stimuli on the five senses of smelling, tasting, seeing, touching, and hearing. The Bhagavad-Gītā 2:58 is sometimes cited here: "One who is able to withdraw his senses from sense objects, as the tortoise withdraws its limbs within the shell, is firmly fixed in perfect knowledge." The transition from the world of the senses to the inner world of the spirit is a major theme in most Hindu spiritualities. That is why in India the figure of a turtle is engraved in the floor just inside the temple or in the ground just outside. When we enter the temple, we are to leave behind attention to sensuous and worldly concerns and be attentive to the presence of the Divine.

If we continue to perceive sounds, smells, skin sensations, and the like, we are to become indifferent to them. *Pratyāhāra* means the withdrawal of the mind into itself rather than the normal interaction of the mind with the sense-organs and the sense-objects of the external world.

The final three *aṅgas* of the yoga path are called the "inner limbs," as they involve meditation proper. They are *dhāraṇā, dhyāna,* and *samādhi.*

Dhāraṇā, the sixth limb, is concentration of the mind on one point. Sometimes *dhāraṇā* is called simply "concentration" or "attention" and treated as the step just prior to meditation practice rather than a stage of meditation itself. It means a constant focus of the mind on one object and tenaciously bringing the mind back to that object whenever it wavers. The result is calm; when the mind is focused on one thing, it becomes composed.

Even apart from meditation we sometimes have the experience of being so absorbed in other activities that we become completely unaware of the passage of time, as when we're reading a good book or listening to music or perhaps gazing into the eyes of our beloved. At that time we are at peace. But *dhāraṇā* is more extreme in its practice of concentration; it is an unwavering concentration *forced* upon the mind even when the mind wants to go elsewhere. It requires hard work to subdue the mind and keep one's awareness channeled in one direction.

The seventh limb is called *dhyāna,* or continuation of attention, a more advanced state of concentration in which the meditator's awareness of self begins to recede through the continuous flow of attention on the object of meditation. It is uninterrupted concentration on an object without distraction. It is to be regarded as a more advanced stage of meditation than *dhāraṇā.*

The eighth and final *aṅga* is *samādhi,* or absorption, the final practice leading to enlightenment. Here continued uninterrupted concentration results in the final withdrawal of normal awareness, the dissolving of the yogi's normal self-awareness into the higher consciousness of unity. The sense of being a doer or meditator has melted away. Patañjali distinguishes here higher and lower states of *samādhi.* The first involves the continued presence of the object of meditation, but nothing else. By contrast, the higher *samādhi* is completely without content. It is pure awareness. It is thus difficult to distinguish the higher *samādhi* from enlightenment itself.[16]

The main attraction to yoga in the Western world is the practice of the *āsanas.* I have noticed over the years how little attention is thus given to the first limb of yoga, its moral foundation. For many people, yoga practice is essentially a physical workout. Others, by contrast, take up yoga as a spiritual practice, as a means to grow in self-awareness and peace. They combine meditation with *āsana* practice. But even many of these yoga practitioners are unaware of the significance of the *yamas* or moral foundation for the spiritual path.

We might raise the question, then, given the fact that so many people find so much value in yoga practice even without practicing the *yamas,* whether the moral foundation is as essential to yoga practice as traditional *aṣṭāṅga yoga* has always maintained. Can a person ignore the *yamas* and still reach spiritual perfection? What if that person were even to display extraordinary powers (*siddhis, vibhūtis*) without having first submitted him- or herself to the rigorous demands of the yoga moral code? Would not such powers be evidence that the highest spiritual goal has been reached without the strict practice of morality?

One of the most notorious alleged transgressions of *yama* practice occurred more than thirty years ago and involved a well-known Indian guru who was the head of the yoga organization in the United States to which I belonged for some time. The guru had made a name for himself, among other ways, by displaying remarkable powers at a well-known midwestern U.S. clinic in 1970. Through years of intense yoga practice beginning in the Himalayas he had attained a very advanced level of meditation and mind control, which in turn allowed him almost complete mastery over his body. In addition to control of his body, he claimed to possess a "perfect control of the mind." As he was able to demonstrate at the U.S. clinic, he could perform some quite extraordinary feats through sheer willpower, such as making his heart stop beating for seventeen seconds without adverse effect. He could increase the temperature of one part of his hand while decreasing the temperature in another part. Perhaps most remarkably, he demonstrated his ability to control objects at a distance. For example, he caused a knitting needle mounted on an axle five feet from him to revolve at will. For many people in his organization such displays of power and mind control were an indication that the swami was a living liberated being, a person who had attained the highest level of awareness, wisdom, power, and holiness, a veritable God walking among us, a man who was therefore beyond all moral reproach.

The swami's godlike reputation was abruptly called into question some years later when a number of the younger women in his organization came forth with allegations of brutal sexual exploitation, including rape.[17] Each of them, it turned out, had been suffering in secret, confused, alone, betrayed by their guru, anguishing, not wanting to believe what had happened. Gradually each woman discovered she was not the only victim, that her spiritual guide, the famous swami, was in fact a serial predator. There is no need here to go into detail, though the court summaries are easily available online, and a number of reputable newspapers and journals have given detailed reports. Before the swami could be brought to court he fled the United States and died some years later in India. Some of the more important figures in his organization continue to deny to this day any wrongdoing on the swami's part; they are unable to bring themselves to accept the women's testimony.

What does the yoga tradition teach about such a guru's display of power and the relation of that power to spiritual liberation? What role do the special powers (*siddhis*) play in the spiritual quest, for example, the ability to move objects at a distance? Are they important? An entire section of Patañjali's *Yoga-Sūtra* is given to a discussion of these *siddhis* or *vibhūtis*. It teaches that such powers are to be expected in one who has attained an advanced stage of mind control. They are a normal and expected phenomenon. They are a natural by-product of advanced mental calm. But nowhere is it said that such powers are necessary for spiritual liberation or that they are even desirable. In fact, the opposite is true. These so-called paranormal powers are said to be a distraction, even a danger, to true spiritual development, and they are to be ignored. The classical yoga tradition is well aware of the misuse of such powers for worldly or selfish gain, leading to the downfall of the yogi. And so, while the *Yoga-Sūtra* does witness to the existence of yogic powers, it is clear that such powers and the mind control that caused their manifestation cannot in themselves be regarded as an automatic sign of spiritual attainment or maturity. *Mind control and selfish desire can coexist. Advanced mind control is no guarantee of moral purity.* Without the control of ego, pride, and desire, there can be no talk of spiritual attainment. A thorough and complete cleansing of one's whole being occurs only when one is completely free of the impulses of the ego and its cravings; even latent impulses, urges to engage in sensual indulgence or to control or use another person for one's own pleasure or gain, must be eliminated.

In Patañjali's understanding, complete liberation is impossible to attain without the ordering of the whole of one's life to moral principles of self-restraint toward others, which in their most positive interpretation might be translated as love, compassion, and charity. But if the *yamas* are treated lightly, whether through the practice of theft, sexual license, or deception, the final goal cannot be reached. There is no bypassing them, even with complete mastery of the other *aṅgas*. The true goal of yoga, then, is this: *the complete harnessing of both the mind and the ego* for the purpose of spiritual realization. Mind control and ego control are not synonymous. Both are required for liberation. Hence the necessity to begin the yoga path with the moral commandments called *yamas*.

This observation is important when we seek to discern whether yoga is compatible with the Christian spiritual life. Although the *yamas* do not mention love, they represent a very high ideal of moral practice and self-abnegation that resonates strongly with the selflessness demanded of the followers of Jesus.

Let's turn now to the idea of transcending the earthly body in yoga and Christianity. I had previously noted the contrast, even opposition, between classical yoga's negative view of the body and the more positive Christian hope in the resurrection of the whole person, both body and soul. But this contrast should not blind us to a surprising fundamental agreement about life in the earthly body. Both Patañjali and Christianity regard *bodily existence in this world as a problem to be overcome*. It is not only true for Hindu practitioners of yoga, but also for Christian devotees of a personal God that life in this earthly body is experienced as unsatisfactory. For it is in the body that we suffer illness and disease. And as our body ages and withers we suffer a gradual diminishment of our physical and mental powers. All this is as obviously true for Christians as it is for Hindus.

We might call this realistic assessment of life in the body a "healthy dualism." *Dualism* is normally a much maligned word in Christian theology. Anthropological dualisms teach that something about us as human beings is intrinsically good and something about us is intrinsically evil and beyond rescuing. It is always the body and soul that are referred to: the soul is good, but the body is evil. Christianity has combated dualistic attitudes of this type from its very beginnings in Gnosticism, Manichaeism, and various brands of Platonism and Neo-Platonism. It even exists in the minds of Christians today whenever they think that the final goal of the spiritual life is for their souls to get to heaven, as if God's promises were for the soul alone and not for the whole human person. Such dualism marks classical yoga anthropology, too, as we have seen. The spirit (*puruṣa*) wants to divest itself of all matter (*prakṛti*). But in contrast to this extreme dualism there is a healthy dualism that recognizes that even with the authentic Christian hope for the redemption and transformation of the whole person in the resurrection, all is not well with the body here on earth below. Besides the gradual decline of the body with the passage of time, there is also the problem that the desires and appetites of our material nature must be brought under control; when left unchecked, they have the capacity to be a distraction and even an impediment to spiritual growth. That is one of the truths of a healthy dualism shared by both Christians and Hindus.

And in further support of this healthy dualism is the awareness that we make every day here on earth; namely, that *we are a spiritual reality that transcends our own body*. We tend to the body and care for it and suffer from it and experience it as an object of our awareness. So, in a certain sense, we are, in fact, *not* the body, as Hindus would say, or using a Christian frame of reference, we might say that we are *more* than just our body. Our relation to our own body is such a mysterious thing, with both positive and negative ramifications of our attitudes to it, that it is no wonder that so many interpretations have been given to it by the different religions and philosophies throughout history.

We see this tension in St. Paul, who articulates both positive and negative attitudes to life in the body. He teaches that as long as we are in the earthly body—not just inordinately attached *to* the body, but actually *in* the body—we are not yet perfectly one with God. He also clearly sees how the physical body can deflect one's attention from spiritual goals. That is why he says, "I buffet my body and make it my slave" (1 Cor. 9:27). But Paul does not ultimately strive after a nonbodily state, as in Patañjali, even though life in the earthly body presents so many challenges. He longs for life with God in the resurrected body, which he calls a building or house built by God, whereas the earthly body is only a tent: "For we know that if the tent, which is our earthly home, is destroyed, we have a building from God, a house not made with hands, eternal in the heavens. For in this tent we groan, longing to put on our heavenly dwelling, if indeed by putting it on we may not be found naked. For while we are still in this tent we groan, being burdened—not that we would be unclothed, but that we would be further clothed, so that what is mortal may be swallowed up by life. He who has prepared us for this very thing is God, who has given us the Spirit as a guarantee" (2 Cor. 5:1–5). For Paul, the earthly body must finally give way to the heavenly resurrection body. But in both cases it is a body; it is not just pure spirit.

Both Hindus and Christians, then, desire to transcend the limitations of earthly embodiment. Yoga's solution is to leave behind the body altogether (an extreme dualism) in the attainment of a pure higher consciousness that no longer generates karma and therefore permits escape from future physical embodiment. Christianity's answer is very different. Its hope is in God's mercy and the transformation and liberation of the whole person that occurs in the full and final encounter with divine love in the freedom of the resurrection. But a healthy dualism, that is, a healthy disciplining of the body, helps us to align ourselves to God's will here on earth.

What, then, is the value of the yoga path for Christians? Patañjali's *aṣṭāṅga yoga* practices, especially the *yamas* and the *niyamas,* and the way these practices are illumined by the traditional commentaries, are enormously impressive in their ethical and spiritual depth. Here it makes no difference whether we give them a classical or a modern interpretation. The *yamas* act as a mechanism to prevent yoga practice from falling prey to self-centeredness and self-interested desire. Many Christians will immediately recognize an affinity with some of these yamic and niyamic principles and practices from their own Christian ascesis and moral ideals. The disciplining of the body, the striving to overcome all selfishness in our interaction with the persons and things around us, the focus on keeping both mind and heart pure, the attempt to avoid sexual license—all these are themes more or less familiar to the spiritual life of the Christian.

If this is so, if there is already such a great ethical and ascetical convergence between yoga and Christian spirituality, then why is it that so many Christians today have been drawn to yoga practice as something additional and helpful to what they already know? What is it that yoga offers that is missing or underdeveloped in Christian spirituality? I believe there are many answers.

First, yoga takes a very holistic approach to spiritual development, since both body and mind are deliberately and systematically brought under control and made to serve spiritual ends. The *final goal* of yoga might be defined in dualistic terms as a separation of the body from the spirit, but the *path* to that goal involves *sustained attention to the body and mind* as vehicles or tools of liberation.

Second, yoga is a path replete with sound wisdom and practical advice. It teaches us to be more attentive to the changing states of our body and mind, to learn the deep connection between physical and mental discipline, between breath and mind, and we are even offered guidance as to which diets are most conducive to spiritual awareness. All our life, in its mental, physical, and spiritual dimensions, potentially falls under the scope of yoga's very *elaborate practical advice.*

Third, there is really nothing like the physical postures (*āsanas*) in Christian practice, not even in Eastern Christendom's combining of hesychastic prayer with certain bodily postures. The yogic use of balance and stretching as a practical means to slow down the mind and enable it to remain in the present moment helps to overcome the restlessness and lack of focus we sometimes experience in meditation and prayer. Physical practice can thus be a way of settling into silence, a bridge from a scattered to a more focused state of mind. We can experience quiet and calm whenever we focus on our physical practice. Those who are familiar with *āsana* practice know the deep sense of peace and wholeness that comes at the end of each session from the practice of *śavāsana*.[18] The harnessing of an unruly mind, then, is as much a benefit of posture practice as is the disciplining of the body in other ways. We learn to be patient with ourselves in *āsana* practice, too, as it sometimes takes months and even years to master a particular posture.

Fourth, many people who are at first uninterested in meditation when they take up yoga practice gradually come to discover its value, especially if they have a teacher who understands that yoga's ultimate aim is spiritual health, not merely physical health. They discover the *calming effect of meditation* and its capability, if done in combination with the *yamas,* to help uproot self-centered awareness. As with all enlightenment-oriented spiritualities, one of the strengths of yoga is the attention it gives to the mind and its habits.

And, finally, through yoga practice Christians learn just how much can be accomplished already in the spiritual life through *effort alone.* With determination and with the practice of the *yamas* as a strong moral foundation, one can orient one's mind toward virtue, selflessness, and inner silence. This does not mean that spiritual and moral perfection or even the final goal of the Christian spiritual life, namely union with God in love, can be accomplished through effort alone; to make such an assertion would be akin to the Pelagianism condemned long ago by the church. But it does teach us that even in a religion of grace like Christianity we might learn to give greater attention to effort than we are normally accustomed to doing.

For all the positive value that comes from yoga, there are, of course, limitations of yoga for Christian spirituality. Though ideally practiced under the guidance of a wise and experienced teacher, yoga is basically a self-help discipline. This is true in both its ancient and modern expressions. How much we put into yoga practice determines how much we get out of it. It is not a practice that involves prayer to God, though Christian practitioners often enough use yoga as a tool to center themselves so that they may learn to pray from a deeper place within themselves. But the focus of yoga is normally meditation, not prayer.

As effective as yoga practice has proved itself to be as a self-help discipline over the centuries, the fact remains that from the Christian perspective, with its teaching of the absolute centrality and necessity of divine grace and love, spiritualities like yoga that rely primarily on one's own effort have their particular limitations and dangers. Let me name one of these limitations now. The dangers will come next.

First, in terms of a limitation, since the ultimate goal of the Christian spiritual life is union with a God of love, yoga can only take a person so far. Yoga practice may help to purify the mind and heart, but it does not teach people how to give their hearts to God or to open themselves to God who is Person. In yoga there is no asking or entreaty to a personal God. Yoga does not involve interpersonal or interactive practices with a God of grace and love. Its entire focus is on disciplining the mind and body, in order to make possible an awakening to a non-interactive inner spiritual reality. There is *no relationship with a God of love* here, no prayer, no abandonment to divine love or to the sovereignty of the divine will. Yoga may uncover a unity of higher consciousness hidden within an individual, but it cannot bring about a unity of love between persons.

We might reflect a bit on why it is that no amount of human effort by itself can create union with a personal God or, for that matter, with any human person. It belongs to the very definition of persons, whether divine or human, that they are able to freely choose to reveal themselves and to bestow their presence upon another. One of my teachers in India, the great Jesuit philosopher and indologist Richard De Smet, used to point out that even a child can withhold its mystery from another. We cannot willfully break into intimacy with another person, let alone single-handedly cause a union of love. We may love another person, but we cannot be united with that person unless the individual freely opens him- or herself and offers him- or herself to us. There has to be a mutual unveiling and self-gift of one person to the other and even a mutual surrender. From the Christian perspective, not only are we called to surrender to God; even God surrenders to us on the cross, thereby unveiling the depth of divine love. God does this for the purpose of eliciting or winning our love and to perfect us in love. The cross is an event by which both divine love and divine patience are unveiled.

Persons, then, reveal themselves through what they do. If they do not act we cannot know them, we cannot know if they are good or evil, and we cannot know their will and intent. It is not enough to go within ourselves in meditation to try and uncover a personal and interactive God. In meditation we might discover something of the mystery of divine presence and divine peace, but we will learn little of God's dynamic love and active personhood. In meditation we do not find much evidence for God as loving Person. In meditation we can never discover historical events that are the signs of God's personhood and love. Meditation practice cannot uncover the life, death, and resurrection of Christ, events that reveal in a special way the depth of God's love for us. These events must be proclaimed to us if we are to know about them. Simply going inside ourselves will not discover them.

This is where grace comes in. Divine grace is often understood in Christianity to be a kind of medicine given by God to help restore or heal (*gratia sanans*) our disordered will and to help us overcome sin. Although this is indeed a genuine function of grace, it is not the only meaning and perhaps not even the primary meaning of the word. For the fact is, even if sin had never entered the world, God's grace would still be necessary for us to grow in awareness of God's love, because of the sheer unknowability of God as Person. Access to the inner mystery of a person must always come to us as a gift. Divine grace is a kind of gift, but it is a necessary gift. We can finally only come to know God if God freely chooses to reveal Godself to us. Intimacy with God is otherwise beyond our reach. Our effort and longing can only prepare our heart for union with God; it cannot cause God to enter into a relationship with us.

Moreover, the love and mercy of God are freely offered to all people, even to the sinner and to those who do not even seek to know God. Such love cannot be earned even by the pious. There is no point in trying to earn a love that is already freely offered. Even in modern yoga teaching with its goal of union with God, we hear nothing about an unmerited grace or rescue offered to those who are not even seeking spiritual liberation.

Now, as to the two dangers of yoga practice I mentioned above, the first is this: the danger of self-preoccupation, even narcissism. This danger exists despite the fact that one of the primary goals of yoga practice is to overcome attachment to the lower self, of giving the ego-centered self too much importance and attention. Nevertheless, in self-help spiritualities like yoga there is always the temptation to quantify and manipulate our spiritual development, always focusing on ourselves rather than on God. There is the risk of dwelling too much on our mental states, on our spiritual progress, and on our success in mastering more and more difficult *āsanas* and stages of meditation: I did this, and this happened to me. Then I did that, and that happened to me. As if the whole of one's spiritual life were the result of one's own doing. A sense of pride, then, can easily creep into yoga practice. The possibilities of self-deception in the spiritual life, of the prideful ego reasserting and rebuilding itself even after strenuous disciplines of self-denial, are almost endless.[19] But in Christian spirituality our gaze is ideally fixed more on God and on our neighbor than on ourselves and our spiritual attainment. We are to lose ourselves in love of the other, but not as a strategy to attain a high spiritual state. We love the other, because the other is intrinsically worth loving.

In Christian spirituality a healthy relationship with God is measured by obedience to God's will, by striving after a pure heart, and by the practice of charity toward others. It is not measured by altered states of consciousness or by the measurability of psycho-physical phenomena or by the manifestation of paranormal powers. It is gauged by the degree to which we grow in love, humility, and charity.

In yoga, as we have seen, it is possible to neglect the moral foundation altogether, the *yamas,* while practicing whatever other *aṅgas* we choose. When this happens, when morality receives little attention in yoga practice, chances are there is also no sense of moral accountability before God or of recognition of God's lordship. The "God-within" of contemporary yoga is not a fully personal God, who would—even as a God of love—hold us morally accountable for our actions. And yet it is still possible for us to bring our Christian understanding of God's lordship to the practice of yoga.

The second danger of yoga practice is that we might thereby be opening ourselves to the influence of the demonic, especially when we practice meditation. I was recently asked to respond as a Catholic practitioner of yoga to the charges frequently made by evangelical Christians—and sometimes by Catholics, too—that yogic and other Eastern forms of meditation open practitioners to the influence of demonic powers.

Far from denying this possibility, I find worth recalling that the same threat of the demonic is well attested to also in the Christian tradition of prayer. Jesus, who sets the example of prayer par excellence for Christians, was himself assailed by demons. Some of his more saintly followers through the ages, people of prayer such as St. Anthony of the Desert (251–356), St. Ignatius of Loyola (1491–1556), St. Teresa of Avila (1515–1582), St. John of the Cross (1542–1591), and St. John Vianney (1786–1859), give witness to attacks and temptations by demonic forces. Should we therefore stop praying, because men and women of deep and persistent prayer have attracted the attention of the demons? The answer is obviously no. Nevertheless, in both prayer and meditation, one might expect the assault of dark forces.

But in a certain sense I've not really addressed the issue. For the evangelicals are, in fact, asking an important, but slightly different question. What they are asking is whether meditation, in and of itself, practiced alone, independently of prayer, makes us more susceptible to falling under the sway of the demonic than when we pray. For to be assailed by demons, as happens in prayer, is not necessarily to fall under their influence. But does meditation expose us even more, make us even more vulnerable to the power of the demonic?[20]

Let me make clear before I proceed that I do not find meditation to be valuable only insofar as it is connected to the practice of prayer, for example, in the sense that meditation practice can help us to enter into a deeper center of our person, our "heart," from which we might learn to pray more deeply and more purely. As much as I am convinced of meditation's value as a help to prayer, I also find meditation valuable in itself, independently of prayer, as a method that sharpens our awareness of who we are, making us more aware of the false self that we have created and that must finally dissolve in the presence of truth.

I do think that those who do not believe in the demonic are more vulnerable to its subtle attacks. Such yoga practitioners are not on guard. Why should they be? After all, Patañjali's *Yoga-Sūtra* says nothing about the demonic and its possible influence. So one's susceptibility to the demonic will be determined by the beliefs or lack of beliefs one brings from Hinduism and Christianity to the practice of yoga and meditation. The issue is not really whether meditation makes us more vulnerable to the demonic than does prayer, but rather how aware we are of the reality of the demonic in the first place, whether we meditate or whether we choose to pray. I think the answer has to do more with the overall faith context of meditation and prayer than with its practice alone.

Also, many yoga practitioners I've met who have not taken yoga's moral foundation very seriously are sometimes a bit too proud of their achievements as practitioners and teachers. They are too focused on themselves. Their egos are therefore sometimes very big. They are therefore especially vulnerable to the whispering flattery of demons who would lead them astray. But a Christian who practices yoga should be more prepared to recognize the influence of the demons, since that person knows of their existence and influence from the Gospels and from the whole of the New Testament.

I remember almost twenty years ago how the first time I mentioned the word *yoga* in one of my theology classes, many of my students, most of whom were Christian, could not stifle their laughter. They thought the whole idea of practicing yoga was strange and exotic, something that people of other religions did. Only one student out of about seventy that day had ever tried yoga. But nowadays almost every hand goes up when I ask which students have practiced yoga. Things have clearly changed. Yoga is more prevalent now than ever among people living in the West. If my students end up going deeper into yoga than simply practicing *āsanas*, they will learn just how much the wisdom of ancient India can spiritually nourish them, even here on the other side of the world, in twenty-first-century America. This is a lesson I learned all those years ago in India, and one that I continue to learn through my practice today.

12

A Catholic Holy Man

I had hoped to one day meet Father Bede Griffiths (1906–1993) after discovering his autobiography, *The Golden String* (1954), during my time in the New Mexico monastery. Along with Thomas Merton he was one of the most famous Catholic monks of the twentieth century. It would be ten years before I finally met Father Bede in his ashram in India. In the meantime, mostly during theology studies in Germany, I had read some of his other works: *Christ in India* (1967), *Vedanta and Christian Faith* (1973), *Return to the Center* (1976), *The Marriage of East and West* (1982), and *The Cosmic Revelation* (1983). These books were written by a Catholic priest and monk from England who lived almost forty years in India. Father Bede's works bore witness to the spiritual riches of other religions and their significance for Christian spirituality and theology. He wrote out of his experience of living among the great religions of India, of how India had transformed him. He had been drawn to India because he felt there was something missing from the contemporary Western world, a natural movement within that had become stifled even in Christianity. He had gone to India, he famously wrote, "to discover the other half of my soul."[1]

It was in India that he came to value Hindu and Buddhist forms of meditation for Christian spirituality. From Hindu monks he learned a greater simplicity of life than anything he had experienced in the West. It was also in India that he became convinced that people of other religions had come to experience the ultimate reality in very different ways than Christians had done and that these experiences had led to a real transformation and holiness.

Reading about all this awakened in me a desire to know more about Hinduism and Buddhism. It was the main reason I had come to India. Among other things, I wanted to learn about *enlightenment,* which is such a key word in Hindu and Buddhist spirituality. Many Hindu schools of thought, along with all forms of Buddhism, have proclaimed for thousands of years that spiritual freedom can only come when enlightenment is attained, when right awareness dawns, when we are finally able to understand the true nature of self and world, no longer filtering reality through our egos and desires. We eventually become free from the burden of the lower self and discover ourselves to be connected at a deeper level with the ultimate reality. Here was a different spirituality than I had come to know in Christianity. I had already learned from the Psalms that all creation gives glory to God, that is, that the majesty and goodness of the Creator are reflected in all creation, but the Psalms did not speak of God as our true Self or as the hidden Ground of all that exists, a mysterious presence of the Infinite within ourselves deeper than our own subconscious. In Griffiths's words:

> What is this "transcendent Mystery", this "ultimate Truth", this "universal Law"? These are words we use to express the inexpressible. This is the whole problem of life, which continually baffles our reason. The ultimate meaning and purpose of life cannot be expressed, cannot properly be thought. It is present everywhere, in everything, yet it always escapes our grasp. It is the "Ground" of all existence, that from which all things come, to which all things return, but which never appears. It is "within" all things, "above" all things, "beyond" all things, but it cannot be identified with anything. Without it nothing could exist, without it nothing can be known, yet it is itself unknown. It is that by which everything is known, yet which itself remains unknown. It is "unseen but seeing, unheard but hearing, unperceived but perceiving, un-

known but knowing" (Bṛhadāraṇyaka Upaniṣad, 3.8.2). This is the mystery upon which both Indian and Chinese thought lighted in the sixth century before Christ. They call it Brahman, Atman, Nirvana, Tao, but these are only names for what cannot be named. We speak of "God", but this is only a name for this inexpressible mystery.[2]

The religion outside of Christianity that Bede knew best was Hinduism. During our first discussion at his ashram, he advised me to approach Hindu doctrine and spirituality from a chronological standpoint. He saw Hindu history as a magnificent unfolding of wisdom that had been taking place over a period of thousands of years, starting with its beginnings more than three thousand years ago. This development, he was convinced, could not have been accomplished without God's revelation and grace. Hinduism was about going beyond the mind and senses and discovering the divine presence in our heart and in the heart of all reality. This was an experience made possible by God.

There was also the discovery of divine love in Hinduism, according to Bede, starting with the Bhagavad-Gītā (200 BCE) and gathering force through Hindu history. Teachings of divine love and grace become dominant in most Hindu spiritualities, so that in the course of time we note a greater and greater convergence between Hindu and Christian teaching. And yet important differences remain, he said. The strength of Christianity is, of course, the man Jesus Christ, the Divine Word made a human being, God uniting himself with the human race. Through Christ, a man who really suffered and died, God gave a dignity to all human suffering and death. In Christ's resurrection we learn further that all created reality is destined to be transformed and integrated into the divine life, to share in God's infinity and eternity. Individuals in their entirety, all human relationships, everything having value from the perspective of divine love will be saved.

People sometimes overlook just how well versed Bede was in the Catholic theological tradition. The man who was writing about the value of other religions for Christians had already carefully studied the patristic theologians and Aquinas as well as contemporaries like Karl Rahner, whose work he greatly admired. He also had a good sense of church history and was able to distinguish between true and false understandings of magisterial authority. He was sometimes critical of the exercise of authority from above. But clearly his greatest contribution to the church was in showing his Christian readers how much they stood to gain spiritually through exposure to other religions. At Bede's memorial service, the local bishop, Bishop Gabriel of Tiruchirapalli, said, "Dom Bede Griffiths is a great gift to the Indian Church. He is a saint."[3]

Father Bede taught that the time had come for Christians to explore what God had given other religions. In *The Cosmic Revelation* he writes: "Today we are aware of the presence in other religions of a wisdom and experience of God which challenges the Church. I feel that we are really entering a new epoch. For almost two thousand years the Christian Church grew up with the understanding that it alone was the true religion; that there was no religion outside Christianity which was not fundamentally false, or at best no more than a natural religion. Only today, in these last few years, have Christians begun to discover the riches which God has lavished on other nations."[4]

I had never before encountered such an open and welcoming approach to other religions in my theological training in Germany. It went even beyond the teaching of Vatican II (1962–65), in which the new Catholic understanding of other religions had been articulated. The Vatican II document *Nostra Aetate* had clearly affirmed the spiritual value of Hinduism, Buddhism, and Islam, but it did not go so far as to say that these religions were founded on revelation, unlike Judaism and Christianity. But Bede stated this explicitly, and in doing so he gave the religions a higher value than the council had done.

Father Bede read the world in light of Christ, and he evaluated the world religions in view of what God had revealed in Christ. Moreover, he taught that all humanity was saved in Christ. In an interview published near the end of his life, he says, "The grace of Christ is present in some way to every human being from the beginning to the end. Normally it comes through their traditional religion . . . In India sometimes you meet the most Christlike people among Hindus, and there is no doubt that the Presence is there."[5]

A nd so now the time had come to finally meet Father Bede. I had written him from Germany about the possibility of spending some time in his ashram. I promptly received a welcome letter. A few weeks before my arrival in India, I also received a postcard from Bede informing me that he would be making a short visit to Europe and would therefore, unfortunately, not be returning to the ashram until a few days after my arrival. I should wait at the ashram for his return. I was surprised that he had taken the trouble to write.

It was only a few hours' journey from the village of Palayam to Bede's Saccidananda[6] Ashram, which was located out in the countryside along the banks of the Kaveri River. The ashram, its liturgy, and its contemplative way of life were adapted as much as possible to the culture of India without compromising its Christian foundation. The monks wore the saffron-colored robes of Hindu *sannyāsis*, and many of the hymns sung at Mass were in Sanskrit. Liturgy was celebrated cross-legged on the floor, and the Christian symbols that adorned the ashram were in the style of south Indian art and architecture. The nucleus of the ashram community was comprised of Father Bede and a small number of other monks who were his disciples. Numerous visitors from around the world passed through the ashram in order to meet Bede. Some stayed many months. I myself lived there three weeks.[7]

I was immediately impressed by Father Bede's spiritual presence, his humility and gentleness, the quality of his homilies at Mass, and his capacity to inspire a high level of spiritual conversation among the ashram guests. He was clearly a man filled with joy, wisdom, and love and was therefore a living embodiment of Christ's presence. He was one of the most nonjudgmental people I have ever met. And he was also an excellent listener. I had the opportunity to spend a good part of two afternoons with him in his hut. We talked of interreligious dialogue and of similarities and differences between Hindu and Christian understandings of the divine-human relationship. There is much that I no longer remember from our conversations, but I do recall one thing in particular that remains with me. Bede emphasized the need to pass beyond all words and concepts about God in order to attain to the direct experience of the Divine. He was not saying that the words we use about God are useless or could be dispensed with. The words used in Christian creeds and theology preserve the memory of God's activities in history and the significance of those activities for our salvation. They properly orient us to who God is and what God demands of us. But we cannot stop at words and concepts, as necessary as they are in mediating the truth about God. Even words and concepts that are true are limited. We are made for the experience of unity with God, even in this life. And the experience and reality of God are much richer than can be put into words.[8] I think Bede felt the need to impress that on me in particular, because of my recent theological studies in Germany. He also spoke of a wisdom shared by the different religions, despite all their real and important differences. The great religions of humankind all teach that we must finally pass beyond the limited world of the senses and of reason to attain the experience of the higher truth within. On this point Bede recommended that I read Seyyed Hossein Nasr's *Knowledge and the Sacred*.[9]

One of the great challenges today for Christians is to open ourselves to what God is teaching us through other religions without compromising the importance of Christ. Bede Griffiths and Thomas Merton are exemplary in this regard. Unfortunately, Merton spent less than two months in Asia before his untimely death in 1968, although he had been reading extensively in Asian religions, especially Buddhism, Sufism, and Taoism, throughout the 1960s and had been corresponding with people of other religions. For those who have read their works, it is clear that neither Griffiths nor Merton fell prey to relativism or indifferentism. Neither of them taught that all religions are making the same experience and just describing it differently. Neither taught that all religions are equally valuable, although all the religions, according to Griffiths—at least all the major world religions—do have great value. Perennialists[10] are sometimes accused of taking the approach that the religions all finally teach the same thing, but in most cases this is an incorrect assessment. To assert, as perennialists do, that common themes of wisdom have emerged from within different religions is not to make the additional claim that all the religions are really saying and experiencing exactly the same thing. There are both similarities and differences already on the level of experience. But in all true mysticisms there is at least one striking commonality, say the perennialists; there has to be the annihilation of all the mental impurities and the death of the lower false self. It is the contemplative, the person of persistent prayer or meditation, who understands this inner connection of the religions better than anyone, certainly better than the professional scholar of religion devoid of such experience.

It should be added that Father Bede's theological interests were not limited to interreligious dialogue and the meeting of the mysticisms. He welcomed liberation theology to India with its emphasis on the empowerment of the poor and marginalized. In a conversation near the end of my stay at his ashram, he told me that he considered Aloysius Pieris, the Sri Lankan Jesuit theologian and scholar of Buddhism, and more famously one of the leading advocates of Asian liberation theology,[11] to be "the best theologian in Asia." He did not say that Pieris was just the best among the liberation theologians, but the best theologian in Asia—period. And yet he felt it was a mistake that many of the liberation theologians in India had begun turning away from the rich mystical and wisdom heritage of Hinduism and Buddhism. He felt that both liberations were needed, the interior transformation as well as the social.

Father Bede suffered a massive stroke in January 1990 that nearly killed him. In a remarkable interview,[12] he describes this experience as an awakening to a deeper sense of God. "It was a death of the mind," he says. Soon after the stroke, as he was coming back to his senses, he felt a powerful need to "surrender to the Mother. It came very clearly: 'Surrender to the Mother.' And I made this act of surrender, and a kind of wave of love overwhelmed me." He called out to a nurse, "I'm being overwhelmed with love! I don't know whether I can survive it!" He adds, "What my experience taught me was that when everything else goes you discover this love which is in you all the time. It's then deep down there, and you know nothing about it. But let everything go, and it comes." He says this experience gave him insight into Jesus's experience on the cross. When Jesus faced death, darkness, nothingness, "he was taken into total love. That is the experience of death. Behind all death is this tremendous power of love." Normally our mind controls everything, and we don't know about the love within, which is there all the time. He goes on, "But sometimes you have to be hit on the head, you see, to awaken you . . . and you are no longer afraid of death or accidents or illnesses. They're all incidents which Love can use to reveal itself . . . What you face in death is unconditional love. That is the Judgment: unconditional love, which is very demanding. It doesn't let you do what you like. Love demands love."

Father Bede suffered additional strokes a few years later that finally brought his earthly pilgrimage to an end. I consider myself fortunate to have met him, if only briefly. It was he more than anyone else who taught me to be open to the work of God in other religions.

Part II

13

My Muslim Family

Iarrived in India as a student, thinking my time there would be fully focused on learning Sanskrit and studying Hindu thought. I would not have time for anything else, I thought, since I would be there only a year. And though I had come to India with an almost monkish approach to studying Hinduism, I soon found myself engaged to a woman who had been raised in the Muslim faith.

I almost didn't get to meet Mariam. I was ill the day Father Victor arrived at the ashram on his motorcycle to get me. He was the priest who had prayed over me at Palayam a few weeks before. He was still in India, back from the missions in Papua New Guinea. As a priest, he was allowed to return to his homeland for a few months every three years. After visiting his family in Tamil Nadu, he had made the trip north to Pune to visit friends and families he had known from his seminary days. "You have to meet this Muslim family," he had told me. "They're special. You'll like them." Victor had been one of about ten seminarians who used to spend Sunday afternoons at the home of Mariam's family. They would bring guitars and sing songs, and Mariam's mother, Khatijah Shaikh, always prepared a feast. Now, years later, the Catholic priest had come to the ashram to pick me up and take me to the same Muslim home. "Tomorrow I'm going back to the missions," he told me, "and I won't be back in India for three years. Let's go see the Shaikh family before it's too late." Victor's idea was that I should have a family while in India. The Catholic priest recommended this Muslim family.

But when Victor arrived on his motorcycle, I told him straightaway that the visit to the Shaikh home would have to wait until another day, because I had fallen ill. The last thing I wanted to do was ride a motor-cycle across the city in the hot sun. I apologized to the priest for his having come all the way to the ashram to get me.

"You go," I said. "Give me their address, and I'll look them up when I'm feeling better."

"You'll never find them," he said. "They're on the other side of the city. Let's go now. We'll be back in less than two hours."

"I'm too sick," I said. "I'm not going."

"Just get on the bike," said the priest, forcing himself to smile, though he was clearly growing impatient with me. "When we get there, I'll make them understand that you can't eat. I'll make sure to tell them you're sick. Let's get going."

After Victor's many assurances that this would be a simple trip across town and back, I climbed behind him onto the motorcycle, and we took off. I hoped to meet the Muslim family briefly and be back within an hour, even though Victor had said two. But fifteen minutes later the bike broke down. We pushed it several blocks to a garage. It felt like it weighed a ton. I was frustrated and angry that I had come along. *I should not have come*, I thought to myself. *This is crazy.* And by that time I had absolutely no idea where in this huge city I was or even what direc-tion from the ashram we were.

An hour later a mechanic had the motorcycle working, and we were off. We swerved through heavy traffic, avoiding pedestrians, stray dogs, slow-plodding cows, and herds of water buffalo. Victor eventually pulled off onto a narrow street, on one side of which were balconied apart-ment buildings several stories high. On the other side of the street were narrow lanes dividing rows of small blue and gray cement houses, most of them single story, all situated tightly adjacent to one another. Beside the lanes were other lanes, and still other lanes were behind them. Here and there a solitary tree rose up between the buildings to provide much needed shade. Our Muslim family was in one of those houses in one of those lanes. Victor was right; I never would have found it on my own.

We were an hour late for our visit and drenched in sweat. I was praying we might head back soon. When we arrived in the neighborhood, children were playing everywhere outside, old people were sitting on chairs or benches in front of their tiny houses in the shade of overhanging roofs, and from inside a few homes I could hear the sound of a television.

Many people stared at me as I walked with Victor down the lane, some of them grinning as they looked me up and down, not only because I was a foreigner, but because I was dressed in a green pajama-like outfit that I thought would make me blend in with the local population. I was wearing the khadi cloth of the poor, something Gandhiji's followers might have worn. I had not been paying attention after my arrival in Pune to what people were actually wearing. What I should have noticed was that in the modern big cities of India, most educated men wore Western clothes with buttoned shirts and trousers with cuffs. It seemed I was the only one dressed like a traditional Indian, and a poor one at that. I had brought my Western preconceptions with me to India, which had prevented me from seeing what was right before my eyes. I found out later that my future mother-in-law used to wonder to herself whenever I came, *Doesn't he have anything else to wear?*

When I stepped into the Shaikh house on that first visit, the family was waiting for us. Snacks and fresh fruits had been heaped on silver trays on a table in the middle of the room. Father Victor greeted everyone in Hindi and gave hugs all around. Everyone in the room was smiling. They had not seen Victor in three years. He explained that I was an American student who had only recently arrived in India and was staying with the Christian sisters at an ashram in Shivaji Nagar. I was studying Sanskrit and Hinduism. He conveyed this in Hindi to Mr. and Mrs. Shaikh and then translated it into English for me. But when Victor spoke to the son and two daughters, it was in English, a language they knew as well as Hindi, from their schooling. The son's name was Shabbir; he was a tall, lanky, handsome business student at a local college. His two sisters, Mariam and Hameeda, a few years older in their midtwenties, were also college educated. They wore colorful Indian outfits called *salwar kameez*, that is, a tunic over baggy trousers, with the shoulders and chest covered by a *dupatta*, or long scarf. They were not covered from head to foot with the black chador like some of their more conservative cousins in the next neighborhood. The sisters looked a lot alike, it seemed to me, both of them slender with the typical thick black Indian hair, but Mariam was smaller framed, and there was something about her face that drew my attention. She was small, an inch or two over five feet, a few inches shorter than I. The mother of the house, Mrs. Shaikh, a small woman with dark hair tied in a long braid running down her back, smiled quietly at Victor and me and then disappeared into the kitchen to prepare hot tea. Victor announced that due to illness I would not be able to eat. This elicited various responses of concern.

Abdul Shaikh, the father, was a wiry man of medium height with slightly slouched shoulders, the cause of which I was to learn only later. His face was slender and serious, with prominent cheekbones, and his white hair looked a bit out of place on a face with no wrinkles. I learned later that his hair had turned gray before he had reached thirty. After shaking my hand, he stood quietly off to the side, but he kept his eyes on me. He and Victor conversed privately in Tamil, their mother tongue. When I glanced at Mr. Shaikh, he would flash a smile at me and then look away. I took note of his shyness. His dark eyes, penetrating and intelligent, would meet my own, dart away, then return. He was the kind of man who seemed to quietly take in everything. He had earned the respect of his neighbors, I learned later, because he had not given in to impulsive speech or engaged in gossip. His general silence was born of a natural reflective disposition as well as the experience of long hardship. Life had come close at times to breaking him, but he had survived.

Mr. Shaikh's story of how he ended up in Pune is a remarkable one. It all started in 1950 with a theft that took place aboard a train traveling up the western coast of India, from Kerala to Bombay.

This was just a few years after India's independence. On board the train was a teenager from Kerala named Yesudas[1] Ratnam Pillai. He had boarded the train somewhere in one of the southern states and was now traveling to Bombay, the great teeming city on the Arabian Sea into which thousands of migrants from all over India had been streaming in search of work. It was a two-day journey. Only eighteen years old, of slight build, quiet and shy, with slightly hunched shoulders, Ratnam had never before visited this part of India. In his compartment he struck up a conversation with another young man who was also on his way to Bombay, and in the course of their trip the two became friends. The teenagers even made a pact: since neither of them had ever before been to Bombay, they would look out for each other as they searched for work. They would stick together as a team.

Only a few hours before they were scheduled to arrive in Bombay, the train halted briefly in Pune, a large city in western Maharashtra. Ratnam asked his new friend to keep an eye on his trunk while he made a quick visit inside the station to buy tea and breakfast for them both. Inside the trunk were all Ratnam's possessions: his clothing, money he had saved, and a number of medicines, pharmaceutical books, and literature on home remedies. For some time Ratnam had been making a living as a pharmaceutical salesman, selling medical literature to passengers riding long-distance trains.

Upon returning to his train compartment only minutes later, Ratnam made the unhappy discovery that both his companion and all his possessions were gone. He never saw either again. The teenager was left standing in his compartment with nothing but the clothes on his back and a few rupees in his pocket. He knew not a single person in the sprawling city, nor did he speak Marathi or Hindi, the two local languages. He was now completely alone in an unfamiliar part of India. It is difficult for me to grasp the shock he must have felt when he discovered that he had been betrayed, that everything he owned was now gone. In my mind's eye I imagine Ratnam frantically searching the station for his "friend," racing in vain from one platform to another, finding no trace of him anywhere, and finally coming to the gradual realization that he had been duped. In a daze, he slowly steps out of the train station into the tumult of the big city, standing for a while on the busy unfamiliar street, under an indifferent sky, surrounded by strangers, pondering what to do next, where to go.

By the time he stood outside that train station in Pune, Ratnam had been traveling on his own for three years already, having run away from home at fifteen. He had been raised in Alleppey and Trivandrum, cities on the Kerala coast not far from the southernmost tip of the subcontinent, where the Arabian Sea, the Bay of Bengal, and the Indian Ocean all come together.

The state of Kerala, where Ratnam grew up, is famous for many reasons. In part because of its proximity to the equator and to the sea it is almost everywhere lush and beautiful, with pristine beaches and spectacular green wooded mountains cradling stately tea plantations and innumerable spice gardens. Black pepper, cardamom, turmeric, ginger, nutmeg, cinnamon, cloves, and paprika are all grown here and have accounted in large measure for Kerala's fame and for its being the chosen destination of travelers from many distant lands for more than two millennia. Marco Polo arrived in Kerala in 1292 on his return to Venice from China, and in 1498 Vasco da Gama docked anchor in Calicut in search of "Christians and spices." The Christian Keralites are especially proud of one particular traveler from antiquity. According to tradition, St. Thomas the Apostle, a direct disciple of Christ, the "doubting Thomas" of the Gospel of John, arrived in Kerala as a missionary in the year 52 CE. For Keralites it is an indisputable fact that Christianity in India represents one of the oldest bastions of the religion found anywhere in the world. If they are right, then the church in Kerala is almost as ancient as the churches of Jerusalem and Rome. By the time St. Peter arrived in Rome[2] from Palestine, St. Thomas would have already been living in India for at least five years. Though Christianity in Kerala is almost two thousand years old now, Christians today still constitute only a mere 20 percent of the state's population. The great majority of Keralites remain Hindu. Yet Kerala is the state with the highest percentage of Christians in all of India; a full one-fourth of all Indian Christians live there.[3]

The name "Ratnam" means "jewel" in Sanskrit, and "Jesudas" means "servant of Jesus." He was born on Christmas Eve. His full Catholic baptismal name was Ratnaswami Jesudas Michael Pillai. "Pillai," the surname, is common to various groups of south Indians, both Hindu and Christian. In India, last names can be revealing. To know a person's last name often means to uncover not only the religion and even Hindu caste to which they belong (or originally belonged), but also the part of the country from which the family originally came. So when one Indian asks another, "What is your good name?," they are often hoping to learn more about the person than what name he or she goes by. If your last name is Chattopadhyay, then you are a high-caste Hindu from the Bengal area. If your last name is Fernandes or D'Souza, you are a Catholic from the western coast of India, and your ancestors were probably missionized by the Portuguese. Your original caste name and social status in the Hindu community have disappeared altogether and have been replaced by a Portuguese name. If your name is Pillai or Pillay, you are from Tamil Nadu or Kerala, and if you also happen to be a Hindu, you are a member of an upper caste.

Ratnam's father was Mutthaiah Pillai, who had grown up in Ramanadachampudur, a small village even farther south in Kerala than Trivandrum and Alleppey, near the city of Nagercoil. This was where Ratnam was baptized into the Catholic Church before the family moved north to Alleppey. Nagercoil is only twelve miles from the little rock island off the southern tip of India where Swami Vivekananda (1863–1902), one of the great heroes of modern India and the first Hindu missionary to the West, meditated for three days on the future of India and its place among the nations of the world.

Ratnam's ancestors on his father's side were originally all Hindu, but some had converted to Catholicism three generations before he was born. The story behind the conversion is not clear. The only thing remembered now is that the great-grandfather and the entire village to which he belonged for some reason converted to the Catholic faith. And so the south Indian relatives today, who are scattered across the states of Kerala and Tamil Nadu, follow either Hinduism or Catholicism. Some

of the clan members who remained Hindu chose to change their surname from Pillai to Ganeshan, after the popular elephant-headed god,
to avoid being confused with their Catholic relatives.

The Hindu relatives in south India have remained quite traditional
in some respects. Though they receive Catholic kin into their homes,
they serve them food only on special plates and utensils reserved for non-
Hindus, who they regard as ritually unclean, because they eat meat.
If they were to use the same plates and utensils as their Catholic relatives, they would inevitably pollute themselves, perhaps leading to a bad
rebirth.

Mutthaiah eventually moved his family to Alleppey, because of its
large Catholic population. There he opened a business called St. Joseph
Candle Works, which manufactured and sold candles and brass liturgical items to local churches and stores.

Ratnam's tale of suffering began at the age of eight when his mother,
Mariam, after whom my own wife is named, died giving birth to Ratnam's
little sister, Leela. She was only in her twenties. She also left behind a
four-year-old son, Arul. I know nothing at all about Ratnam's mother,
except that she had been raised a Hindu and converted to Catholicism
before the wedding, which means she and Mutthaiah had entered into a
love marriage instead of an arranged marriage. Beyond that, no one can
recall for me any word she spoke or anything she did. All that remains is
the memory of her love. Years later, as a family man with his own children, Ratnam, now called Abdul, would reminisce how loving his mother
had been to him and how much he had longed for her after she died.

Mutthaiah was devastated by the loss of his young wife, but his children needed a new mother, and so he soon married a tiny woman named
Ponnamma. Unfortunately for the children, so the story goes, the new
stepmother was self-centered and quarrelsome. She would eventually give
birth to three children, and she openly favored them over her three step-
children. Even though the family was not in financial need Ponnamma
often sent Ratnam and little Arul out of the house early in the morning
with a large trunk full of candles. They were told not to return home
until every candle had been sold. Because he was the older of the two

boys, Ratnam was the one who carried the trunk atop his shoulders. The two boys walked all day long, moving from church to church and store to store, knowing that every candle sold would bring them that much sooner back home. Sometimes they would not return until evening. The trunk was so heavy that Ratnam bent under its weight, and as a result he suffered from a bad back and hunched shoulders for the rest of his life.

Eventually Mutthaiah, still grieving over his first wife and unhappy with the second, took to drink and became more critical and impatient with his sons. The stepmother continued to harass them. Finally the day came when Ratnam could take it no more. In a moment of anger he threw a fire stoker at his stepmother, hitting her in the head. He knew he would receive a beating for this when his father returned home, so on an impulse he made a decision that would change his life forever: he simply took to the road and never looked back. And he had no particular destination in mind.

For the next three years, Ratnam traveled alone by foot, by bus, and by train throughout all the southern states of India. He never sent letters home. His family knew absolutely nothing of his whereabouts or if he was even still alive. Ratnam worked his way through Kerala and then into Tamil Nadu, Andhra Pradesh, and Karnataka. Since he was a gifted student, he learned the spoken language and written script in all the states he visited. Even before he began his travels, Ratnam already knew Malayalam from growing up in Kerala and Tamil from his own ethnic background. He had also studied English and Sanskrit at the local Catholic school. Years later he would translate Sanskrit verses (*slokas*) from Hindu scripture for his Muslim children. Now, while traveling from place to place as a young man, he also learned Telugu and Kannada. By the time I met him, he had also taught himself to read Arabic, the latter so that he could read the Qur'ān in the original. He learned to speak Marathi well, and he also became fluent in Hindi. All told, that makes nine languages that he mastered to varying degrees, though he never attended school after the age of fifteen. He was easily one of the most intelligent people I've ever met.

I wonder what Abdul's life might have been like if he had not been mistreated at home and run away. He might have gone on to secondary education. I think he might well have become a physician. He loved learning about all kinds of medicine, whether Āyurvedic, homeopathic, or allopathic. In their neighborhood years later, working out of their grocery store, Abdul and his wife, Khatijah, used to give advice to sick people as to which medicines they should take and what diet they should follow. If the people were too poor to pay, then my parents-in-law would just give them medicine for free, without expecting to be paid back. Sometimes in India even today physicians will pay for medicine out of their own pockets to help the poor, even if they themselves do not earn much. Most physicians I've met in India don't seem to be in the profession primarily for the money. They have compassion for the poor.

It must have been difficult for Ratnam, all those years of wandering and selling pharmaceuticals. He rarely spoke about it. Other people in his situation might well have regaled family members and neighbors with embellished tales of adventure, danger, and heroism, but Ratnam revealed little. He was a quiet, humble man. His children were left to imagine what it must have been like to be a homeless boy on the road, traveling alone, avoiding danger whenever it presented itself. But they received few clues from their father.

The only story I ever heard from those three years, and the one Abdul was most fond of repeating, was about his miraculous healing. Sometime during his time on the road his whole body had become afflicted with festering sores. No medicine had helped. One night he had a dream that if he were to bathe in a pool of water, he would be healed. The next day he came to a Muslim shrine whose ablution pool was large enough for him to immerse himself. According to his account, while dipping himself in the water countless tiny fish swam up to him and began nibbling at his sores. When he rose up out of the water, he was covered with blood. The imam at the shrine bandaged his wounds. The sores disappeared and never returned. In retrospect he saw this as a sign that God was calling him to Islam.

•　　•　　•

Outside the Pune train station, Ratnam had every reason to despair, having just been robbed of everything he owned. His only hope now was to find out whether any Keralites might be living in Pune, since he was himself from Kerala and spoke Malayalam. It was well known that Keralites tended to be successful in business, and many had migrated to other parts of India. Perhaps he might be so fortunate as to meet someone who would offer him a job.

He was eventually led to a Malabari Keralite, a Muslim named Abduka who owned several restaurants in Pune. Abduka was a well-known figure in the city. Not only was he a successful businessman, he had also founded the Kerala Muslim Jamaat (Association) in Pune, which exists to this day. Abduka was highly respected as a hardworking and honorable man. He was also merciful. He took in Ratnam, the Catholic, and gave him a job in one of his restaurants. Because Ratnam was intelligent and honest, Abduka eventually entrusted him to work at the money counter of his main restaurant. It was there that Ratnam met the love of his life, Khatijah. She was one of Abduka's nieces.

Abduka lived in a *haveli*[4] with his two sisters, two brothers, and their families. One of his sisters was Fatima, who gave birth to five children, the fourth of whom was Khatijah.[5] Khatijah had been born in the palace compound of the Kolhapur Maharajah,[6] about 150 miles south of Pune. Her father, Murtaza Baig, husband of Fatima, was from Meerut in north India, and a *nawāb*, a member of the Muslim nobility and land-owning class. As a young man Murtaza had left home to serve in the British army, after which, for reasons that remain unclear, he traveled to Kolhapur, where he was put in charge of the Maharajah's stables and helped train his horses. Somewhere before or during his time in Kolhapur, Murtaza met Fatima and fell in love. Because she was from a different Muslim social group than Murtaza and from an altogether different part of India, namely Kerala, his family opposed their marriage. When Murtaza married Fatima, anyway, he was disowned by his family. He never returned home.

My wife and her siblings still remember their grandmother Fatima as a widow. She moved into their home after Murtaza passed away.

Fatima was a proud and independent woman. It was said that the only person in her life she had ever submitted to was her husband, Murtaza, who was himself a strong and possessive man. When they were first married, he would leave home in the morning after commanding her to lock the door of the house from inside. She was not to go outside until he returned home at the end of the day. He wanted no other man to see her beauty. To test her fidelity, he would sometimes return home at midday and disguise his voice as another man, calling from outside the door for her to open up. She never did.

My brother-in-law Shabbir recalls as a little boy watching his grandmother Fatima, now very old, sitting on a stool. "She liked chewing *paan*," he said. *Paan* is a betel leaf paste mix that is popular across India. "She used to take out grandfather's 'Tommy helmet'[7] and use it as a spittoon." Fatima was apparently not the sentimental type. She eventually died a painful death in her old age while confined long term to bed. Bedsores caused gaping wounds in her flesh. In her last days she cursed God so loudly that her relatives and neighbors all feared for her salvation.

Khatijah was fourteen when she and Ratnam first met. She used to stop by her uncle Abduka's restaurant on her way to school every morning to pick up candy and money. Spirited and good-looking like her mother, Fatima, Khatijah was not lacking in confidence. She had been spoiled by her father, Murtaza. He believed that Khatijah was the most special of his four daughters, since she had brought a blessing upon the family, being the last daughter born before the arrival of the only son, Habib. In India it is sometimes believed that the daughter born just before a first or only son has somehow contributed to the brother's arrival into the world. The clever and spoiled Khatijah took advantage of her special status. Before her father left for work in the morning she would sometimes not let him go until he promised to bring home an extra treat just for her when he returned in the evening.

Khatijah's childhood was happy and uneventful until the day her father began coughing up blood. After a few months, the catastrophe descended on the family that all had feared: beloved Murtaza, the strong, reliable bedrock of the family, passed away, leaving behind a widow with five children. Fatima was now completely dependent on her brother, Abduka, for her family's survival. Her five children, in order of birth, were Ayesha, Hussainbi, Khatijah, then the only son, Habib, and, finally, the youngest sister, Noorjehan, also called Nuri. By the time I arrived in India, all were still alive except Ayesha, who had died of cancer.

It was sometime after her father had died that Khatijah stopped by as usual at her uncle Abduka's restaurant and there met Ratnam for the first time. One can easily imagine the initial flirtation between the two teenagers, the shy smiles, the fleeting exchange of words that eventually blossomed into love. In such a strict society, a young Muslim girl did not have much freedom to interact with a young man like Ratnam outside of her brief visits to the restaurant.

After a year of growing desire, Ratnam and Khatijah could wait no more. Ratnam approached Abduka for permission to marry his niece. The patriarch readily agreed, on the condition that Ratnam first convert to Islam. This was not a problem for Ratnam, for he felt that God had led him to meet Abduka and become a Muslim. He also remembered his miraculous healing in the pool outside the mosque.

In order to become a Muslim, Ratnam needed to do two things. First, he had to allow himself to become circumcised. Second, he needed to recite with faith the Muslim creed, "There is no God but Allah and Muhammad is His prophet," in the presence of two Muslim witnesses. After converting, the young man changed his name from Ratnam to Abdul, which means "servant of Allah," and his last name to Shaikh, which is a common Muslim name around the world, meaning "leader."

Unfortunately, before Abdul and Khatijah could marry, Abduka died of a heart attack, and Khatijah's mother, Fatima, not always the easiest person to get along with, suddenly chose to oppose the marriage on the grounds that Abdul, the fresh convert to Islam, was not a true Muslim, on account of his having been raised a Christian. She said she had not objected to the marriage before, only because she had not wanted to oppose her brother Abduka, the provider for her family. Fatima was able to rally support against Abdul among her relatives, and, as a result, Abdul was not only commanded to keep away from Khatijah; he was also immediately relieved of his duties in the restaurant and cast out into the street.

In a way it was not surprising that the relatives who turned against Abdul had shown such disgraceful behavior. Abduka had always said that his siblings were lazy and useless. He observed with disgust their wanton lifestyles; some of the men were womanizers, and all of them approached business with apathy and were reckless in their spending. Abduka watched all this with concern, knowing that his little empire faced the certainty of eventual ruin. "After I die, just watch what happens," he said. "They will run the business into the ground and end up selling even the tiles in the *haveli* to make money." The *haveli* had been ornamented with imported tile from Italy. Abduka's prediction came true. After he died, his youngest brother, Mohiddinkaka, went through whatever money he could lay his hands on. It was said that he was fond of buying stylish clothes and showing off one expensive new wristwatch every week, and that he threw money at any woman he found sexually desirable. He eventually sold and even gambled away all the restaurants one by one. Finally, in dire straits, he was forced to remove the tiles from the *haveli* and sell them one at a time until there was nothing left. This is the one prediction Abduka made that everyone remembers years later, how even the tiles were sold. Mohiddinkaka would do anything but put in a hard day's work.

Not being one to easily capitulate even after having been forced out into the street, Abdul persisted in his desire to marry Khatijah, even appearing beneath her window each night to sing Hindi love songs. He had a beautiful voice. This could not have been easy for one so shy. Khatijah would tell her children years later how much those songs meant to her, even as her mother, Fatima, tried to send the young suitor away. Knowing that he would not win over the young girl's relatives, Abdul's only hope was to convince Khatijah to run away with him. For days he waited in vain for a response. Every night he sang the love songs. Still there was no answer. In near despair he finally managed to send his beloved a simple note: "All the others have betrayed me. Will you betray me, too?" That was enough to persuade Khatijah to overcome her indecisiveness. The next day the fifteen-year-old girl slipped out of the *haveli* and fled with her nineteen-year-old husband-to-be. This was made possible only with the help of one of Khatijah's male relatives, whose identity remains unknown even to this day. He must have liked Abdul very much to have taken the risk of smuggling Khatijah out of the house.

The young couple wed at a local mosque. Soon after the wedding ceremony, a full four years after he had run away from home, Abdul finally wrote a letter to his family back in Kerala to let them know that he was alive and where he was living. "I have married a Muslim," he wrote, "and have converted to Islam myself." His doting younger brother, Arul, who had suffered more than anyone else from his older brother's long absence, was furious that Ratnam had become a Muslim. Family ties now counted for nothing. Mutthaiah, the father, was even more scornful. He wrote to Abdul, "Now that you have disgraced us and converted to Islam, you are hereby cut off from the family. We never want to see you or hear from you again. All the inheritance—the land, the business, the house—will go to your brother, Arul."

And so in his heart Abdul bade farewell to his family. He accepted his banishment as the necessary price to pay for the woman he loved and for submission to the one God. He accepted without protest that he would never see his father or his brother and sister again.

But many years later, a full twenty years after he had left home, Abdul one day received a telegram from Arul. "Papa is dying and calling for you. You must come immediately." Abdul took the next train to Kerala and reconciled with his father on his deathbed. He also made peace with his stepmother and with Arul, even though his brother continually tried to persuade him to return to Catholicism. Arul never could accept that Abdul had embraced Islam of his own accord. "It's all your mother's fault," he used to tell Mariam and her siblings. "She forced him to become a Muslim."

"No, he had already made up his mind even apart from marriage," Mariam answered.

"That's why Arul Uncle never liked me," Mariam tells me. "I challenged him. I wasn't arguing that one religion was better than another. All I was saying was that my mother was not to blame."

Those first years of marriage were a struggle. Teenage romance had to face up to the harsh realities of life. Abdul and Khatijah could not rely on help from anyone. They lived wherever they could; eventually they were taken in by Khatijah's older sister, Ayesha, and her husband. Eventually Khatijah came up with a plan to rent an abandoned boxcar that had been moved from the train station to downtown Pune and use it as a store to sell baked goods. Through sheer hard work the young couple was able to eventually buy their own little home and storefront. Their bakery became a success.

During those early years, Abdul contracted pneumonia and had to be hospitalized. Because he had little money he was admitted to a poor person's hospital and put into a ward with tuberculosis patients. Three of them died the first week he was there. In the hospital Abdul contracted TB himself, and, as a result he suffered for the rest of his life from poor lungs. This is what eventually caused his death many years later.

A year after they were married, Razaak, the first child, was born. He was succeeded two years later by my wife, Mariam, after whom came Hameeda and Shabbir.

All four children were sent to private Christian schools. It is a tribute to my parents-in-law that they valued education. "I will be forever grateful to my parents for giving us an education where we could learn English," Mariam told me. "If I didn't know English, you and I could never have communicated."

She's right, of course, but there's one more person to whom we must be grateful: the train thief. If he had not stolen everything from my father-in-law, he never would have gotten down from the train that day and settled in Pune, gotten married, and had a daughter named Mariam, who I would one day marry. I am therefore grateful to him and for having learned the remarkable story of my father-in-law, Abdul.

·   ·   ·

The one person missing during that first visit to the Shaikh home was Razaak, who was a few years older than Mariam and was the eldest of the four children. To this day no one ever seems to know where exactly Razaak is or when he might show up next. He just appears without warning, without explaining where he's been, spends enough time to have a meal and make simple conversation with whoever is around, and then just as suddenly he disappears again, sometimes for days. I can say without exaggeration that I have heard so many interesting stories over the years about Razaak and what he's up to when he's out and about that they could fill an entire volume. His natural charm and people skills have enabled him to borrow money almost at will. And I have never met a man so totally unconcerned about losing money. One day his pockets are stuffed with wads of rupees, and the next day he is broke. He lives recklessly without wasting any thought on the future. There are endless rumors as to the various ways he borrows his money, but no one knows for sure.

The next hour of my visit with Victor to the Shaikhs was spent getting to know Shabbir, Mariam, and Hameeda. I was impressed by their overall level of education and the many informed questions they asked about life in Europe and the United States. They were unusual Muslims, I eventually learned, certainly the most educated Muslims in the neighborhood and among the few who knew fluent English. Many Muslim families in Pune, if they were not well-to-do, sent their children to Urdu-speaking Muslim schools, institutions that did not prepare them well to integrate into Indian society or to find good-paying jobs. It has often been remarked that a lot of Muslims in India do not value education enough, and that it's their rigid religion that gets in the way and pressures them into settling for an inferior education at Muslim-run schools and ending up with low-paying jobs.

But it is not just the lack of quality education that keeps many Muslims down. In an article published a few years ago in the *Los Angeles Times*, Asra Nomani, an Indian-born Muslim woman living in the

United States, attributed Muslim poverty in India to widespread anti-Muslim discrimination.[8] In her article she referred to a recent government report that had appeared under the direction of a former Indian chief justice, Rajender Sachar, who was not himself a Muslim. Summarizing the document, Nomani stated that "Muslims were now worse off than the Dalit caste, or those called untouchables. Some 52 percent of Muslim men were unemployed, compared with 47 percent of Dalit men. Among Muslim women, 91 percent were unemployed, compared with 77 percent of Dalit women. Almost half of Muslims over the age of 46 couldn't read or write. While making up 11 percent of the population, Muslims accounted for 40 percent of India's prison population. Meanwhile, they held less than 5 percent of government jobs." Nomani's many conversations with Muslims in India had revealed "bureaucratic, housing, job and educational discrimination."

Muslims in India sometimes feel like outsiders or second-class citizens in a country that is four-fifths Hindu. Mariam tells the story of interviewing with a Hindu business owner for an accounting position. She had just graduated from college. The interview was going well until she revealed that her name was Mariam Shaikh. She could tell instantly by the owner's shocked reaction to her Muslim name that she would not get the job. "But at least he was polite," she said. "He told me immediately after hearing my name that there was no position at the moment, after all, but he would notify me when one opened up." He did not insult her, but he also did not call back.

It is well known that religion has the capacity to bring out both the worst and the best in people. It produces both saints and bigots. I have heard harrowing stories of my in-laws' store in Pune being destroyed in religious rioting, while Mariam, Hameeda, and their mother huddled behind the closed doors of their home. Muslims were targeted all over the city. But fortunately, my experience in India in recent years has led me to believe that more and more young people, especially those who are most educated, have grown weary of religion's divisiveness and wary of politicians with religious and sectarian agendas. Whether Hindu or Muslim, they tend more and more to regard members of other religions as sharing with them a common humanity. These are not young people who have given up their faith. They are not secularized former Hindus and former Muslims; they continue to identify themselves as practicing Hindus and Muslims. But now they judge all religion, including their own, by its ability to inspire people to do good, to practice justice and mercy, and to build solidarity with all human beings. This humanizing of religion has great affinity with the teaching of Jesus, even among those who have never heard of him. For me this is strong evidence that the Holy Spirit is at work outside the boundaries of the visible church. The Spirit of God is the Spirit that brings unity and love.

Looking back on that first visit, I am so glad that Father Victor convinced me to take that motorcycle ride, as ill as I was. It would not be long before the Shaikh family would be more than friends; they would become family.

14

A Secret Love

I was attracted to Mariam from the moment we met. This surprised me, as my mind had been moving mostly in the realm of spiritual realities with all kinds of questions: Was the God revealed in Hindu scriptures, the ultimate reality and hidden Ground of the world, also in some way the God in whom Christians believed? Did Hindu enlightenment have anything to do with the Christian experience of divine love? Where did meditation and prayer converge? Now all these questions were suddenly put on hold in the presence of Mariam. Everything about her was physically stunning: the thick black hair framing her intelligent and sensitive brown face, her slender and delicate frame, her deep and perceptive eyes. But her appearance alone would not have been enough to cause me to fall in love and commit. It was the kind of person she was that had made the difference. I soon discovered that behind the physical appearance was a great spiritual depth and pure heart, a quiet dignity and inner strength, a generosity and passionate sense of justice. I soon learned that she was a person with great compassion for people, especially the poor, and animals. She would give generously and without hesitation, a giving that has continued unabated even to today. If someone is in pressing need, she says, then we should just give without thinking too much about our budget, and things will somehow work out. It doesn't always turn out that way, to be sure. Sometimes the wolf has been at the door.

Those were just a few of the qualities that struck me during our earliest days together. And when she first met me, she didn't flirt, unlike other Indian girls I had met. She didn't place her hand on my arm when we talked, as one girl had done. And she had clearly spent a lot of time thinking about a lot of serious matters, like society's inequalities and gender relations, justice and injustices she had seen, and relations between the religions. As far as the way people treat one another goes, there was not much she had not thought about.

She loved to read, and she was at home in silence. At school sometimes during recess, she later told me, when the other students were playing games, she would go off by herself to sit quietly, to commune with God who was palpably present in nature.

There's one story about Mariam that made me realize how independent she was. Only fourteen, on the cusp of womanhood, she announced to her parents one day that she would never marry. There was no use arguing about it, she said; she had thought things through and had made up her mind. Even before reaching puberty, she had noticed how the Muslim men in her neighborhood always seemed to control their wives. The man could always do whatever he wanted, but the wife always had to ask her husband's permission to do anything, whether buying new clothes, making a visit to her mother's home, or taking the children on an outing to the park. If her husband said no, then the wife had no recourse but to work on him slowly, through whatever it took: flattery, coaxing, and sometimes persistent nagging, to eventually get him to give in.

Not all men were controlling of their wives, Mariam later told me, but most marriages were sufficiently male dominated to make a girl like herself wary of entering into matrimony. "The Muslim women I grew up with were very strong," she said. "They had to put up with so much. They had to fight for everything they wanted. The man said no to everything. Even if they didn't end up having a fight, the woman still needed to get the man's permission. But I didn't want to be in a marriage like that. Why would I want to get married and ruin my life?" She saw a lot of unhappy marriages, and at the family store she heard from wives about the beatings they had received from their husbands. By around the age of nine, Mariam started noticing how distraught women, sometimes with a black eye, would show up at her parents' shop and ask to buy ten aspirin at once. But a woman with a headache would normally ask for only one aspirin. "Why do you need ten?" she would ask. If she didn't get a straight answer, she would tell the woman—sometimes it was a teenage mother—to wait for a moment. She would then fetch her mother, who would take the woman aside and talk her out of suicide.

There was also another problem with getting married that loomed in the back of Mariam's mind: Muslim men were allowed to have as many as four wives at once. Her own brother, Razaak, would eventually have four wives, and they lived in different parts of the same city, each with her own children. All four families were unhappy. There were no exceptions. The kids hardly ever saw their father, and the wives had very little time each day—and night—to share Razaak. "And," Mariam added, "it's not fair to the older wife when a man marries a younger woman. He will love the younger one more, even if the Qur'ān says he shouldn't."

One time a family friend, a wealthy businessman, gave hints to Mariam that he wanted to take her as his second wife, though she was only a teenager and less than half his age. Mariam complained about him to her mother, who from then on stopped taking Mariam on visits to his home. But the man's wife got wind of her husband's intentions, and for a while she was unfriendly to Mariam. She knew it would be hard to compete with a younger woman for her husband's affections.

Mariam knew, too, how in other ways Muslim marriage law favored the man. A Muslim woman could marry only a Muslim man, but a Muslim man could marry a Muslim, a Christian, or a Jew. And if a husband wanted to divorce his wife, he needed only to pronounce the word *ṭalāq*[1] three times, and the divorce was final.

Those were some of the reasons why this headstrong fourteen-year-old girl informed her parents that day that she had come to the decision never to marry. It is perhaps difficult for Westerners to appreciate just how radical was this decision. In India it is very rare for a woman to deliberately choose to remain single, because it is the desire of almost every woman to have children. It is as mothers that women expect to find their greatest fulfillment. But sometimes, in extreme cases, a woman will act heroically and choose to forgo marriage for the sake of her parents, if she has no brothers to take care of the parents in their old age. In India it is normally the responsibility of the sons to take care of the parents. When a daughter gets married, she leaves her mother and father and moves into the home of her in-laws, but her married brothers will remain at home. They and their wives are expected to provide for the parents. If there are no sons in the family, and all the daughters marry, no one is left to care for the parents. So sometimes one of the daughters will sacrifice herself and choose not to marry, so that her parents may not be left helpless.

Even though Mariam did have two brothers, she explained to her parents that by remaining single there would be even greater certainty that they would be well taken care of in their old age. "Just treat me like a son from now on," she said. And she added that if her father and mother were to agree to this arrangement, they in turn should stop thinking about marrying her off.

Abdul listened patiently and with some amusement to what he considered to be his daughter's nonsense, and then quietly but firmly informed her that, despite her intentions to the contrary, the day would certainly come when she would marry. He was ultimately right about this, of course, but not in the way he expected.

Mariam's marriage proposals had started coming in around the time she turned fourteen. At a certain age a girl attending weddings—and there are lots of weddings going on in India, all the time—suddenly starts getting noticed by mothers of marriageable young men. The mother may not be so bold as to approach the girl directly, but she will ask other people about her, where she's from, how old she is, whether she has already been promised to another man. In Mariam's case her first favorable proposal—from a twenty-year-old son of a banker—came in when she was fourteen, through a friend of the family. Although her mother reluctantly gave in, Mariam persuaded her against it, since she wanted to continue her education.

How exactly do parents go about finding a suitable mate for their son or daughter? In Indian society, families will often learn about the availability of a marriageable boy or girl through a network of neighbors, relatives, and friends that sometimes extends beyond the neighborhood into other parts of the city and even into other regions of the country. Information will gradually trickle in about the other family, about their financial situation and moral state, what secrets they might be trying to keep hidden, and whether their son or daughter is upstanding and responsible. Official overtures are then sent out, and finally the big day comes when the boy and his parents come over to visit the girl and her parents at their home. That way both families can get a better sense of each other, and they also get to see the two young people close up. The boy and girl are sometimes total strangers, seeing each other for the first time on the day the boy's family comes for the visit. In more conservative families, like Mariam's, the girl is not allowed to even look at the boy at their first meeting or look into the face of her future in-laws as she serves them tea for the first time. Mariam had already protested how unfair it was that the boy could look at the girl while the girl could not look back at him. But her mother demanded that she keep her head down, so as not to embarrass the family. As the girl serves tea to the boy's parents they size her up, looking for signs of genuine deference to elders and an eagerness to please. If the girl ends up becoming their daughter-in-law, then God willing, she will bless them with many grandchildren. If the visit on this day of introductions goes well, then a formal marriage proposal will be sent from one family to the other. If the proposal is accepted, negotiations will be conducted for the dowry, and preparations will be made for the wedding ceremony.

The word on Mariam was that she was not only good-looking, but also intelligent and hardworking, the kind of daughter-in-law any family would love to show off, provided she did her work quietly without talking back to her husband or her parents-in-law. Mariam rose every morning at five thirty, opened the family store herself—she had been doing this since the age of ten—then helped her mother in the kitchen grinding lentils. After that she ironed her clothes, picked up her lunch, and then walked a full hour to the Catholic school at the edge of the city. After school there was the long walk back home again, sometimes in rain or heat, and when she got home she worked in the store until almost midnight. She never seemed to get enough sleep. But she loved school more than anything else, even if she didn't always find time to do her homework. She won awards every year at school for academics and art. Sometimes she was late to school and missed the annual awards ceremony entirely, because of her work at home. When that happened, she learned only from her friends which awards she had won. The teachers would call out her name onstage, and she would not be there. "One of the reasons I didn't want to get married," she told me, "is that they wanted to marry me off so young, and I wanted to keep going to school. I even wanted to go to college. I wanted to study art." She clung to this hope even while her more submissive Muslim cousins in the adjacent neighborhood, clad in the black chador, were being married off in their teens one by one.

One day around the time Mariam turned fourteen, her mother, Khatijah, informed her that a family would be coming to their home the following week with their twenty-year-old son to see whether the two would make a good match. Mariam protested that she was not ready to get married, but her objections were ignored. The boy, they said, had a very good job, and so he was a good prospect: Mariam would be financially secure for the rest of her life. School was less important. "It wasn't just that I wanted to stay in school," Mariam said. "I wasn't ready to get married and have a bunch of kids. And I didn't even know about sex. When you grow up in India, most girls are never told about sex. It's not a subject that you talk about. You don't ever have that big talk with your mother. It's understood that you'll find out everything about sex once you're married." That often means you'll be educated on your wedding night with a perfect stranger.

When the day came for the arrival of the suitor and his family, Khatijah fixed her daughter's waist-length hair into two braids and had her put on her finest clothes. Immediately thereafter, when no one was looking, instead of waiting for the arrival of her future in-laws, Mariam slipped out of her home unnoticed. Her parents didn't know where she was, but they were certain she would be back home in time to receive the visiting family in whose home she might be living for the rest of her life.

The boy's family arrived on a sweltering afternoon in the hot season, but the young girl they came to see was nowhere to be found. This was a great embarrassment to Mariam's parents. It was the kind of thing that simply does not happen when two families meet for the first time to consider the marriage of their children. The girl doesn't simply disappear. Too much was at stake.

"She's coming," Abdul assured his visitors. "Something must have happened to detain her, but she's definitely coming."

Some time elapsed, and still Mariam didn't come. More time passed. The situation became more and more awkward. An hour went by, tea and snacks were offered, polite conversation was made, the young man waited eagerly to see his prospective bride. Still no Mariam. Abdul excused himself to go look for his daughter. He went from house to house inquiring about her, but no one had seen her. Two full hours passed. Since Mariam had a reputation for being respectful to her elders, the boy's family was willing to wait. Meanwhile Abdul kept excusing himself to search for his daughter.

While Abdul was walking in the lane outside his home he did not know that his daughter was just a short distance away, watching him through a peephole from inside the house of a Hindu family. The Hindus were in sympathy with the young Muslim girl who would not marry. They knew she wanted to stay in school. For two hours Mariam watched her father step in and out of their house looking for her. He was visibly agitated. Agitation eventually turned into exasperation. Meanwhile a Hindu friend, Karuna, kept bringing Mariam glasses of water to keep her hydrated.

Finally the visitors had had enough. If this young girl would not even bother to show up to meet her future parents-in-law, what kind of girl was she really? She would obviously not be a good match for their son.

She would not be obedient. And so they rose to their feet and thanked Abdul and Khatijah for the tea and snacks and conversation, but they were clearly upset and offended by this girl's poor behavior. It was clear that there would be no formal marriage proposal extended to Abdul and Khatijah's daughter. Mariam had brought disgrace upon her family.

The visitors had barely left the house when Mariam returned. As she stepped through the doorway she could not conceal a grin that revealed how deliberate had been her absence that afternoon. Her father, understanding immediately what had happened, motioned for her to come to him. As soon as she was within reach Abdul's hand darted out and slapped her across her face with such force that it left finger marks on her cheek. Mariam was not surprised by the slap. She knew it was coming. But that was better than a slow death in a loveless marriage and the end of her schooling.

The scene repeated itself two more times in the coming years. The visiting family arrived with hope and then left frustrated, never to return. After the third humiliation, Abdul was in tears. "Why are you doing this to us?" he asked Mariam.

"I keep telling you. I'm never getting married. I'm thinking of becoming a Catholic nun."

But the proposals kept coming, now for her younger sister, Hameeda, too. Both girls were convent educated and hardworking. Twice it happened that marriage proposals were sent by two brothers to marry the two sisters. That means the sisters could have lived out their lives in the same house. But Mariam and Hameeda respectfully declined. At least they belonged to a family in which they could say no. Many Muslim girls had no choice but to agree to marry the man their parents had selected.

Mariam eventually attended college, but her father did not allow her to study art. Instead she took up accounting. After graduation, she landed a job as an accountant for a construction company. She had the freedom now to leave her neighborhood to travel by bus across the city, but all her pay went to the family. After work, she would return to the family store and work late into the night, just as she had done as a girl.

By the time Mariam reached her midtwenties, her neighbors and even some of her relatives would taunt her as being an "old maid," who, weirdly, chose not to marry. "Why would I want to get married and be unhappy?" she answered. "Don't you see me smiling?" One of the reasons gossip swirled around her was that so many women in her neighborhood were trapped in unhappy marriages. Having no opportunity to earn money for themselves, they were in complete financial dependence on their husbands. And if their husbands beat them or had mistresses on the side, there was nowhere for them to go. For some of these women, then, their only sense of empowerment came at the expense of another woman's greater misfortune. Mariam was said to be that unfortunate person, an old maid at twenty-six.

That is about the time I arrived in her neighborhood.

I loved talking to her. We talked about everything, but especially about the very different lives we had lived, our different backgrounds and religions. I felt I could talk with her forever. Even today we never run out of things to talk about.

But it is not all just harmony between us. There have been many times in our marriage when Mariam has taken me aside, her soft eyes flashing with anger, and told me that I could have been more understanding with a particular person or might have shown greater generosity in a given situation. "Don't wait for me to do it first," she'll say. "You should do it on your own." Her words sting, but that's because she tells me what I need to hear, not what I want to hear. It is sometimes not easy being married to a woman with such high standards of sensitivity to others. I think this is one of the greatest advantages, spiritually speaking, to being married. We hear truths about ourselves that we'd rather not hear, but that we need to hear, anyway, if we are to grow spiritually. Even learned monks and priests can deceive themselves into believing that the adulation shown to them by others is a sign that they are in fact very spiritual and important. But some of them would be better off married.

A bit later on that first afternoon, I met her again as I walked down the little lane back toward her house. She was heading to the family store, to replace Hameeda for a few hours. I was startled by the purity of her face in the sunlight. And I was also taken by her lovely womanly form as she walked. When she saw me, she smiled and asked politely, "Have you had anything to eat yet?" I don't remember what I answered. I probably stammered something incoherent.

Our afternoon of conversation came to an end, and it was time to return to the ashram. Everyone—Mr. and Mrs. Shaikh, Shabbir, Mariam, Hameeda—all of them insisted that I come back again soon, and for regular visits. I said I would like to.

As I was riding the motorcycle home with Victor I found myself in a state of mild euphoria. *Here I am in India,* I thought to myself, *and it has never once crossed my mind that I might be spending time with Muslims.* How unexpected. This was a whole new world. I wondered what I would learn about Islam. And the Shaikh family was so refined and welcoming. Yes, I would have to come back, but I wasn't sure when.

But a week later I returned to the Shaikh home, and the four of us—Mariam, Hameeda, Shabbir, and I—talked away the whole afternoon.

A short time passed after my first two visits, and I fell ill again. And so I did not expect to see the Shaikh family for a while until I recovered. I was fully into my studies now. One day I was walking back to the ashram after Sanskrit lessons. It would be a long walk, since my lessons were in a different part of the city. The street was streaming with late afternoon rush hour traffic, noisy with the whir of scooters and the rumbling of buses and trucks and above everything else the piercing blare of high-pitched horns. As I walked, I was lost in thought, my mind reflecting on questions about Śaṅkara and Hinduism and the meaning of nonduality. As I was thinking and walking I watched my sandals kick up dust that sparkled in the sun. I paid little attention to the traffic as I walked. I did not notice that a black-and-yellow motor rickshaw had pulled up alongside me. "Hey!" called out a young woman's voice. I looked up. It was Mariam, the beautiful young Muslim woman, her dark brown eyes looking straight into mine, her teeth shining white with a mischievous smile. Her elegant *salwar kameez,* black and maroon, flowed gracefully over her slender body like water. She was returning home from work. "How have you been?" she asked.

"I've not been keeping well. But I've been meaning to visit you all." I had not come the previous Sunday.

"Do you still have our number?"

"Yes," I said. "It's in my room, but could you write it down again, anyway?"

She reached into her purse and pulled out a scrap of paper and placed it on her lap. As she wrote, her head bowed in concentration, I took a long look at her. Her thick black hair parted at the nape of her neck. It reminded me of a sculpture I had once seen in a Berlin museum. And then my eyes fell on her delicate brown hands as she wrote. I was awed. Her fingers were long and elegant. I had never seen such beautiful hands before. I drank in her form, the hands, the face, the brown skin, the black hair, the stylish clothing.

"Here," she said, as she handed me the paper.

"When's a good day to come?" I asked.

"How about Sunday again?" she answered. "Come have a meal with us."

"OK, I'll call you."

"Good," she said. "Now take care." She smiled once more, signaled to the driver to continue, and was gone. I would have loved to talk longer.

As I walked back to the ashram there was only one thought in my head. "Do not fall in love," I kept repeating to myself. "Do not be an idiot. You're not here in India to fall in love; you're here to study." But I could not stop thinking about those hands and that face and that haunting voice. I knew I was in trouble.

•   •   •

I remember exactly when I truly realized that this was it, that she was the one. It was the following Sunday when I returned to the ashram after paying her family a visit. I sat down in my room and my hands began to tremble. I had seen Mariam only four times by then, three times at her home and once in the rickshaw. But when I was alone in my room, it suddenly came to me that I would marry this woman. It was not so much a decision as a realization. It was a quiet certainty that caught me off guard. From the standpoint of reason it didn't make much sense. I had not been in India very long, I had all my research still ahead of me, I didn't have a job, and in general I barely knew her. And yet the certainty was there, and it didn't come as an end result of carefully weighing pros and cons. It didn't feel like a decision at all, in fact; it was more like I was being informed of something from within, and now it was just a matter of getting on board.

I wrote her a marriage proposal right then and there and gave it to her in an envelope the next time I saw her, not explaining what it was. I thought it would be better that way. She should read my message quietly, without my being there. It would come as a shock to her. A letter would give her time to think and decide, if she needed to. We had known each other, after all, only a few weeks.

When I next saw her, she said, yes, she would marry me. But then she asked, "What took you so long?" She told me later that it had not taken long for her to fall in love with me.

So ours would be a love marriage, not an arranged marriage. Arranged marriages always involve a man and a woman of the same religion, and if they're Hindu, of the same caste as well. The marriage is arranged by the two families. In most cases the two people entering an arranged marriage know each other only a little or perhaps not at all. They might be total strangers. Love marriages, by contrast, are decided by two individuals, often against the wishes of their families. With love marriages the man and woman—or the "boy" and "girl," as they are usually called in India before they get married—know each other very well, they have fallen in love and perhaps secretly dated, and they will try to win their parents over to officially "arrange" what has already been decided by the young couple. This sometimes works, but it is rare, and only if the boy and girl are from the same social group. The biggest obstacle to love marriages is when the two people are from different castes or even different religions; then no arranged marriage is possible. I will return to that later in the book. The overwhelming majority of marriages in India today are still arranged. This is true for Hindus, Muslims, Christians, Parsis, everyone. But it is slowly starting to change in the big cities now. More and more young people are marrying outside their religion and caste.

Since India is the country where almost anything can happen, I cannot resist telling the story of a love marriage that came to be between two people who had never even spoken a single word to each other before the day he proposed to her.

Such was the case of a Hindu couple we know. They first saw each other at a bus stop in Pune. Every morning Sushama was on her way to college, and Arun was on his way to the office. But neither of them knew even that much about the other, even after months of furtive glances and the occasional meeting of eyes. She thought he looked quite handsome and gentle; he for his part found her very beautiful. She thought he looked great in white shirts; he thought she had a wonderful taste in saris. But they were both too shy to speak to each other. She recalls how she longed to see him every day at the bus stop, because of his good looks and gentle face. He, too, looked forward each morning to exchanging secret glances with her. They would smile, and then one of them would board the bus and be gone until the next morning. Such fleeting encounters repeated themselves for months. "Some days he didn't show up at the bus stand," she recalls. "I'd get so sick and depressed that I had to cut classes and go home."

Finally, one day he could no longer hold himself back. "Will you marry me?" he all but shouted. Those were his first words to her.

"Oh yes!" was her immediate reply.

They did not even know each other's name yet. But Arun and Sushama have been married now for more than thirty years. And they are from different castes.

We faced some serious obstacles, the biggest of which was Mariam's parents. It had not taken them long to realize what was going on. I would now come to the house more often, officially to give her brother Shabbir German lessons, but the evening always ended with all of us—Mariam and Hameeda included—talking for hours. We never ran out of things to talk about. The parents, I think, started to notice the way I looked at Mariam when I spoke to her. That's probably when the alarm bells first went off inside them.

I should add that Mariam's parents never once treated me with hostility when I visited their home. The most critical time was when it first dawned on them that my primary reason for regular visits to their home was not in fact to give German lessons to their son Shabbir, but rather to spend time in conversation with their daughter Mariam. They realized that our relationship could lead to marriage. At that point Mr. Shaikh sat Mariam down and told her, "I don't want you talking to that American boy anymore." She said nothing in reply, but during my next few visits to her home, she avoided me while I was with Shabbir. A bit later, her father, not yet convinced that I did not have designs on his daughter, instructed Mariam to tell me I was no longer welcome to even come to their home. "I can't do it. You tell him," was Mariam's reply. She knew her father could not bring himself to tell me, hospitality to strangers being such a sacred tradition in all the religions of India.

What Mr. and Mrs. Shaikh wanted to prevent more than anything else was their daughter converting to Christianity. But the fact is Mariam had considered converting even before she met me. Her appreciation of Catholicism had grown during her years at Catholic school. The cloistered sisters had loved her without ever trying to convert her or even giving a hint of conversion. "They did not judge us, they did not condemn us for belonging to a different religion, and they did not try to convert us. They just loved us schoolgirls," she said. She was drawn to them by their love. The sisters never spoke disparagingly of other religions, not of Islam or Hinduism or Protestantism. That impressed Mariam a lot. Nor did the seminarians who came to her house. They never spoke ill of other religions, and they never talked about whether one religion was better than another. But Mariam does remember the time Father Victor, still a seminarian, spoke of the way Christians understood God's love. It was an unconditional love, he said. No strings attached. You can't earn such love. God's love was offered freely, like a parent to their child. That made sense to Mariam. Good parents love their child unconditionally, and they suffer when the child goes astray. How much greater God's love must be than the love of a human parent. Catholicism had not given Mariam faith in God. Islam had already done that. "Islam gave me an unshakable faith in God," she said. But the emphasis on such radical love is what attracted her to Christianity.[2]

We thought it would be best for me not to come for a while until things died down a bit. We would therefore need to meet secretly. I asked if she could come visit me at the ashram. I had already told the sisters about her. They looked forward to meeting her.

For the next few months things were difficult. Mariam could come visit me in the morning on the way to work, but only for fifteen minutes. She had to travel out of her way to reach the ashram. And so we were able to meet only once every three or four days. I remember how hard it was not seeing her. I would count the days and the hours until our next meeting. Then she would appear, smiling radiantly, and we would sit for fifteen minutes, trying to get in everything we had been saving to talk about. Then she would be gone, and the old longing would begin all over again and the counting of days and hours till we would meet. All people should have this kind of ardent desire for God, too, if we are to become one with Him. So say the lovers of God in all the religions. It is a mutual desire for oneness. The Song of Songs in the Hebrew scriptures, like much Hindu literature, uses the ardent longing of separated lovers as a metaphor for the love between God and the devotee. It is in

God, the supreme Lover, that all loves are ultimately rooted and ultimately find their fulfillment.

It was around that difficult time of fleeting encounters when Mariam took up again the practice of yoga at the famous Ramamani Iyengar Memorial Yoga Institute, not far from the Christian ashram where I lived. She had learned yoga years before while attending Catholic school. Going to the yoga institute was an opportunity for us to meet for two hours once a week, even if talking was not allowed during practice. We could at least look at each other while stretching and balancing and standing on our heads.

It would be more than a year before we married. Mariam insisted that we first get the blessing of her parents, no matter what. In the meantime, Hameeda and Shabbir worked on their parents, putting in a good word for me at every opportunity, though the issue of marriage did not explicitly come up.

Just a month before we married we decided it was time for me to formally ask for Mariam's hand in marriage. Shabbir had told his father in advance that I wanted to speak with him about something. He must have known why. He was in the house when I approached him, and Mariam was there, too. Mr. Shaikh had not seen me in a while. I just came straight out with it; I told him I wanted his permission to marry his daughter.

He did not hesitate for a moment. He told me in a calm voice, "You can marry her if you become a Muslim." I told him I couldn't. Mariam said, "I don't want him to become a Muslim. I want to become a Catholic."

"You be quiet!" he snapped at her. "Is this what you've been doing behind my back?"

Nothing was resolved that day. I was very upset when I left the house. I feared I might lose Mariam. How did I know her father wouldn't try to marry her off to some other man, now that he knew the full truth about us? I had heard such stories before, and they worried me.

It eventually helped that Shabbir came up with the idea of us taking a train to Kerala to meet Mr. Shaikh's brother, Arul Raj. He was a Catholic; maybe he would support my marrying Mariam, especially since she wanted to become a Catholic. Uncle Arul and Mariam's father were still close, though divided by religion. Shabbir's idea was worth a shot. Shabbir and I took a train south and returned a week later. Arul Raj got to know me, though he was wary at first. Educated people in India are often aware of the high divorce rate in the West. But in India, for the most part, when you marry it's forever. For the next few days, Arul Raj asked me a lot of questions about my intentions and my character. But even on the day we departed he was still noncommittal. He didn't promise me anything. Later I found out that he wrote a letter to his brother, Mr. Shaikh, in which he stated that I was a very upstanding and sincere person and that by all indications I would make a good husband for Mariam.

While I was away in Kerala Mariam took her father aside one day and had a long talk with him. She convinced him that he must finally come to terms with the inevitable. She told him as gently as she could that if he did not finally accept our marriage, she would have no choice but to elope with me. But that would bring shame upon the family, an option she really didn't want to take. And besides, she added, had not her father himself abandoned the faith of his upbringing, Catholicism, to convert to Islam for the sake of love? But in her father's mind, this was really no argument, since Islam was the superior religion. Converting *to* Islam was a good idea; converting *from* Islam was a bad idea. Mr. Shaikh ultimately realized there was nothing he could do to change his daughter's mind. Mariam ended up pleading with him. "Please say yes, Abba (Papa)! Please!" In other families, daughters were sometimes married against their will to a man they did not want. But Mr. Shaikh loved his daughter too much to do that, and he could see that there wasn't much he could do to stop the wedding, but his heart was broken.

It was Mariam's discussion with her father that had made the difference, plus the letter of support from Arul Raj, and so I was eventually accepted as the future son-in-law. We were of different religions, my in-laws and I, but we all believed in one good and gracious God, and that belief turned out to be important. It was at the heart of our identity. We were believers. That was a good foundation for our relationship. And our relationship strengthened over time into real love.

15

Tiwari and the Wedding Invitation

Not long before we were married, Mariam and I visited a printer in Pune's "old town" to pick out a wedding invitation. We settled on a colorfully painted card that displayed elaborate twisting flowered creepers bordering an empty white rectangular area, inside of which we were supposed to place whatever words would be suitable to proclaim our love. We reflected for some time on what we might say. What message did we want to give to those invited to our wedding? Should we choose words of our own making or play it safe and quote the wisdom of some famous poet or sage or holy text? Since at the time I was studying Hindu scripture I suggested we might borrow some lines from the Bṛhadāraṇyaka Upaniṣad (ca. 600 BCE), in which a Hindu man, Yājñavalkya, speaks to his wife, Maitreyi. The passage runs as follows:

> It is not for the sake of the husband that the husband is dear, but the husband is dear for the sake of the Self. It is not for the sake of the wife that the wife is dear, but the wife is dear for the sake of the Self. (Bṛhadāraṇyaka Upaniṣad 4.5.6)

I interpreted this to mean that the husband and wife find God (the "Self," Brahman, the Lord within, our true Center) in their devotion and love for each other. Inasmuch as they give themselves to each other they learn to die to self-centeredness and thereby find God. After hearing those words and my explanation, Mariam enthusiastically agreed, and so it was decided. The passage seemed to unite so well human and divine love. And even though we were not Hindu, many of our guests would be, and so the Upaniṣad quote seemed perfectly appropriate. But I must also confess that I was feeling a bit pleased with myself at the time for knowing Hindu scripture well enough to be able to locate the perfect passage for my wedding day. My friends back home in the United States, reading the wedding invitation, would be very impressed by my knowledge of Hinduism, I thought to myself.

Later that day I returned to the ashram and paid a visit to Yisudas Tiwari,[1] whose room was a few doors down from mine. A retired professor from Serampore College in Bengal, Yisudas was well known in Protestant theological circles in India. His background was unusual. He had been raised in Agra in a devout and learned Hindu home with great reverence for classical Sanskrit works, and he enjoyed a considerable command of the Sanskrit language. But as a young man he caused great pain to his family by converting from high-caste Brahmin Hinduism to Protestant Christianity. In this decision he had been influenced by the writings of C. F. Andrews, an Anglican clergyman and friend of Gandhi, and by his reading of the New Testament. It was only many years later, Tiwari confided to me, that he came to realize what a great "shock" his conversion must have caused his father and the Brahmin community. One could sense a certain pain in his voice even years after the fact as he related the story to me. He expressed no regrets about his conversion, only that embracing a new religion had caused his family so much pain.

Soon after the conversion, Tiwari's father arranged a meeting between Gandhi himself and the young convert to Christianity, with the hope that the encounter might persuade the wayward son to return to the faith of his family and caste. The conversation was still fresh in Tiwari's mind decades later, as he related it to me. "Gandhiji asked me why I had become a Christian. I told him that Jesus had become my guru and savior. Then he asked me, since I was now a Christian, if I hated Hinduism. I told him no; I said I would always love Hinduism.

Then he said to me, 'Then be the best possible Christian you can. Make Christians better Christians; make Hindus better Hindus.'"

Tiwari went on to a career teaching the history of religions to Christian students, and in the seven months I lived with him at the ashram, I never once heard him bad-mouthing the religion of his upbringing. He could even be playful in reflecting on his Hindu roots and how they continued to influence him. Once, on a major feast day for the Virgin Mary, he said with a chuckle, "I *love* goddesses; I could worship a great number of them!" But he could also be stern and impatient and very direct, especially when Sanskrit was being mispronounced by those at the ashram who should know better. "It's not *MA-ha*!" he would almost shout. "It's *ma-HA*!" (*Mahā* means "great," as in "Mahatma," or "great soul.")

I think Tiwari and I shared a special closeness because of my impending marriage. Almost all the other community members, most of them nuns, were celibate and unmarried. Tiwari's own wife had passed away some years before, and he still missed her dearly. He never tired of talking about her, and he was fond of quoting verses from Kālidāsa's ancient Sanskrit poem "The Cloud Messenger," about separated lovers in sweet and agonized longing for each other. He could at times be both wistful and humorous.

And so I walked into Tiwari's room after returning from the printer. There he was, the elderly scholar now in his seventies, white-haired, ascetic, and dignified, as always in his simple room at the Christian ashram sitting behind his desk working on the Gospel of John. He was in the process of writing a commentary on Christ's farewell discourse to his disciples. I was excited and confident in the knowledge that this expert of Hindu scripture would appreciate, even relish, the text I had found for my wedding day.

"Yisudas!" I exclaimed. "I've picked out the verses for our wedding invitation. Do you want to hear them?"

He smiled broadly and his face lit up. "Yes, I'd love to."

And so I began: "It is not for the sake of the husband that the husband is dear—" But Tiwari, the accomplished scholar and expert in

Hindu scripture, immediately cut me off with a scowl. "You dope!" he shouted. "This is a verse about a man who is about to renounce his wife. He's *leaving* her. But you're getting *married*. You can't use it for a wedding invitation. Hindus will think you're *stupid*." And then, with a small dismissive wave of his hand, he muttered to me in a low voice, "Why don't you stick to your own scriptures?" I was stung by Tiwari's bluntness, and I apologized for my error, thanked him for his advice, and, feeling thoroughly humiliated, quietly left his room.

And so I did as Tiwari had instructed; I went back to my own scriptures. And this is the New Testament passage Mariam and I ended up using for the wedding invitation: *"Love bears all things, believes all things, hopes all things, endures all things."* It is from Paul's First Letter to the Corinthians, chapter 13 (the great chapter on love), verse 7. Since most of the wedding guests, being Hindu and Muslim, would not know what a Corinthian letter was, we simply identified the quoted passage as being from "the Holy Bible." The response was very good. A Hindu yoga teacher told us she didn't know the Bible had such beautiful passages in it. And so I am grateful to Tiwari for having saved me from public humiliation brought on by pride.

16

Wedding Day Fiasco

A week before the wedding, I stood with my father-in-law in his store. "Will you be coming to the wedding?" I asked.

He paused, looking straight at me, his eyes welling up with tears. "I can't," he said quietly. It was hard enough for him to see his beloved daughter convert to a different religion; it was further agony not to be able to attend her wedding. He knew that if the word got out that he and his wife had given away their daughter at a Catholic church there would be problems with some of the more conservative relatives and friends.

Mariam and her father had always been close. As a three-year-old, so the story goes, she refused to eat dinner until "Abba" came home late at night from work. It was from her father that Mariam had learned to read and do math at five, so that she might compete for admission to Catholic kindergarten. With her father's help she enrolled at a Catholic school run by cloistered sisters. Mariam also learned from her father how to tend his roses. She was the one who put in long hours at the store, even on school days. Mr. Shaikh had many reasons to be proud of his daughter. So many people praised her: the neighbors, the relatives, and the teachers at school. And here was her father now, fighting to hold back his tears. I did not deserve to intrude on this relationship, and I did not know how to react to a man older than I who had never shown emotion to me before, whose face was now so sad. All I could do was tell him I would save him a piece of the wedding cake. With great effort he bravely smiled.

A few days later my mother-in-law sternly advised us not to return to the house after the wedding for at least six months, as there might otherwise be trouble with the Muslim relatives.

Mrs. Shaikh had reason to be concerned about Mariam marrying outside her religion. Mariam's cousin Yasin had eloped with a Hindu girl a few years earlier, and things had not gone well with the relatives, to say the least. The boy and girl were just teenagers, and even though they had practically no money, they were determined to get married, no matter what. So one day they took off. For them the most immediate goal was to escape the relatives who would certainly be out combing the city for them. Both families were absolutely against a marriage across religious boundaries. Hindus and Muslims simply do not marry each other, unless one of them converts—and it is almost always a conversion from Hinduism to Islam rather than the reverse.

And so when both sets of parents are against an interreligious marriage, the young couple has no choice but to run away. In India this is an act of desperation with extreme consequences. First, it brings moral disgrace upon the families involved, making it more difficult for the other siblings to get married, especially the sisters. As a consequence, those who would marry against the wishes of their parents are sometimes disowned and thereby lose all financial and social support. They are regarded as dead by their families. Sometimes the hearts of the parents will soften when a grandchild is born, but often the parents remain unmoved. Mariam told the story of a Brahmin girl she knew who had married a Muslim boy. "Even after she gave birth to a boy, her parents would not see her."

So when Yasin's parents learned that he had eloped with a Hindu girl, they enlisted other relatives to track them down before they could leave the city. They knew immediately where to look. Some of them took off for the train station, and the others fanned out to the city's main bus terminals. Within a few hours the boy and girl were located, just as they were about to board a bus that would have taken them out of the city to freedom. They were literally dragged back to their homes. Within a few days the girl was married off to a Hindu stranger, and Yasin had one of his legs broken with an iron bar by his own father, to prevent him from running away and searching for his beloved. The two young lovers never saw each other again. And so, because of stories such as these, my mother-in-law warned us not to return anytime soon to the neighborhood, because the Muslim relatives might react angrily to Mariam's conversion to Christianity. It's not that they didn't like me as a person; it's just that I was leading a Muslim woman away from the one true faith.

I never knew until much later why it was that my future brother-in-law Shabbir always insisted on accompanying me by foot out of the neighborhood, even though I had a bicycle. "Let's walk," he'd say, and ten minutes later he would see me off, waving to me as I pedaled off into the night back to the other side of the city. It was, I learned later, for my protection. There were worries that some of the more conservative relatives might confront me.

At our first prenuptial meeting with the parish priest, an elderly Indian Jesuit, we discussed preparations for the wedding at St. Xavier's, the downtown church built by German priests more than a century earlier. In the course of our hour-long conversation we settled on the wedding date and which friends or relatives might be considered as witnesses, and whether we fully understood the seriousness of our marriage vows. All throughout the conversation the priest had assumed that Mariam was a Catholic, most likely because "Mariam" is a name common among Christian women from the south; it is not just a Muslim name. At the end of our little conference the priest turned to Mariam and asked, "So what is your full name?"

"Mariam Shaikh," she said softly.

"*Shaikh?*" he asked, clearly surprised. "A *Muslim?*"

Mariam nodded.

"*Will there be trouble?*"

We assured him there would be no trouble, but we really didn't know.

The reason the priest had asked whether there might be trouble was because of an incident that had taken place in Pune only weeks before. An Indian-Iranian Shiite girl from downtown had run off with her Catholic boyfriend. I knew the girl's brother, Muhammad; he was Shabbir's friend. I had been teaching German to both of them for a number of months. He was from a conservative Muslim family. His father had two wives. When the girl ran away from home, the relatives could not find her, and after visiting the boy's home and not finding her there, they concluded that she must be hiding in the Catholic seminary located near the boy's home at the outskirts of the city. And so they would search for her there, even if it meant turning the place upside down.

A throng of Muslim men approached the seminary brandishing knives and swords. They demanded that the girl be handed over. Some of the priests and seminarians blocked the Muslims at the seminary entrance and attempted to calm them down and convince them that the girl was not inside. (The girl was in fact hiding elsewhere in the city.) But to no avail. The Muslim men insisted that they be allowed to search the place. The priests refused. Tempers flared. The Muslims threatened to search the seminary by force.

"Wait just a moment," said one of the priests. He was one of the highest authorities in the seminary. "I'll be right back."

The Muslims thought the priest was going to submit and turn the girl over to them. Instead he returned with a rifle. He was an avid hunter, a man who enjoyed going out into the hills to hunt rabbits. When he approached the Muslim men, he discharged three shots into the air as a warning not to proceed any farther. The Muslims dispersed and did not return. When I first heard the story, I thought to myself, *Well, at least it wasn't the spiritual director who fired the shots.*

Another incident took place not far from where Mariam lived, some months after we had married. It reveals the desperation of young people in love who are separated by social barriers. This time it involved two Hindus instead of a Muslim and a Hindu. The boy and girl were very young, only sixteen, but they had grown up together in the same lane and now wanted to marry. Though they were both Hindu, they were of different subcastes, not high caste versus low caste, but rather two subcastes that were not so very different. To their dismay the parents on both sides refused to allow the marriage. They were opposed to intercaste marriage. Perhaps it was just caste pride at work in the families instead of religious conviction, one caste being slightly higher than the other. The boy and girl persisted with their pleas for many weeks, but without success. Tired of hearing the constant pleading, one of the parents finally stated in no uncertain terms that the two would *never* be allowed to marry, so they should just drop the idea once and for all. There would be no further discussion.

The next day the boy and girl went missing. It was obvious that they had run away. But where did they go? And where *could* they go? And how could they start a new life together when they had no money? And, besides, they were so young. For two days both families scoured the city for the young couple, but they found no sign of them. It was only on the third day that the bodies of the two, tied together with a sari, were found washed up on the banks of a river outside Pune. They had committed suicide by jumping off a high bridge. Neither could swim. They had tied themselves together to be united at least in death. The bodies were brought back to their neighborhood in the back of a flatbed truck. Word of the double suicide quickly spread to neighboring lanes. The families of the young lovers, weeping and cursing what had happened, were inconsolable, and the neighbors publicly mourned the loss of the two. Finally, out of grief, the parents of the dead boy and girl called a Hindu priest, who agreed to perform a wedding ceremony over the two corpses. The understanding was that the souls of the two would at least be united until their next embodiment on earth. So the boy and girl corpses were dressed in wedding garb, the ceremony was performed, and the two were cremated—on their wedding day.

My own parents in the United States were surprised when I wrote them that I was going to get married. They did not know I had even been seeing anyone. They were happy for me, but also a bit apprehensive, as I was still a student in India with no imminent job prospects in the States, and I was years away from completing my doctorate. There was no certainty I would ever land a job once I returned to the West. Getting married at this time of my life didn't seem to make a lot of sense to them. And they would not come to the wedding for understandable reasons. My father had never traveled by plane before, and he was reluctant to fly across oceans and continents all the way to the other side of the world. My mother, by contrast, was not afraid of flying, but she was not attracted to the idea of going to India. Everything she had ever seen on American television about India reminded her of poverty, disease, and natural calamities. The media preferred to show India's problems rather than its achievements. At the time, my mother could not fathom my love for the country.

The final weeks leading up to the wedding remain a blur. I recall Mariam and I getting in and out of rickshaws, endlessly crisscrossing the city to distribute the wedding invitations, prepare the reception hall, order the cake and everything else connected to the reception—silverware, food, and drinks—pick out the right music, find a photographer, select the wedding dress, and get measured for my suit. There was nothing romantic about those days; we were almost entirely on our own with the preparations, always exhausted, just trying to get everything done in time for the wedding day. My brother-in-law-to-be, Shabbir, volunteered to do what he could to help. I dropped Mariam off a few streets away from her home every day just after dark. Only a few people there knew about the wedding: Hameeda and Shabbir and a few close friends who could be trusted to keep our secret.

It was now the morning of our wedding day. We would be married by midafternoon. But there were still a few things to do. First, I had to make sure that the soft drinks were properly delivered to the reception hall. Then there was the mattress. I took a rickshaw to my apartment to see if it had arrived. When I got there, I saw it lying on the bedsprings, but there was a problem. The mattress was only two feet wide by three feet long, big enough for a small child, but not big enough for two newlyweds. There had obviously been some misunderstanding. I tucked the mattress under my arm, got back in the rickshaw, and headed back across town.

The man at the mattress store insisted this was the size my brother-in-law had ordered. I asked him how that could be, since the mattress was for me and my wife. It was our wedding day, after all. The owner shrugged his shoulders. "I do have one mattress left," he said, "but you'll have to pay for that one, too." I had no choice. He signaled to his man to take the larger mattress to our apartment.

Now it was early afternoon, and I was finally finished with everything. All the wedding preparations were in place. For the first time in weeks I felt I could relax. A friend had offered me the use of a little room on M. G. Road[1] within walking distance of the church. It was an hour before the wedding, just enough time to compose myself. The warm December sun was shining down peacefully on the city, pedestrian traffic had thinned out, since most of the shoppers had gone home to rest, and the shops were beginning to close down for the afternoon. My suit was draped neatly over a chair. All the turmoil of the days leading up to the wedding was now dissipating; all that remained in this last quiet hour was to collect myself and to prepare mentally for the transition to a new state of life, with all its unknown responsibilities. I settled down in a chair in the shade of my room to consider one more time the enormous implications of married life.

At that moment the silhouette of my brother-in-law Shabbir appeared in the doorway. "How's it going?" he asked, with a broad smile. He was upbeat.

"Pretty good," I replied. "One hour to go, and all I've got to do is get my suit on and walk over to the church and marry your sister."

"You still need to do one more thing," Shabbir said.

"What's that?" I asked.

"You need to get a haircut."

"Shabbir," I said, "I don't need a haircut. And even if I did, there's not enough time left."

"Yes, there is," he replied with a confident grin. "I've made an appointment for you." He was positively beaming.

"What do you mean?"

"There's a really good barbershop on East Street, and they're waiting for you right now. I was just over there. Your hair looks okay, but they'll make it look really good, since it's your wedding day. If we leave now, we'll easily be back in time for the wedding."

Since East Street was only a few blocks away from where we were, and since I did not want to disappoint my soon-to-be brother-in-law, I agreed to go, but we had to hurry.

After a short ride in a rickshaw, we got down and entered the barbershop. The first thing I noticed when I stepped through the doorway was that the place was absolutely packed with men and boys, some standing, others sitting. At the opposite end of the room in front of a giant mirror six barbers were busy at work. Every one of the barber chairs was occupied, and many more people were awaiting their turn.

"It's full," I said to Shabbir. "Let's go."

"No," Shabbir answered. "I just talked to the owner; he's expecting you."

We approached the owner, who was standing at the cash register. After a brief conversation with him in Hindi, Shabbir turned to me and said, "There's been a misunderstanding. The owner says that you can have a haircut right now only if the other people here agree to it. We need to take a vote."

"What do you mean, take a vote?" I asked.

At that moment the owner began waving both his arms in the air and cried out, "May I please have your attention, everybody! Please, may I have your attention!" All activity stopped, the barbers held their combs and scissors in midair, and all attention focused on the man with the waving arms.

The owner continued, in English and Hindi, "This man here"—he touched my shoulder with his hand—"is from America. He is going to marry this man's sister"—he touched Shabbir's shoulder—in *one hour*. The wedding is in just *one hour*! He needs to get a haircut. But there isn't much time. Should we let him go ahead of you all?"

I wanted to run and hide.

I am not exaggerating: the place erupted in cheers. "Yes, let him get the haircut! Let him go first! It's all right!"

After a few minutes, one of the chairs in front of the big mirror was free. As I settled in and the barber placed a sheet over my shoulders I felt many eyes fixed on me. Shabbir explained in Hindi what kind of cut I needed. The idea was that a simple touch-up would do.

Barbers in India, even working with scissors, are very quick, much faster than anyone I've seen in America. And that's why, before I could recognize there was a problem, it was too late; the damage had been done. The barber was giving me a new look, starting by cutting all the hair away from my forehead.

"Shabbir!" I said. "Tell him to stop!"

Shabbir translated, and the barber stopped cutting immediately. But my hair could not be rescued. To remedy the problem the barber decided he would innovate; he combed the hair on the sides straight back, and before I could protest how silly I looked, he reached for a metal can and delivered a heavy dose of hair spray guaranteed to keep the new look in place. And it was now too late to wash my hair before the wedding.

Shabbir took a long look at me. "Sorry," he said in a quiet voice. And as if to reassure me he added, "It doesn't look *that* bad."

All I could think about now was getting to the church on time.

Our rickshaw pulled up to the church just as the bells began chiming. Moments later a car pulled up. Mariam stepped out in a white wedding dress, her face veiled. She had spent the whole day with a Sindhi family in a different part of the city, letting them help her get ready for the wedding. The main reason she was with them instead of with her own family was to keep the wedding a secret from her Muslim relatives and neighbors back home. Because she was raised a Muslim in a conservative neighborhood, she could not be seen putting on a white Christian wedding gown at home. There might be trouble; perhaps the ceremony would be disrupted, or maybe Mariam's parents would be ostracized by their Muslim relatives for allowing their daughter to convert and marry in a Catholic church. She had to find a different place to prepare for the wedding. And so she had left her home at the same time she did every workday morning, so as not to arouse suspicion. Already there had been talk in the neighborhood that she might one day run off with me, but so far it was only speculation. No one really knew what was going on between us.

The Sindhis had invited a Goan lady to do Mariam's makeup. Mariam protested that she never wore makeup. "But it's your wedding day," everyone said. "You have to look special." The Goan Catholics are among the most Westernized of all the Christian communities in India. Originally from the tiny state of Goa on the western coast, they are now also found in other cities like Pune and Mumbai. The Goan Catholic community as a whole has inherited many of the customs of the Portuguese missionaries who converted them to Christianity centuries ago. The Portuguese understanding back then was that to be a true Christian, one had to not only believe in Christian doctrines and learn the Lord's Prayer and Hail Mary, but it was also necessary to abandon everything Hindu, including Hindu customs and Hindu names, and take on European ways. This attitude is, of course, very different from today's "inculturation" approach, in which alien customs and practices are allowed, even encouraged, as long as they do not contradict Gospel teaching and values. But hundreds of years ago the Goan Hindus who converted to Catholicism were introduced to beef. And for the first time they began consuming alcohol, which eventually became a staple at all celebrations, both religious and secular. The new converts were even forced to change their names to those of the Portuguese: D'Souza, De Silva, Fernandes, Rocha, Rodrigues, Lobo, Pereira, Furtado, Vaz, and Mascarenhas are common in Goan Catholic parishes. Goan Catholics also took to wearing Western-style clothing, which meant for women a simple dress instead of the elegantly draped sari or tuniclike *salwar kameez*. Goan women also tended to wear a good deal of makeup for public functions. And so when Mariam spent the better part of her wedding day with a Goan lady, it was clear that she was going to make Mariam as beautiful as possible, but by Goan standards, which meant administering a serious application of makeup.

As Mariam was getting ready her mother appeared unexpectedly. "I just had to see you in your wedding dress," she said. She would not be coming to the ceremony.

As we met outside the church Mariam and I sized each other up. "What happened to your hair?" she asked in amazement.

"Shabbir talked me into getting a haircut," I answered. "Things didn't go so well."

Then she removed her veil, revealing lips bright with red lipstick and deeply rouged cheeks. "What did they do to your face?" I asked.

She said nothing. She had not wanted makeup, anyway, but neither did she want to offend anyone. As we walked up the aisle of the church together Mariam wiped her lips and cheeks with a tissue while I ran my fingers through my hair, trying to loosen up the new look.

Though our wedding took place in India it was not very different from any of the Catholic weddings I had attended in the West. The parish church itself had been built by German Jesuits in the nineteenth century, and it was in every way European in design and structure. Only the artwork was Indian, displaying huge paintings of episodes from the life of St. Francis Xavier, after whom the church was named, as he arrived by ship in Goa, ministered to the Indian people, and finally lay prone on his deathbed. The language of our liturgy was English, which is not unusual in large city parishes whose members are often comprised of people from various parts of India speaking very different languages. English becomes the convenient common language for those worshipping, although masses are also celebrated in the regional language. Perhaps the one element that most distinguished our wedding ceremony in Pune from Catholic weddings in the West was that most of the people present that day were completely unfamiliar with Catholicism and its rituals.

The guests were of different religions: Christian, Muslim, Hindu, Parsi, Sikh, one Jew. This is normal at Indian weddings, to have guests

from such different backgrounds. The Muslims present were young
friends of Mariam who had kept our secret. Each of the different groups
kept to itself for the most part, except the Christian sisters from the
ashram, who mixed with everyone. The Brahmin family with whom I
had lived for so many months did not come. They would not be seen at
a public function with their servants, for in their eyes that would have
demeaned them. And the servants did not come, either, though they had
also been invited, for fear of arousing the displeasure of their employers.

After a while a few of the guests told us quietly that the food was
too spicy to eat, even for Indians. Others began telling us the same:
the main meal was, unfortunately, inedible. We apologized and urged
everyone to help themselves to the wedding cake. What we didn't know
was that part of the cake was somehow spoiled or had been contami-
nated. As a result, a number of guests became ill from food poisoning
while at the reception. Others showed symptoms after they returned
home. We learned this only some days later. We ourselves were spared;
we don't know why.

When the reception ended, it was time to clean up. The teenage
Goan boys we had hired through a friend arrived drunk. Instead of
washing dishes, they began throwing plates and glasses against the
kitchen walls, just for the fun of it. Mariam's brother Razaak arrived
soon afterward and threatened them into submission.

We left the wedding hall and traveled to our secret meeting with
Mariam's mother. She smiled when she saw Mariam, but she looked a
bit sad. It was her daughter's wedding day, and she had not attended.

We arrived at our apartment exhausted. All our efforts had not re-
sulted in a perfect wedding day. Almost everything had gone wrong.
Mariam was in tears. We finally looked at it this way: we had hit rock
bottom on our wedding day. Things could now only get better.

It did not take long to notice the disapproving looks of strangers on
the street even after we had married. Many must have thought I was
a Westerner with an Indian girlfriend and no long-term plans. The

remarks, the catcalls that we heard, were always expressed in Hindi or Marathi, the assumption being that only Mariam would understand them. They were therefore directed at her, and they were always from other men. She ignored them. "What did he call out?" I would ask. Her answer, always the same, was "Never mind" or "You don't want to know." But as soon as our firstborn arrived, held securely in his mother's arms with me at her side, the insults and insinuations came to a complete and abrupt halt. Instead we encountered smiles and approving nods from both men and women of all ages. If we had a child, after all, we were probably married; our relationship was therefore judged to be legitimate.

It is years later now, and we are back in India. It is still three weeks until the monsoon arrives, and the heat is stifling. We are almost feverish by midafternoon, and our ceiling fan has gone dead. The power will not return for at least three hours. Until then, our apartment balcony windows are thrown open to the hazy molten sky and to swirls of fine yellow dust that settle lightly on our bed and table. Time passes so slowly in the absence of television; for now, with nothing else to do, Mariam and I willingly surrender to dreamlike remembrances of days long ago when we first met, in this lovely sprawling city in Maharashtra, the place where we fell in love. We recall how I proposed to her in less than three weeks' time and how she answered, "What took you so long?" How her parents resisted, how her brother and sister fought for us, and all that happened on our wedding day. Even though the future was uncertain we were at least in beloved India. Life was simple then, and sometimes full of adventure. Even when money was scarce we always somehow managed to travel. When Mariam was pregnant and sick with our first child, even then we took the old rickety bus to Aurangabad and then another to Ajanta. We walked all day in and out of Buddhist caves, and she, as always, did not complain. Inside one ancient cavern I looked at her as she stopped enraptured before the painted mural of a young woman combing her long black hair, surrounded by her devoted maidservants, and I thought how she was even more beautiful than that woman and even more loved. I look at her now and see the same young woman after all these years. Her face still radiates such kindness; isn't that the word people always use about her?

Is that what first attracted me to you, those deep and compassionate dark eyes, or was it your gentle voice that I seemed to recognize from another world and time? Or was it your slender and seductive form, hips swaying as you walked toward me that first time?

17

A Muslim Prayer of Petition

A few months after we were married, we moved from an apartment building alongside the noisy Bombay–Pune Highway in Shivaji Nagar to Deccan Gymkhana, a Hindu neighborhood in a more pleasant and serene part of the city. Our new apartment was almost hidden from view by luxuriant flowering trees, creepers, and bushes. All day long we were treated to the sweet melody of birds we only rarely glimpsed through the thick foliage.

December is an idyllic time to be in Maharashtra. By October the monsoon's storms have given way to the calm of the dry sunny season. Every day the skies are a deep cloudless blue, the breezes are balmy and soothing, and the butterflies are fluttering happily from flower to flower. When the sun sets and darkness descends, the starlit nights are cool enough for you to wrap yourself in a colorfully embroidered Kashmiri shawl and take a leisurely stroll around the neighborhood, past old stone bungalows encircled by silhouettes of stately banyan trees. In short, you think you've died and gone to heaven.

It was in those few months after we married that Mariam became pregnant. In November Brian arrived, and he immediately became the center of our life.

It was on one of those perfect days in December that Brian suddenly stopped eating. He was about a month old. His appetite had been good, but on this particular day and for no apparent reason he simply stopped nursing. When we took him out of his crib in the morning, he turned his head away from Mariam when she brought him to her. We were surprised, but at first we thought nothing of it. A little later his mother tried again, and as before Brian refused to nurse. We checked his temperature, but he had no fever, and he didn't seem to be in pain. In every way he was his usual good-natured self. This continued all day long, so that by midafternoon we began to be more than a little concerned, and by late afternoon we started to panic. I suppose this reaction is not unusual for first-time parents. Birds and animals know instinctively what to do the moment their young come into the world, but people have to be taught how to care for their babies. No one had ever told us what to do if a healthy baby simply refused to nurse. We were completely unprepared and baffled by what was happening to our son.

We waited impatiently for Mariam's mother to arrive. Every day for several months after Brian was born she came to our apartment to give Mariam a full body massage with spices and oils. It is an old Indian custom that both mothers and newborns receive a daily massage after the delivery, if they can afford it. The massage is usually given by an older woman—perhaps a relative or a friend of the family—who has the time to come by every day. The massage is supposed to strengthen the bodies of both mother and child. Sometimes the new mother will even move back to her childhood home for up to six months, to be cared for by her own mother, after which she returns to her husband.

Mrs. Shaikh typically arrived at our apartment just before noon after traveling across the city in a motor rickshaw. She always showed up at our door dressed in a simple sari, part of which she draped over her graying hair, a normal gesture for a modest woman going out in public. In one hand she carried a large bag full of spices and oils for the massage; in the other she carried a bag with several metal containers of freshly cooked rice, chapatis, vegetables, and either shrimp or chicken or goat curry. After the massage was done, we enjoyed lunch and leisurely conversation, after which Mariam, her mother, and Brian would travel back across the city to the neighborhood where Mariam grew up. Occasionally I would travel to the neighborhood with my family, but usually I stayed behind to read and write. When the sun began to set in the early evening, it was time to put aside my work and flag down a rickshaw to rejoin my family across town. After dinner and visits to neighbors and relatives, we would finally return home together around midnight. It was a simple life that repeated itself on a daily basis, and we were happy.

But now our baby was not nursing. On that particular day my mother-in-law happened to arrive quite a bit later than usual, although I don't remember the reason why. When she arrived at our door in late afternoon, she saw from our faces that there was something wrong. "What's the matter?" she asked.

"Brian won't nurse," replied Mariam. "He hasn't had anything all day."

Mrs. Shaikh chuckled and shook her head as she walked past us into the apartment. She said something in Hindi.

"What did she say?" I asked Mariam.

"She said, 'O you people of little faith.'"

Next she picked up Brian, held him in her arms, and looked at him with the love and understanding of a doting grandmother. Then she instructed Mariam to fetch a metal spoon and a string. After Mariam handed them to her mother, the older woman wound the string around the ladle portion of the spoon, over and over. Then she told Mariam to squeeze some of her milk onto the spoon. Next she went to the kitchen and lit the flame on the stove. She held the spoon with the milk and string directly into the flame, and as she did so she said a prayer in Arabic. Mariam and I looked at each other with skepticism. Though Mrs. Shaikh didn't know exactly what the prayer meant word for word, since she didn't speak Arabic, she had faith that it would work. She had been taught the prayer by her mother, who had learned it from *her* mother, and who knows how many generations before that from mother to mother. Each time the prayer was passed on, you were taught that this is exactly the prayer you say in Arabic when someone has cast a spell on your child, preventing him or her from eating. You say this standard prayer to God, and you say it with faith and with the understanding that God is more powerful than anything or anyone in the world, whether man or demon. You don't need to know the meaning of the individual words.

As I watched the milk in the spoon heat up in the flame, boil into bubbles, and finally evaporate, I noticed with some amazement that the string did not burn, even though it was being licked by the flames of the fire. After the milk had completely disappeared, Mariam's mother unwrapped the string and threw it away. Then she turned to Mariam. "Try nursing him now."

Mariam took Brian to her breast, and he immediately nursed.

A year passed, and we had gathered at Mrs. Shaikh's home again, where she had just prepared dinner. Brian was now a bit over a year old, sitting quietly on a stool. He had eaten nothing all day, and when his grandmother offered him rice and dal (lentils), he refused, even though he normally looked forward to his nani's food. Mrs. Shaikh assessed the situation and immediately concluded what was the matter. Someone must have put a spell on Brian again. So she took a large metal pot and filled it with water and placed it on the floor near her grandson. Then she took a handful of salt in her fist and waved it in a circle over Brian's head, all the while reciting the same prayer in Arabic that she had recited the year before. As she prayed she took care not to let a single grain of salt fall from her hand. When the prayer was done, she threw the salt into the vat of water, carried the pot to the back of the house, and then poured the water down the drain. After watching her mother's little ritual, Mariam brought Brian the same rice and dal that he had refused only minutes before, and this time he ate it without hesitation. No one had asked him why he had not eaten all day, and he didn't seem to notice the prayer that had just been spoken over him by his grandmother.

Of course there is no way of knowing for sure if someone has indeed cast a spell on your child or who did it or why. None of that matters finally; what is important is that in times of distress, the Muslim goes to God and says with faith a prayer that God has revealed. If nursing infants are involved, then spoons are used; if the children are older, you use the salt and the pot filled with water. It is not said that spoons or pots are definitely required for the prayer to be effective; it's just that this is the way things have always been done.

After the incident with the spoon, I wrote a letter to a Benedictine monk and professor I knew back in the United States, Father Kilian McDonnell, describing what I had seen. Father Kilian was a well-known Catholic theologian and scholar, a professor who was very active in ecumenical dialogue, that is, in the theological exchange between different Christian churches. He was also a specialist in the theology of the Holy Spirit and the gifts of the Spirit. Though he was not a participant in the dialogue between Christianity and other world religions, he was very interested in my experience in India. I sent him a letter describing the incident involving Brian, my mother-in-law, the prayer, and the spoon, and I asked him what he made of it. He wrote back essentially the following: As Catholics we shouldn't be surprised that the one God, the God of all creation and a God of love, would answer the prayers of anyone, regardless of religion, who turned to Him in genuine need and humility. Indeed, as Catholics we should even expect such things to happen from a God who does not withhold grace to any person who comes to Him with a humble heart and in real need. It certainly didn't matter to what religion a person happened to belong. But the string and the spoon, he said, he didn't understand what that was all about!

18

My Son's First Word

It was almost as if Brian had taken a vow of silence. He was well over a year old now and still had not pronounced his first intelligible word. At first we were not concerned; from his earliest days he had been making happy gurgling and cooing sounds, and he was almost always smiling. He seemed in every way like any other contented baby, stirring with joy in the presence of doting family. If he cried, it was only because he was hungry or ill. On the rare occasions when he was agitated, a visit to a Catholic church or the local Hindu temple would immediately quell his crying. I proudly carried him around the city as he took in the swirling, noisy world of urban India. I was often struck by how his infant face would radiate such an extraordinary sweetness. Strangers sometimes approached him on the street, touching his hand and speaking to him in Hindi or Marathi or English. He smiled back at them kindly.

One day I carried Brian inside a little grocery shop in Pune where we were approached by a Muslim fakir, a wandering mendicant who had renounced the world for God. He was clad in a long green tunic and sported a long beautiful beard. He interrupted his conversation with the shopkeeper when he saw Brian and exclaimed, "My goodness, what a beautiful child!" I felt honored that a man of God would praise my child, and I thanked him warmly.

But another month passed and then another, and still Brian did not speak. We were wondering when he would finally speak that first word.

At last the eventful day arrived. It was early evening, and dusk was slowly settling over the city. I had walked a mile from our apartment to purchase vegetables at an outdoor market, located near a busy intersection in front of an old bookstore, where I regularly purchased literature on Hindu philosophy and spirituality. Brian, as usual, was with me, his tiny arms and legs sticking out like a bug through the openings of the baby backpack. We made our way slowly through the throng, passing vendors sitting cross-legged on the hard sidewalk behind wicker baskets heaped high with fruits and vegetables. Now and then I stooped low to hand money to vendors as they held aloft carrots and okra on their scales. The sun had disappeared below the horizon now, its fading rays starting to throw trees and buildings into spectacular silhouettes. The vendors began lighting their kerosene lamps.

I was not quite finished buying vegetables when Brian suddenly extended his tiny arm, pointed his finger at a man standing closest to us in the crowded market, and cried out excitedly, "Buddha!" And then he swung his finger in the direction of another person and again called out, "Buddha!" He did this over and over the next few minutes, calling out the word *Buddha* to everyone passing by. No one else seemed to notice the little boy's excited shouts of "Buddha! Buddha! Buddha!"

I did not know what to make of this, but it seemed important enough for me to hurry home to tell Mariam and ask her what it meant. My "Wise Woman of the East," as I sometimes playfully call her (she does not like the title), would know what to make of Brian's exclamations. When I stepped through the door of our apartment, she was in the kitchen, waiting patiently for the vegetables, but she did not expect to find me almost breathless with excitement.

"Brian just spoke his first word," I announced.

Mariam's eyes got big. "He did? What did he say?"

"He said 'Buddha.'"

"What?"

"He's calling everybody in the market 'Buddha.' You know, 'Buddha! Buddha!' Does 'Buddha' mean anything in Hindi besides, you know, the Buddha?"

"No," said Mariam. "It only means the Lord Buddha. What was he doing when he said 'Buddha'?"

"He was pointing his finger at different people one by one."

"Oh. Are you sure he said 'Buddha'?"

"Yes, I'm sure."

Brian never cried out "Buddha" again, but Mariam and I still recall the event from time to time, knowing that we will never understand what had happened. Perhaps it meant nothing at all. Maybe Brian just happened to put two syllables together that sounded like the word *Buddha* as he pointed to the people all around him.

Or perhaps there was another explanation. One kind of Buddhist might offer a clarification that, from a certain perspective, would seem perfectly obvious. It might go something like this: In his previous life Brian had been a Mahāyāna Buddhist. One of the central teachings of Mahāyāna Buddhism is that every being endowed with consciousness has buried deep within the pure Buddha mind or Buddha nature. One must awaken to this inner nature, if liberation is to occur. Thus when Brian was pointing at all the people in the market and calling out "Buddha!," what he was really doing was declaring to them their hidden Buddha nature. He did this through a spontaneous transmission of knowledge from his previous life as a Buddhist, a knowledge that would soon be buried and forgotten in the present life through his reeducation and indoctrination into another culture and religion. But on the basis of this explanation one might also conclude that Brian must not have been a very good Buddhist in his previous life; otherwise he would have been reborn as a Buddhist in this life. Instead he was reborn into an inferior religion called Roman Catholicism!

19

Shivapur and the Miraculous Stone

One of the most famous Muslim shrines in the western Indian state of Maharashtra is in Shivapur, a small city (*pur*) originally dedicated to the Hindu God Shiva. On our visit back to India, we reach Shivapur in no time, since it is less than an hour by van from Pune. The shrine (*dargah*) contains the remains of the Sufi saint Qamar Ali Darvesh,[1] who, according to tradition, lived here almost eight hundred years ago. Architecturally, Shivapur is quite unspectacular, to say the least, and there is nothing that might draw us back one day except the shrine itself.

Everything in Shivapur revolves around the *dargah* and its pilgrims, and because of its idyllic setting in a wooded area near a flowing creek, it has long been a popular destination for Muslim families from the surrounding area. When Mariam was a girl, a visit to the *dargah* meant an all-day outing with relatives, prayers offered to the saint for various favors, and always a picnic in the woods. The shrine was brightly painted then, and the grounds were immaculate. The crowds were much smaller, and access to the *dargah* was simple. The clan would drive up in a small caravan of motor rickshaws and park just outside the shrine. One could pass in and out of Shivapur and the shrine area without difficulty.

But times have changed. Today, Shivapur charges a ten-rupee entrance fee for all out-of-town motor vehicles, whether carrying pilgrims or not. Our driver negotiates our van slowly through motor and pedestrian traffic, ignoring along the way numerous men standing in the middle of the street signaling to us with flailing arms to steer our vehicle into their paid parking areas, as if we were long-awaited visitors.

About a ten-minute walk from the shrine we squeeze the van in between two vehicles parked alongside the road. A Muslim man with a long black beard and skullcap steps quickly out of his little stall under the trees and sternly informs us that we are occupying one of his parking spaces and that we may continue to do so only if we agree to purchase one of his flower garlands (*sehrā*) to drape over the saint's tomb. Mariam and her nephew Abid look at each other quizzically. Parking anywhere in Shivapur had always been free. We are now being charged to park near the tomb by a shopkeeper who has only recently set up business?

What size garland would we have to buy? asks Abid. Perhaps that small yellow one over there? The vendor shakes his head, no, looking at me. Perhaps a larger one, then, for a hundred rupees? No, answers the shop owner, again looking straight at me, the foreigner: we will have to purchase the largest one for two hundred fifty rupees. This is preposterous, given the fact that admission to the shrine itself is completely free. Abid instructs the driver to back out into the road and find a different location, and so we end up pulling into a new spot a bit farther away from the shrine where we end up paying nothing.

After getting down from the van on this late afternoon, we wend our way down the macadam road in light rain under the partial shelter of shade trees, sidestepping puddles as we go. As we walk I continue to learn about Islam from Abid. He informs me that such garlands as we have just seen are used not only to drape Muslim tombs but are also standard at Muslim weddings. Both bride and groom wear a garland that extends from the crown of the head down to the knees. Some garlands are so tightly woven that the couple's faces are hidden from view. The flowers are parted only after the ceremony, when bride and groom gaze upon each other for the first time as husband and wife. The thickest, longest, and most expensive *sehrās* weigh over twenty pounds.

My teenage niece, Neha, usually too shy to speak to me, turns to me now as we walk down the street and advises me in a soft voice to keep an eye on my camera, because of possible pickpockets. Continuing down the muddy road, we follow a crowd of pilgrims past numerous tiny commercial stalls selling flower garlands and CDs proclaiming the greatness of Islam until we come at last to the shrine compound.

We find ourselves at the bottom of a steep stone stairway leading upward through trees to the *dargah* proper. Here we must remove our shoes, even though the worn steps rising before us are damp and grimy. Abid, always organized and observant, shows the shoe keeper exactly which pairs of shoes and sandals we are leaving in his care. The old man, who sits cross-legged on the ground in the open air, oblivious to the lightly falling rain, nods his head wordlessly and stacks the sandals and shoes atop one another to keep them together. I have no idea how he keeps track of them all. There are hundreds of pairs here, many indistinguishable from others. I wonder what kind of life he might have lived had he been given the opportunity to get an education. Who knows? With his intelligence he might have one day become an engineer or a university professor instead of the guardian of shoes.

The foot traffic on the stone stairway is crushing. People are shoulder to shoulder moving in both directions, up and down, in no apparent order. We are concerned not to lose the children in the crowd. But I find myself momentarily separated from my relatives and do not find them again until I am able to push my way to the top, where they are waiting for me.

We step into a walled outdoor courtyard at the center of which is the shrine, a simple whitewashed building under a domed roof. Slender towers point upward to heaven at each of the four corners of the shrine. Leafy shade trees line the edge of the compound, offering beauty and shelter to visitors and providing a foretaste of the paradise to come. Numerous metal spouts jutting out of a stone wall at the edge of the compound gush forth cool water for pilgrims to wash hands, feet, and face. At this particular moment little boys and girls are performing the ablutions together. It is clear from their splashing and laughter that not all of them are washing with the solemnity expected of adults. But no one is bothered by this.

Behind me at some distance I hear a dull thud as if something heavy has fallen to the ground, and a few minutes later the sound is repeated.

Adjacent to the place where the children are washing is a tiny shrine office whose open door affords a view of a tall man sitting inside at a desk. Like so many other Muslim men he sports a beard and skullcap. He is the overseer of the shrine.

Outside the office, on a large plaque attached to a wall, the story of the saint is retold in English and Hindi. It may be summarized as follows: Hazrat Quamer Ali Durvesh (so the name is spelled on the plaque) was born in Pune, though his family originally came from Delhi. When he was a young man, his beloved brother died, leaving him so disconsolate that he lost all interest in worldly life. He turned to God and found consolation in constant prayer. "He served the people," adds the sign. How often have I noted this at other Muslim *dargahs:* the saint is not just close to God, but he also makes himself available to address the problems and concerns of the people in his vicinity. After some time, Qamar Ali left Pune and came to Shivapur, but no reason is offered as to why he visited this particular place. Once here, however, he is said to have liked the scenery and the numerous mango trees so much that he ended up making the town his home.

It happened one year, according to the story told on the plaque, that the countryside was afflicted by a severe drought. "By his prayers and grace of God a fountain started flowing here." No details are offered. Another time, with the cloud of famine hanging over the land, the saint was himself slowly starving to death. His younger brother somehow learned about this and sent him money, but Qamar Ali Darvesh gave it all to the poor.

His prayers were apparently very effective, and the saint lived a very ascetic life. It is said that he did not sleep at night nor did he eat anything or drink even a drop of water all throughout Ramzān, the holy month of fasting. By then four disciples had submitted themselves to his spiritual guidance. He advised them to perform hard work to gain control over themselves and their desires.[2] Qamar Ali also helped end human sacrifice in the area, but the plaque does not explain the particulars of this evil. People gradually began coming from miles around to pay their respects to the saint, still a young man, and seek his advice, and he treated them all equally, regardless of their religious or societal standing.

The sign notes the presence of two large stones near the shrine. I see only one now. The large stone is said to weigh seventy kilos, over 150 pounds. It is to be lifted by exactly eleven people forming a circle around the stone, each using only one index finger. The smaller stone, which I did not see, is to be lifted by nine people.[3] Any other number of people will be unable to raise the stone. For the big stone, you cannot have twelve men instead of eleven, and you can't use more than one finger each. If you innovate, the stone cannot be lifted.

The raising of the stone always follows the same procedure. The men form a circle around it and bend down to place their index fingers at the base of the rock. Women are not permitted to participate, however, though I have been unable to get a clear answer as to why this is. People just shrug their shoulders in answer to this question. This is the way things have always been done here; that's all. After taking a deep breath the men begin lifting the stone while crying out together, "Ya Qamar Ali Darve-e-e-e-sh,"[4] trailing out the last syllable until one of the men runs out of breath, at which point the stone can no longer be held aloft and falls to the ground with a mighty thud. The goal is to lift the stone high above the heads of the circle of men.

I first saw the raising of the stone years ago. My friend Tim from the United States was with us at the shrine. Though it was taken for granted that he was not a Muslim, the men surrounding the stone invited him to join in, anyway. I watched as he and ten Muslim men raised the stone high into the air.

Neha said she saw a television program about this shrine a year ago. It reported that a demon used to trouble the local people. But Qamar Ali Darvesh was able to trap the demon inside the stone, where it now suffers torment each time the stone crashes to the ground.

Mariam tells me she has never once seen the stone fail to be lifted high into the air, even during her many visits to the shrine as a girl. But today is different. Sometimes the stone is lifted six or seven feet into the air, as it is supposed to, but more often than not, attempts to raise it that high are unsuccessful. Many times the stone cannot be lifted higher than knee level. I think I might know the reason for this. It seems that whenever the stone cannot be lifted high into the air, the circle of lifters is composed of rowdy teenage boys and young men. Their wild laughter leads me to believe that lifting the stone has degenerated for them into mere amusement. It is no longer an encounter with the power of God or the saint's prayer of intercession.

I tell my young nephew Adi that the plaque does not give the saint's dates and ask if he can please ask the man in the office about this. Adi goes inside, and a moment later the caretaker emerges from his office, but he waits at the door for me to approach him. He sizes me up warily and asks, "What is it you want to know?" in heavily accented English.

"Hello," I say. "Do you know when the saint died?"

He answers, "Six two three Muslim time." I calculate 623 on the Muslim calendar as 1245 CE. At what age Qamar Ali died and under what circumstances the plaque offers no information. But it adds that the saint's death anniversary celebration (*'urs*) takes place every April or May. I cannot imagine what the crowds must be like then.

I find myself the object of interest of a number of people in this crowded courtyard. "You write fast," says one young man, smiling, as I enter information in my notebook. "Why are you doing it?"

I tell him I want to write about Muslim *dargahs* for a book.

"What country are you from?"

"America," I answer.

"What do you do there?"

"I teach at a university."

There is no further response from the young Muslim. He continues to study me quietly and does not intrude on my writing with further questions. He has spoken to me as one human being to another, and there is no mention of religion. We are united by respect for the saint and submission to the one God of creation. The holiness of the saint transcends all religious differences. The young man speaking to me has no interest in ingratiating himself with me, to gain some favor from a citizen of a powerful Western nation. Nor does he feel the need to instruct me about the greatness of Islam.

I leave the plaque and return with my camera to the place where the stone is being lifted, hoping to take some pictures. A circle of young men tries to lift the rock, but without success. It tumbles to the ground after rising only a foot in the air. I move closer to get a better angle. Another young man behind me standing with his friends tells me I ought to join the circle myself. I say, no thank you; I'd just like to take pictures. Then he says something to me in a mixture of Hindi and broken English, so rapidly delivered that I can't make out what he's saying. I do not respond. He and his friends say something more that I can't comprehend, and loud laughter erupts. I feel uncomfortable. Are they making fun of me? I move quietly away to a different place in the crowd to take pictures.

A middle-aged man says to me in Hindi, *"Aur ah-gay"*—keep going. In other words, get closer to the stone to get a better picture. Another man taps two other men on the shoulder and asks them to move out of my way, since I have a camera. They readily oblige. After a short time, the young man who was mocking me with his friends approaches and says softly, "I am sorry if I offended you. Please forgive me."

"It's all right," I say, looking him in the eyes.

Outside the shrine, in the open courtyard, families have spread bedsheets on the square to prepare for a picnic. My relatives are waiting for me at the perimeter of the open area, looking over the wall at the dried-up creek bed at the bottom of a steep hill. Garbage is strewn everywhere in the creek and the adjacent field. There is even trash scattered across the courtyard where we stand. The courtyard walls are in need of repair, its green and white paint chipped away. Small piles of rubble lie at the base of the wall.

"This place is in very bad shape now," says Mariam sadly, looking at the garbage scattered below. "When I was a kid, it was immaculate, just like the Christian shrines. I don't know what's happened. You never used to get your feet dirty walking barefoot around the shrine."

The only explanation I can think of is greed. With all the money being collected from the pilgrims as they enter the city, it seems strange that none of it is used to preserve the structure of the shrine or to keep the premises clean.

Inside the little shrine building the saint's tomb is piled high with white lily and orange marigold *sehrās*, far higher than at the Babajan *dargah* in Pune. Many men and boys are kissing the tomb or resting their forehead against it. Some are sitting on the floor, so as to remain in the saint's presence. Others are laying garlands across the tomb. Women are not allowed inside, unlike with the shrine in Pune. They may advance only to the various wide entrances to the sanctum and may not cross the threshold.

Tabassum asks me later if I noticed the lamp hanging in the tomb area. I concede that I had not. "It has been burning continuously for eight hundred years," she says, "whether or not people add oil to it. And if you are bitten by a snake or animal and go to the *dargah*, you are well."

It is difficult to sift fact from fiction in regard to the life of Qamar Ali Darvesh. One hears a number of purported facts not included on the plaque outside the shrine that describes his life. If true, they help answer a number of questions. It is said, for example, that unlike other family members, the young boy was very pious and even studied under a Sufi teacher from the age of six. From early on he was known for both his compassion and his ability to heal others. He died at eighteen, but no cause is given, as far as I have been able to find out. On his deathbed the young saint instructed that a large stone be placed near his shrine after his death and that the stone should only be lifted by eleven men using only their index finger and only when invoking the saint's name. Qamar Ali Darvesh did not explain why the number eleven was important or why only one finger was to be used. More important than anything else was the spiritual message. By the lifting of the stone under such unusual circumstances people should know that nothing is greater than the power that comes from God. And everyone should know that God loves all people, regardless of their religion or caste. Anyone may participate in lifting the stone, regardless of their background. When we lift the stone, we are to remember God's love for all.

I want very much to believe this version of the story.

Although I had observed the lifting of the stone several times over the years, I had never tried doing it myself until January 2011, when I brought a group of American students with me from my university back in the United States. The day we arrived in Shivapur it was late morning, and the large crowds had not yet gathered. Above us large fox bats hung upside down from the trees, like heavy fruit. We watched as a circle of men raised the stone high above their heads, before it plummeted back to earth. One of our students, Stephen, stepped into the circle with ten Muslim men, who had encouraged him to take part. But the eleven men could not lift the stone higher than a few inches. Stephen immediately recognized what had happened: he had forgotten to recite the words. So he rejoined the circle, this time with me by his side. And yet the stone fell back to earth again after barely rising above the ground. This time it fell in my direction, landing at my feet. I was perplexed by this, especially since I was confident that the stone would be lifted. But then I remembered that I had made exactly the same mistake as had Stephen only moments before: in concentrating on the stone, I had forgotten to recite the words. The oldest man among the Muslims noticed what I had done and said to me firmly in broken English, "One breath for all words. No stopping." In other words, take a deep breath and don't forget to call out to the saint.

So we tried it one more time, now without Stephen, who had graciously stepped aside for a Muslim man. As we chanted together, "Qamar Ali Darve-e-e-sh!," we were finally able to raise the stone above our heads. It felt as light as a pebble. Later Stephen and other members of our group joined in, calling out the saint's name, and each time they effortlessly lifted the stone.

Perhaps one day scientists will offer an explanation as to how the stone is raised, drawing solely on their knowledge of energy and physics. But I doubt that they will be able to explain why the stone cannot be lifted without calling on the saint, why the circle must be composed of only eleven men, and why the stone falls in the direction of the one who does it incorrectly.

As we were returning by bus from Shivapur on that trip, Mariam, who was also with us, wondered aloud whether women, too, might one day be given the opportunity to lift the stone, since the miracle is supposed to be a sign of God's love for all people, and not only for men. Why not give women a chance? The Muslim women who come to the Shivapur shrine simply accept without complaint that they are excluded by sacred tradition from lifting the stone, just as they take for granted that as women they may not enter the sanctum where the saint is buried. But did Qamar Ali Darvesh explicitly forbid women from raising the stone? It is well known that many Sufis in India and abroad have stretched the boundaries of traditional Muslim law and piety for the purpose of promoting a more tolerant and inclusive spirituality. Why not here at this Sufi shrine, too? Mariam speculated about the possibility of women slipping into the shrine compound under the cover of night and raising the stone high above their heads, not so much as a sign of their own accomplishment, but rather as a sign of their full equality and empowerment before God. What would be the reaction of men who were to find out about this? How many would be compelled to rethink their understanding of women's relation to God and men? How many, by contrast, would regard the lifting of the stone by women as a kind of blasphemy that must be punished? For women to gain full equality in Islam, says Mariam, they will have to boldly take the initiative and be willing to suffer for their convictions.

Seeing—and feeling—the stone being raised that day caused me to come to a deeper appreciation of God's presence in the lives of Muslims. What stood out in particular was that the raising of the stone was connected to a Muslim saint of great humility and lowly stature, a young man who had practiced selfless charity toward those in desperate need, a man, finally, who recognized that God's love and mercy were not restricted to one group or religion. That Qamar Ali Darvesh had displayed so many Christlike qualities made it easy to believe that God might be using him, even centuries after his death, as a bridge to bring together Muslims and people of other religions.

20

Khatijah's[1] Death

The abandoned palace city of Amber[2] was an unexpected treat on my family's new trip north to Rajasthan, a place we reached after stops in Delhi, Agra, and Jaipur. Although its place in Indian history has faded, Amber has a long and distinguished past; records indicate that it was already thriving by the end of the tenth century CE. The city had also been for centuries the seat of power of Kachwaha Rajput rulers[3] until construction of the new royal city, Jaipur, began in 1727, only seven miles to the south. Jaipur, the now new city of kings, would itself attain historical significance as the center of one of Indian history's most important alliances: the Hindu Rajputs and the Muslim Moghuls. This was an alliance of convenience and necessity for the Rajputs, who needed to curry the favor of the more powerful Moghuls in order to flourish.

Jaipur is one of the three cities that make up what is commonly known as the "Golden Triangle," the other two being Agra and Delhi. The Golden Triangle is the largest tourist draw in all of India, largely because of the Taj Mahal (in Agra) and countless other stunning architectural monuments such as the Red Fort and the Qutb Minar (both in Delhi), the latter being the highest minaret in India.[4] Moreover, Jaipur is world famous for the production and sale of gemstones. And so to travel to the Golden Triangle is to be transported back in time to an age of almost unparalleled achievement in art, architecture, and power.

Before traveling to Jaipur, we knew next to nothing of Amber, and yet it might be considered one of India's architectural wonders. The Taj Mahal in Agra, with its perfect setting of exquisitely designed tombs, mosques, arched walkways, and manicured lawns, may be more beautiful, more exquisitely symmetrical and harmonious, but it does not compete with the pure physical achievement of Amber with its many citadels and lofty fortifications stretching from one mountain ridge to another. Its austere distant ramparts rising into the sky reminded me of photos I had seen of China's Great Wall.

To reach the palace, Amber's jewel, our silent Hindu driver, Debilal, steers the van up a steep twisting cobblestone street, hemmed in on both sides by high rugged stone walls. It was not so long ago that one could make the slower but more regal ascent to the palace aboard an elephant, but such transport has now been temporarily discontinued without explanation. At the top of the hill, outside the main gate, a large crowd is gathered around numerous travel buses, cars, and rickshaws. Here the wealthy and educated mingle with the poor and unlettered. Many have come on a sightseeing outing, others to worship at the Shila Devi Temple;[5] most have probably come to do both. As we approach the imposing arched entry gate, young men are already hurrying toward us with postcards and inexpensive jewelry, the latter especially popular with the local village girls, who haggle tenaciously to procure the colorful trinkets. In appearance, these girls are very unlike the young women of the big cities, for none of them wear Western-style jeans, but instead the traditional wraparound sari or the tuniclike *salwar kameez*. Many are poor and thin. Most are illiterate. A few of them whisper in groups or giggle with their hands over their mouths upon seeing Mariam in slacks and blouse. She is the exotic one here.

The climb is steep, but every few yards affords a fresh view of magnificent surroundings, both natural and constructed. Above us, perched majestically on a towering cliff, is the Jaigarh Fort, looking down protectively upon the palace and its visitors. The fort has never been conquered by any invading army.

Though the sky is overcast with a threat of rain, the mood of the crowd is boisterous. The opportunity to go on an afternoon outing is a special treat for those villagers accustomed to the grueling work of tilling fields, gathering fuel, and tending herds.

After entering the spacious palatial compound, we find ourselves at the bottom of a steep stone walkway leading up to the famous Hindu temple. Our guide is Rani, a well-educated and smartly dressed young Hindu. He has recently married. He is slender, and his serious face displays sharp intelligent features and dark eyes. He bends down to the ground, devoutly touches the dust with the fingers of his right hand, then brings the dust to his forehead. We are standing on holy ground. Rani informs us in advance that to enter the temple we will need to leave outside not only shoes and sandals, but also belts and wallets, as "animal skin" is not permitted inside. We decide to hold off on entering the temple for at least an hour until we have first visited the various halls, courtyards, and high turrets of the palace proper.

After a short climb up a narrow winding stairway, we reach the walkway of a high outer wall and pause to survey our surroundings. For miles we see parched and rugged mountains bearing massive stone walls and countless edifices, further evidence that one of India's greatest virtues is patience. I find it difficult to imagine the effort, time, and toil required to transport the material to build even one such structure. In India one man designs a palace and begins its construction, over a period of many years another completes it, and finally a third and his descendants inhabit it and adorn it with exquisite works of art.

Half a dozen long-legged and fierce-looking monkeys suddenly scamper up over a wall and dash into a stone-pillared hall behind us. Just as suddenly they come to a halt and sit motionless on the smooth floor. Two small children, perhaps brother and sister, walk toward them to get a closer look. Rani, ever alert, shouts at them to get back; these monkeys might attack.

From tunnels and staircases hidden from our view we hear the raucous shouts and unrestrained shrieks and laughter of teenage boys and girls. To carry on like this in the presence of elders even in modern India strikes many as disrespectful. Uniformed guards displaying long wooden *lathis* (batons) bark at the young people to behave.

•   •   •

After some time, the sky darkens and a cool wind sweeps through the palace. The mountains become partially obscured by a yellowish-brown cloud of dust. The mood is suddenly somber.

Abid, who normally accompanies our every step, has been off by himself for some time. He approaches me now, but something is different about him. His face shows concern as he speaks his first words to me in a low voice, almost a whisper. "Uncle," he says, "I've just received a phone call from Pune." His mother, Tabassum, has relayed an urgent message that is initially difficult to grasp or believe. Abid appears at a loss to continue. "There's something about my *dādī* (grandmother), Mariam Aunty's mother. They say she's *died*. I'm trying to call back and find out more." If the message is correct, Mariam's mother, Khatijah, has just died.

I am stunned to hear this and remark that perhaps there is some mistake. Not wanting to draw Karina's attention to her grandmother's possible death, Abid continues to speak in a hushed tone to me while punching in the numbers of his cell phone. "I don't want to tell Mariam *foopoo*[6] just yet or Karina," he says. In the meantime Mariam, Karina, and our guide, Rani, have climbed to the highest lookout of the palace and are waiting in vain for us to join them. They are enjoying a spectacular view of the surrounding area. A few minutes later they return. Mariam is about to ask us where we have been, but our faces cannot hide that something is wrong.

"What's going on?" she asks.

"I just received an urgent phone call from home," says Abid.

Mariam looks concerned. "I hope it's nothing serious," she says. But she is already thinking that someone might have died. Lots of people die prematurely in India.

I take her aside. "Abid doesn't want me to tell you yet, but I have to." I give her the news bluntly, without first weighing my words. "Tabassum just called. She said your mother died." I repeat this twice for it to sink in. Mariam's eyes tell me that her mind is reeling. I motion with my own eyes wordlessly toward Karina. What about her? Should we tell her? Mariam does not respond.

"I think we should tell her," I say. "She'll be okay. Abid says not to tell her yet, but I think we should." My thinking is that Karina has not been as close to her Indian grandmother as she has been to her other Indian relatives, anyway, mostly because of the language barrier. But I am probably also talking too much. Mariam still needs to process the information about her mother.

Abid now guardedly signals with a nod of his head, because of Karina, to confirm that the original message is correct. Mariam's mother has passed away.

Karina moves a few steps closer to us. She senses something is amiss. "What's going on? What are you talking about?" she asks directly.

Mariam says, "Your grandmother in Pune is very sick and is going to the hospital."

Karina asks, "Is she going to die?"

I interrupt. "Tell her the whole thing. She can take it."

Mariam continues. "We have to go back to Pune. Nani has just died."

Karina's face is now sad. "Why? What happened?"

Her mother says, "Nani has been very sick. Sometimes when she ate food, she couldn't keep it down. So now she's in a better place." Karina has been taught to believe in an afterlife in heaven.

Karina gives us a hug; she is thinking about her grandmother, but she does not cry.

Together, in a daze, we begin descending the stone steps back to the courtyard and main gate. I walk alongside my wife, trying to imagine what she is going through. In the meantime Rani, our guide, has been informed of Khatijah's death. He offers condolences to Mariam. But we now face what seems an almost insurmountable problem. Since in Islam the body is normally buried within twenty-four hours, we will have to leave these parts immediately to reach tomorrow's funeral in time in an altogether different part of India. We must leave Rajasthan for Maharashtra. Our only hope of making it in time is to go by plane. Rani and Abid discuss the quickest way back to Pune and are already making calls on their cell phones. Is there time to book a flight out of Jaipur, and can we reach the hotel in time to pack and still reach the airport in time for our flight? We hurriedly walk past the famous temple entrance, still jammed with worshippers. There is no time to enter now. We climb into the van. Debilal, our driver, looks sadly at Mariam and says nothing. We hastily descend the mountain over cobblestone streets, speed through the barren countryside, and a short time later we are back in Jaipur, negotiating our way through heavy traffic.

Mariam, Karina, and I are dropped off at the hotel, while Abid, Rani, and Debilal head to the airport to get tickets. The flight to Mumbai from Jaipur airport is at eight P.M. We need to be at the airport by seven at the latest. It is already 5:40. Mariam flies into action in the hotel room, forcing all our belongings, including recent purchases, into the suitcases. She enlists me to lay all my weight atop one suitcase as she zips it shut. Just as she finishes packing the last piece of luggage our van pulls up outside the hotel. It is 6:30. Abid shouts up to Karina on the balcony that he has the plane tickets and that we must hurry.

Several hands reach for suitcases, and in a few minutes we are standing on the steps outside the hotel lobby as the van is being loaded. After only six days together with Debilal of what was to have been a ten-day trip to northern India, it is already time to say good-bye. The tall dignified Hindu driver takes Mariam aside, looks her in the eyes, and says in Hindi, "Madam, if ever I have done anything to offend you during this trip I pray that you forgive me." A humble and pure-hearted soul is our Hindu driver.

Mariam answers, "Debilal, you are a kind man. We are honored to have had you with us. We hope you will be with us again for our next trip."

A small old bellhop in a faded uniform has assisted us in taking the luggage to the lobby. He is frail and bent and probably not long for this world. He now learns of the death of Mariam's mother. Although he is a stranger to us, the old man offers heartfelt words of consolation and gives Mariam a long plaintive farewell look. He and Rani wave to us from the steps of the hotel as the van pulls away. My faith in the goodness of the human race is very great at this moment, because of the genuine sympathy and kindness shown to Mariam by Rani, Debilal, and the old bellhop.

We arrive at the airport just past seven o'clock. The airport entrances are protected by stern-looking soldiers in camouflage uniforms wielding black machine guns, but inside the main hall the security and airlines are staffed by friendly and efficient people. We pass quickly through security without incident, but we are still in a daze. In the waiting room at our departure gate a middle-aged woman in uniform approaches me and asks if I am the owner of this black carry-on bag that was left at the security check. It is only then that I realize I had left it behind, inside of which are my camera, camcorder, and all my journals. I express gratefulness to the woman for having averted a private catastrophe.

In less than two hours our plane lands in Mumbai. It will be at least another hour before Tahir arrives with a van and driver. We learn that the funeral is at eleven in the morning, now only twelve hours away. Mariam tells me that although I am not a Muslim, I am allowed to accompany her mother's body to the cemetery. But she, as a woman, is not permitted to go. This is not true everywhere in the Muslim world, but it is the custom in much of India, whatever its original reason. A mother may not accompany even her dead child to burial. The cemetery is off-limits to females. Karina, hearing this, does not hesitate to express her unhappiness at not being allowed to accompany her grandmother to the burial site.

From the airport in Mumbai we set off in the night for Pune in a van crammed full with people and suitcases. For the next four hours we are tossed about by sudden stops and dizzying swerves that make sleep unthinkable. We arrive exhausted in Pune in the middle of the night. But no one thinks of complaining. How can we complain? Our minds are on Khatijah, so suddenly taken away. After we unpack and bathe, Mariam and Abid drink tea to stay awake. Mariam is expected to return to her old neighborhood this very night to join her female relatives. They will recite the Qur'ān until the moment when her mother's body is ready to be taken to the cemetery. In addition to reciting the Qur'ān, the relatives and neighbors, especially the older ones, will reminisce till dawn, recalling Khatijah's life and good works. Her siblings and cousins will fondly remember the days long ago when they first played together as children, chasing each other up and down the narrow lanes. It seems like only yesterday. How quickly one becomes an old person, and how unexpectedly life draws to a close. These people have lived in this city, in this very neighborhood, their entire lives. Most have barely traveled an afternoon's journey from home. And suddenly it is time to depart this world for the next.

Abid, too, will stay the night in Khatijah's neighborhood and return in the morning to fetch Karina and me after we catch a few hours of sleep. Hussainbi Khala will wash her sister's body in preparation for the burial, just as she had prepared her other sister, Nuri, for burial earlier this year. In the hour of Khatijah's interment, when her body is lowered into the grave, unlike the conversation of this night, there will be no sermon extolling the life and character of the deceased. Everything will be about Allah's judgment and mercy.

The first account we hear of how Khatijah died is much too brief, and it lacks all plausibility, knowing what we know about the long-standing feud she has had with her daughter-in-law, Nazreen. Some relatives tell us bluntly that Khatijah died because Nazreen "killed" her. That is the word they use: Nazreen "killed" Khatijah. Nazreen is Razaak's second wife and has lived with her mother-in-law, Khatijah, and tended to her for almost twenty years. But she and Khatijah never got along; they were both strong-willed, and their animosity toward each other hardened over the years as a result of the meddling of some of the relatives, who for some unknown reason chose Nazreen as the object of their bullying and rumormongering. So even now, in Khatijah's death, she is held responsible. A somewhat milder version of the story asserts that Nazreen only indirectly killed Khatijah, because she took her sweet time to fetch the doctor down the lane when Khatijah fell ill. We are immediately doubtful of this explanation, too. Nazreen may not have liked her mother-in-law, but she did everything to make her life physically tolerable, not only with cooking and the constant preparation of endless cups of tea, but also by arising in the night, many times if necessary, to help her to the toilet. And so as the account of Khatijah's sudden death is narrated to us, we learn nothing about the actual cause of what happened, but we are given an earful about Nazreen's alleged moral deficiencies. Because of their obvious bias, these stories must be treated with skepticism.

We eventually piece together from several other sources the following account. Khatijah's health had been on the decline for some time, as we already knew. A few years earlier she had had a colostomy, and for some time she also suffered from high blood pressure and a weak heart. All her doctors had prescribed a diet low in meat, salt, and fat. Because of similar health problems, her own brother, Habib, and his wife, Bibi, had heeded their physician's warnings and are now practically vegetarian, something that is quite unusual for Muslims. But Khatijah never seriously tried to curb her appetite for the things prohibited to her, and everyone knew it. In fact, she demanded to have them each and every day, if possible. Whenever her grandson Abid paid her a visit, the first thing he would do is search her cupboards for any food forbidden by the doctor. He inevitably ended up scolding her during almost every visit. She, in turn, would each time lie to him—most likely with a sly smile— and say that the deadly food was something she ate only once in a very great while, today, of course, being one of those exceptional days.

On the day Khatijah died, she showed no signs of illness. She spent the early part of the afternoon sitting outside her house in the little lane, cheerfully greeting neighbors passing by who had just returned from a wedding in Mumbai. Later that afternoon her son Razaak and her grandson Tahir stopped by for a visit. After some time, Khatijah was overcome by an insatiable craving for *paya*, or curried goat leg. This was one of the meats her doctor had sternly forbidden her to eat, because of its high fat content. But on this particular day she pleaded for *paya*. Tahir gently reprimanded her for demanding something so unhealthy as *paya*. But his grandmother did not relent. She was famous for her strong will. She simply *had* to have that *paya*, and she wanted it now. Razaak finally gave in to her. What is the point, he said to everyone, of worrying about one little meal; let her have what she wants. And so now, seeing that his father, Razaak, had given in to his grandmother's wishes, Tahir took it upon himself to fetch the *paya*. Anything to make his *nani* happy. Razaak bought a special bread with a thick brown crust that Khatijah loved. Someone else brought a guava, one of Khatijah's favorite fruits. Everyone looked on with amusement as Grandmother ate with gusto. She shared her meal with her favorite child, Razaak. Neha and Fardeen were there, too, and watched as their father and grandmother ate *paya*.

Moments after she finished her meal, Khatijah vomited slightly, lost consciousness, and collapsed. Those around her felt she had merely passed out. They rubbed her limp arms and hands, stroked her face, spoke to her. There was no response. Someone hurried to get a physician. Neha and Fardeen, who had lived with their grandmother from birth, and fearing that she might be dying, began to weep and wail. Neha finally passed out. The doctor arrived within minutes and immediately pronounced Khatijah dead. A second doctor arrived and likewise confirmed her death.

The fact that Khatijah's hands were not clenched in struggle meant that she had died within seconds of her seizure. Her heart had simply given out. She had passed away without a struggle after eating one of her favorite meals. That was a wonderful thing, wasn't it? some of the neighbors remarked, to be able to die after eating such a fine meal. But Khatijah's brother, Habib, countered that if only she hadn't eaten that goat meat, she would still be alive today. But Tahir's mother, Tabassum, said that if Khatijah had been denied the *paya* and died anyway, people would have said what a shame it was that she had died after being prevented from eating one of her favorite meals. Either way somebody gets blamed.

Recalling the *paya* incident the following day, Khatijah's sister Hussainbi added that Khatijah had always been the stubborn one in the family. As an example, she described how whenever Khatijah had a serious disagreement with her husband, she would give him the silent treatment for two full days and sometimes longer, until he finally gave in to her, even when she knew that she was the one who was in the wrong. That's the kind of person she was. Mariam was of the opinion that it was simply time for her mother to go, goat meat or not. She had been eating all the wrong things for years, anyway. Everything was in God's hands, and God had decided.

We arrive in Khatijah's neighborhood about ten o'clock in the morning, an hour before the scheduled procession to the cemetery. Gathered outside the family bakery under the shade trees sit fifteen Muslim men in white plastic chairs. All of them are at least middle-aged, most wearing the white *kufi* cap; some sit casually with their legs crossed. One very old and feeble man smokes a *beedi* (a thin cigarette). Our old friend, Mohiddinkaka, is there, the one I call "Dapper Uncle." As Abduka's wastrel of a younger brother, it was he who more than anyone else had squandered away the family fortune in his youth on women and a lavish lifestyle. I recognize him immediately with the hawk nose and high forehead. His hair is now silver and combed straight back, but he is clean-shaven and still as tall, slender, and dashing as ever. He greets me warmly. Most of the men sit quietly, but occasionally one turns to another and mutters a few words in a quiet voice. Younger men and boys stand nearby, some gathered near the street in small groups. Only a few of them wear caps. They, too, speak in hushed voices. Loud talk on this day is disrespectful to the dead and offensive to God.

Abid introduces me to some of the older men. We exchange *"Asalaamu alaikum"* and *"Walaikum asalaam"* many times over. Some of them smile as they greet me, remembering me from many years before. I do not at first recognize Abdul Rahman, my favorite Indian uncle, who has aged so much. His handsome face has grown thin, his beard has become long and white, but his eyes still sparkle with warmth. He embraces me in a long hug and brushes his cheek against mine.

The atmosphere is dignified and quiet. I am given a seat, and soon Abid sits next to me. We discuss quietly what is about to take place and about Muslim faith and funeral practices. When Habib Mamu—the tall, dour-faced patriarch and brother of Khatijah—arrives, Abid and I both arise and offer him our chair, but he declines with a slight motion of his hand, bidding us to remain seated.

Inside the lane an even larger crowd has gathered, mostly women and girls. Some sit while others stand. All face toward the back of the lane, where a colorful broad bedsheet is patiently held aloft by several women to prevent men and outsiders from seeing the deceased woman as she is bathed by her sister Hussainbi. Khatijah's corpse, I learned later, was washed atop an oval wooden table that was carried out of the neighborhood later that day. After the washing was complete, water from the Zamzam well in Mecca was sprinkled over her. Bottles of Zamzam water are frequently brought back to India upon the pilgrims' return.

All the women and girls have their heads covered with a sari or *dupatta*. Mariam is somewhere among them, but I cannot see her. Abid suggests that I seek her out to offer her consolation and strength. "You don't have to worry about Mariam *foopoo*," I say. "She is as strong as a lion."

At last a signal is given for the body to begin its journey to the cemetery. A wave of women surges forward down the narrow lane in the direction of the open street. Somewhere among them Khatijah is being carried by men on a metal stretcher, accompanied by female shouts of "Make way! Make way!" Those who are the nearest relatives to the deceased are urged, even gently prodded, if they have been standing off to the side, to draw near to Khatijah, to take one final farewell look at her. Soon she passes by at shoulder level, wrapped in a light lavender sheet, her face uncovered. A few tufts of hair mixed with white powder protrude from under the sheet covering the top of her head and rest on her forehead. Her eyes are closed and her nostrils are stuffed with white gauze.

The "stretcher" is in reality the bottom half of a rectangular metal cagelike container, which has the appearance of an oversized crib. All four corners have handles pointing forward and backward, to facilitate carrying. Underneath it four short metal legs extend downward to keep the body a foot above the ground when the cage is set down.

A large crowd has already formed in front of the store near the street. Everyone knows exactly the order of the rituals. Men and women separate themselves into two groups, leaving ample space between them for the stretcher to be set down. The body is lowered to the center of the open area. It is now time for those present to bid farewell to their old friend and relative. Those closest in kinship to Khatijah are urged to circle her and view her face closely. Mariam and Tabassum, arms slung around each other's waists, slowly circumambulate the body. A few others, including Abid, follow suit. Others remain motionless as they fix their gazes on the dead woman.

Hussainbi Khala steps forward, bends down to the body, and, without emotion, pulls the shroud over her sister's face, after which she ties the top shut with a string. Khatijah's face will be seen no more until Judgment Day. Near her sister's head Hussainbi places a small purple bundle wrapped in cloth. Inside are sweets for the gravediggers. The body inside the casket lies on a light brown wicker mat. The rounded metal cover is dropped over the body and locked into place. A large broad cloth with green and white designs is carefully draped over it, hiding the body from view. Then a red cloth with simple embroidery at the edges is folded in half and placed atop the first sheet over the part of the casket under which the head and torso rest. Finally, another even larger sheet, brilliant green and completely covered with yellow verses from the Qur'ān, is placed atop the other two.

A man I do not recognize opens a large wicker basket and raises high above his head a long dangling net of white scented jasmine flowers, red roses, and pieces of shiny colored paper. He untangles the net and drapes it over the top two-thirds of the casket. Hussainbi ties the flowers to the casket with strings dyed red and yellow.

The crowd continues to observe silence for a few more minutes until the announcement is made that the body will now be taken to the cemetery. Some of the women begin openly crying. Their friend and companion is taking leave of the neighborhood community. Abid and others step forward and reach down to lift the casket off the ground. Mariam urges me to join them. I take hold of one of the metal handles and am surprised by the weight. Fortunately the casket is not carried by only a few men at a time. Instead many of them step up to help, offering shoulders and hands to all parts of the casket. Once the casket is lifted into the air and begins its trip to the cemetery, an unorchestrated but highly efficient rotation of carriers begins. As the casket is transported down the street, the pallbearers slowly slide their shoulders and hands in the reverse direction underneath it, allowing other men to take their place at the front. Every few steps fresh replacements move to the head of the lines on both sides of the metal coffin. After some time, the men bearing the back end of the casket release their grip and walk quickly to the head of the line located thirty feet ahead of the deceased. Then they walk forward slowly enough to allow the casket behind them to catch up, so that they may begin carrying again. Each time they do so they make sure it is on the opposite side of the casket from where they were the previous time. "First you carry with the right shoulder, then with the left shoulder, then right, then left again," explains Imtiaz, the young rickshaw driver. This sharing of labor expresses the unity and equality among Muslims and also their desire to honor the deceased by doing one last favor for them.

The air is hot and humid at midday, the sky hazy and white. Altogether I count approximately one hundred men and boys in the procession, which takes twenty minutes to reach the cemetery. Along the way some of the men gesture to car and truck drivers to go slowly or to turn down a different street. A few others take it upon themselves to warn of puddles or trash for us to step around. No one seems in charge, however, and few commands are needed as the largely silent procession wends its way down crowded streets. This part of the city, called "Camp," is one of the most densely populated.

We at last pass through the black iron gates of the Muslim cemetery compound. Everyone knows exactly what to do, first removing shoes and sandals before proceeding into a broad empty green hall with a low ceiling. The casket is set onto the middle of the floor. A door to a side room is unlocked into which the men quickly enter and sit down on a row of stone stools. There they perform the ritual washing of hands, forearms, face, nose, ears, mouth, and feet in preparation for prayer, each working quickly, so that others will not be kept long waiting. Everyone who has performed the washing reaches into a pocket and pulls out a handkerchief or small towel to dry face and hands. A small number of men do not perform the ablutions, having recently completed them for *namāz*. Abid tells me that my morning bath is already sufficient, unless I want to wash with the others, anyway, to purify myself. I decline, since I don't know how to do it, and anyway I was not about to pray the Muslim way, since I do not know the Arabic words, and because I will pray silently a Christian *du'ā* (informal prayer). All the while, nobody looks askance at me for not being a Muslim.

Soon two rows of worshippers form on one side of the casket, facing in the direction of Mecca. A pair of young boys stands at attention a few yards removed from the men at the end of the second row, waiting to pray. Abid and another man tell them to move closer to the others. "We're supposed to pray shoulder to shoulder," he whispers to me.

One man leads the others in prayer with *"Allahu akbar!"* (God is great!) two times, followed by a long silence. The stillness is broken by Arabic chanting and by a response from all present that I do not recognize. In contrast to the five daily *namāz* prayers, the funeral prayer involves no bowing or prostration; all those present remain on their feet. The prayer is short, and within minutes the stretcher is lifted and carried out the door into the cemetery grounds. Everyone follows in reverent silence, slipping into the sandals and shoes they had left outside the entrance. Two men lament that in the short time they have been inside washing and praying, their sandals have been stolen. Abid's and my shoes are still there. "Wrong size, I guess," he remarks dryly.

The cemetery is surrounded by high stone walls and thick foliage, beyond which three- and four-story apartment buildings rise. The noise of traffic is constant. The graves are laid out neatly in narrow rows, occasionally interspersed with various medium-sized trees. The graves themselves are simple raised oval or rectangular mounds of earth cov-

ered with plaster; some are painted green, but most are white. Only a
few have headstones with the name of the deceased engraved on them.
Each burial mound has atop it a shallow trough running from end to
end, which is filled with soil that can be used to plant flowers or bushes
to provide shade for the dead. Simply leaving a bouquet of cut flowers is
not permitted.

The cemetery is in a state of visible decline. Most of the tombs are
chipped and cracked with large and small pieces of plaster lying at
their bases. The earth between the graves is unwatered and dusty—the
coming monsoon will remedy that—and almost all the plants on the
graves have withered. But the few that have been attended to are lush
and bright with flowers.

The men carry the casket to the far end of the cemetery where a
rectangular hole four feet deep has been dug. It is surrounded on all
sides by high mounds of dry brown earth, broken tile and plaster, and a
few human bones. None of the grave sites in the cemetery is new. Each
has belonged to a family or cluster of families for generations and will
be periodically reopened to receive the next deceased, provided enough
time—usually six months—has passed for the previous body to have de-
composed. Khatijah will not be buried with her husband, Abdul, because
his grave was opened only a few months earlier to receive Khatijah's other
sister, Nuri. Rather, Khatijah will be interred in a grave on the far side
of the cemetery near one of the perimeter walls, under a tamarind tree.
The relatives feel it would be more appropriate for Khatijah and Abdul,
as wife and husband, to be buried together, but nothing can be done.

The last two previously admitted to the grave where Khatijah will be
interred are her son Razaak's fourth wife, who died in her twenties a few
years ago, and their nine-year-old son, who passed away last year. Both
died of illness. We do not know their names—they lived in another part
of the city—but Mariam met the boy for the first time a few months
before he died. After his mother's death, the boy was brought up by his
grandmother. He fell ill a year ago and could not be rescued, lingering
for weeks before giving up his spirit. He was a quiet, gentle boy, according to Mariam. Everyone wept bitterly when he died.

Khatijah's casket is set down beside the open grave. The flowers and three layers of cloth atop the casket are removed carefully one by one. After the container is opened, the wicker mat, most of which had been rolled up next to the body, is unfurled and draped over the edge of the pit and positioned carefully at the base by two men who have let themselves down inside. The green and yellow cloth, the largest of the three, is raised high above the grave by half a dozen men, providing shade to the corpse as it is lifted from the casket and reverently lowered to the bottom of the grave onto the mat. One of the two men in the grave unties the cloth at the top of the head, and, without uncovering the face of the dead woman, turns it in the direction of Mecca. The large green cloth has been lowered a bit over the grave, providing shade for the dead woman and the two men working, so that if a person would peer into the grave, he or she would have to bend deeply or squat. Most of us do so.

I count nine men who hold the cloth taut a few feet over the grave, providing shade to the lone man who now remains in the grave with the swaddled corpse. A three-foot-long wooden plank is handed down to him. He rests one end of the plank diagonally against the wall above Khatijah's head; the other end he sets securely at the base of the opposite wall. One by one other planks are handed down, where they are joined together faultlessly to create a perfect rooflike shelter for the body. Above the very top of the head an open spot remains where one last wooden plank needs to be placed, but the man in the grave cannot get it to lie flush with the others. The men observing from above call down various suggestions. The man in the grave tries several times, but the board will not fit. Finally three more planks are handed to him, and he places them over each other in such a way that Khatijah's head is finally protected, even if the planks do not lie even.

The man in the grave climbs out with the help of others. The shade-providing green cloth is taken away and folded with care. A large worn metal bowl is then passed around to all those present standing at the grave; each person takes a handful of earth from the ground and drops it into the dish. The bowl bypasses a boy who is standing in back. He races around the crowd to add his handful of dirt.

The top end of the mat, which had been lying under Khatijah's body in the casket, is folded down across the wooden planks into the grave. The bowl of earth is then poured slowly into the hole, and immediately everyone near the grave sets to work. While on their knees they push soil, tile, and even bones and skulls into the grave with their bare hands. I am one of them. Two men hasten the work, pulling on earth with broad hoes. Many of those present rotate with others, pushing the soil down into the hole with their hands. Not a single command has been given. Within minutes the grave is level with the rest of the ground. A few minutes later, the remaining surrounding earth is fashioned into a perfectly oval mound a bit longer than the length of the body. Two bricks are placed together upright at each end of the small mound, and a slender furrow is created between them, after which it is wetted down by a man with a watering can. The red cloth with the embroidered edge is then laid across the earthen mound, and upon that is placed the woven flower net that had been placed earlier on the casket.

With all the activity and congestion at the grave site, it sometimes happens that a man accidentally brushes his foot, which is regarded as unclean, against a neighboring grave. When this happens, he reaches down with his right hand, touches the grave, then brings his fingers to his chest to excuse himself to the dead. (In India, when Muslims approach a cemetery, they also greet the dead with a blessing in Arabic.) One does this likewise with the living when accidentally bumping into another person. One should touch the other's arm and ask forgiveness.

After the burial mound has been created, those present stand in silence while a tiny man with white hair and beard, wearing large glasses and an elaborately woven *kufi* on his head, stands at the grave and recites Qur'ānic verses aloud from memory. He does this for a few minutes only. There is no eulogy for the dead.

The faithful then take their leave, walking quietly and solemnly in small groups across the cemetery grounds and out the main gate into the street. Abid and I remain behind, so that I may take photos of the new grave. Cemetery workers will later create a plaster covering over the earthen burial mound.

After I take pictures of the burial site and we begin walking away, Abid instructs me not to look back at the grave for at least forty steps. He says that after the dead are buried, they cry out to the living not to abandon them in the cemetery. Our silence is an indication to them of death's finality until the Hour, the Day of Reckoning.

As we are about to leave the cemetery, two men sitting under a tree call out to us. They are the gravediggers. Although they have already been paid, they are not compensated well, and so they ask Abid for more money. He gives it to them immediately, both because they deserve it, and because it is one more way of honoring his grandmother.

We wend our way back to Khatijah's neighborhood by foot. It is raining lightly now, and small children, oblivious to death, are dancing barefoot in the street.

After we return from the cemetery to Khatijah's house, we are served hot sweetened tea with sliced white bread and rolls. We eat alongside relatives, friends, and neighbors. No butter or jam is used, so most people dip their bread into the sugary liquid.

Khatijah's closest relatives have gathered together to reminisce, just as they had done the previous night. They recall that Khatijah was her father's favorite child, and that she was also the stubborn one of the brood. Her brother, Habib, remembers how as a little girl Khatijah would sometimes take hold of the handlebars of her father's bicycle and not let him go to work until he promised to bring back candy at the end of the day just for her.

It is custom in these parts that on the day of the funeral, meals are not cooked in the home of the deceased. All the dishes in Khatijah's house have been freshly washed and returned to their shelves and cupboards, in accord with tradition. Food is brought in from elsewhere. The poor are invited into the home to eat alongside relatives and neighbors, the understanding being that this will further add to the merit of Khatijah. There appears to be a certain flexibility in what Muslim families do to honor the dead, but it always involves doing good to others, not just reciting prayers. One common custom is to select a very poor person from outside the family and serve them food for forty days.

Others told me it doesn't have to be a particular person or a set number of days; it can be simply helping the poor in general for a length of time of one's choosing: ten or twenty or forty days or even for the rest of your life. Or you might repair someone's roof or finance the construction of a building to give shelter to the poor.

Mumani Bibi, the wife of Habib, took it upon herself to cook a rice and lentil dish immediately after the burial, while the Hindu neighbors next door, Harisingh Mamu's family, prepared the vegetables. This was especially fitting, since Khatijah, a Muslim, had always regarded Harisingh Mamu as a kind of elder Hindu brother, even tying the *rakhi* string around his wrist, a symbol of sisterly affection for a brother, each year on Raksha Bandhan day.[7] And so when Khatijah passed away, Harisingh Mamu, the Hindu, became very emotional, having now lost his beloved Muslim "sister." At sixty-eight, Khatijah was twelve years younger than her Hindu "brother." Harisingh has been half paralyzed by a stroke for many years now. Once a proud, muscular, and energetic military man, his speech is now slurred; his left leg and arm, useless. He must be carried to the toilet. Khatijah's death has instilled in him a sudden longing to return home to the village of his upbringing near the enchanted "Valley of Flowers," high up in the Himalayas. More than anything else he wants to visit the famous Hindu temple in Badrinath, not far from his home, to lay eyes on it one more time before he passes away. He has grown weary of life. His youngest of three sons, Papu, only in his twenties, died of illness only a few years ago and thereafter his beloved wife, Murkuli Devi. More recently his second son, Devi, succumbed to alcoholism. Harisingh Mamu has seen enough.

Khatijah left behind a small sum, along with a small box of private papers. The money will be distributed to the poor.

The following day, back at Khatijah's home, the entire Qur'ān will be read aloud in Arabic, divided up into thirty sections of equal length, each read by a different girl or woman sitting cross-legged on the floor. The different chapters are read simultaneously by voices that are barely audible to me as I stand in the doorway of the house. Sometimes only two girls are present in the room, at other times as many as nine. The entire holy book will be read in one day on behalf of the deceased.

Abid and I visit Harisingh Mamu, who is still stunned that Khatijah is gone. We promise to drink coffee with him the next day after the early morning prayers at the mosque and cemetery. Khatijah's death is a potent reminder of life's transience and causes Harisingh to turn his conversation more and more to spiritual things, to eternity, to God, to the temple at Badrinath. He tells us about his younger brother, now living in Lucknow, who, as a young man, once desired to become a re- nouncer (*sannyāsi*), that is, a monk, and learn the highest Hindu wisdom at the feet of one of India's four Śaṅkarācāryas.[8] But his older brothers objected on the grounds that no one in their family history had ever before become a renunciant. They sent money to him in Allahabad and commanded him to return home. He married soon thereafter and became an astrologer.

All of us men arrive the following day at the *masjid* (mosque) at around 5:30 in the morning. The city is dark and still. Some of the men are already praying the first of the day's five standard prayers, the *fajr* or pre-dawn prayer. Two lines of praying men have formed, with a third line gradually taking shape by late-arriving stragglers. At the conclusion of the *fajr* the imam sits on the floor, faces the others gath- ered before him, and together they recite a prayer for the dead, all the words spoken from memory. Altogether there are fifty men here and a few small boys, including all the male relatives, except for Razaak. His two sons, Abid and Tahir, are plainly disturbed by their father's absence. How could their father be absent on such a solemn and important occa- sion as prayers for his own mother?

Just before we leave the mosque to go to the cemetery, a man carry- ing a large bowl filled with roasted chickpeas approaches every person present, including myself, and bids us take a handful to eat in honor of Khatijah.

Two tiny women, one in ragged clothing clutching simple prayer beads, the other fully covered in a black chador, sit silently outside the mosque on the bare ground, waiting for alms that most of the passersby will give.

As we approach Khatijah's grave at the far end of the cemetery we see that some men have already been waiting. To our surprise and relief one of them is Razaak, who offers no explanation for his late arrival. But an even bigger surprise awaits us. A woman has come, too, though women are strictly prohibited from visiting Muslim cemeteries. The woman is the aged Hussainbi, who is determined to pray at her sister's graveside, regardless of tradition and its rules. She is standing quietly off to the side, a bit apart from the men, wrapped in a white sari, saying nothing. Most of the men pretend not to see her, and no one dares challenge her to leave. Abid whispers to me, "She's not supposed to be here. Women are not allowed." Yet everyone else seems to take her presence in stride.

Only twelve men are gathered around the grave, which, sometime during the past two days, has received a fresh covering of white plaster. One of the men who had been inside the mosque is now here with his head covered. He recites a long prayer in Arabic for the dead. Meanwhile Afzal, at twenty the youngest of the male relatives, has squatted down near the grave. He removes a few sticks of incense from a bag, lights them, and stands them upright at the base of a nearby tree, in such a way that the sweet-scented smoke wafts leisurely over the grave. He is about to pull out even more incense when Habib taps him on the shoulder and tells him that this is enough. Afzal has no choice but to obey the patriarch.

After some time, the prayer leader interrupts his prayer for the dead, turns to the men, and asks, "What was her name?"

"Khatijah!" calls out Hussainbi, before the men can respond. This will be her only word in the cemetery.

A few minutes more and the prayer is over. Razaak steps up to the grave and is the first to smear light-brown sandalwood paste on it with his fingertips. The cup of paste in his other hand is sent around to all those present, who one by one smear more of the mixture on the mound. Abid does not take part in this. Sandalwood paste, he reminds me, is standard at Hindu rituals as a way of invoking the presence of the Divine. Later he tells me, "Incense and sandalwood paste, that's not Islam. All the dead person needs is our prayers."

I do not respond, but I think to myself that using sandalwood paste is a beautiful way of honoring the dead. After some time I say to Abid, "But as long as it doesn't take away from belief in one God, it's harmless."

"But it might," he insists.

Most of the men here at the grave will walk back to Khatijah's house where Nazreen has been preparing tea. When we arrive there we see that a row of chairs has already been placed outside the home in the narrow lane. We take seats, and Nazreen wordlessly pours the hot brew into the cups of all the men and into Hussainbi's cup. Then she returns to the house to make more.

I take a long look at Hussainbi, the most devout of all Khatijah's siblings, who sits across from me under a roof overhang, engaged in conversation with the men. At seventy she is the only one of four sisters still alive. Ayesha, the eldest, died many years ago, then six months ago Nuri, and now Khatijah. She and her brother, Habib, are the last two left. Hussainbi's red-dyed hair peeks out from under her white sari, which she has modestly draped across her head in the presence of men. Her bony ascetic face is aged and tired. She who has been a widow for forty years is an enigma even to those who know her best. On the one hand, she is the moral anchor of this lane community. She understands that Islam should be more than going through the motions of prayer five times a day. It provides the moral foundation for all of life, for discerning right from wrong. Hussainbi does not hesitate to speak the truth to people who need to hear right from wrong, right to their faces if necessary, whether they like it or not, sometimes eliciting their anger. She fears no one but God, nor does she recoil at the thought of washing the corpses of her sisters. In addition to being the self-appointed local expert on Islamic faith and customs, she has some knowledge of

Sufi wisdom sayings, unlike most Muslims.[9] She is always the same, steadfast in faith, a despiser of gossip, a woman who rarely speaks evil of others, although of late and as an exception to her normal speech, she has strangely pointed out Khatijah's failings as well as her generosity. In speaking of herself, Hussainbi maintains that she is certainly not a moral person, and she states as an obvious fact that she will need the prayers of the saints to get to heaven. In behavior she has always been different from her siblings. As a child she would watch from a distance as the others quarreled and fought. Since the time she was a young girl Hussainbi has been naturally devout. She has also practiced vegetarianism for most of her life, not out of compassion for animals, but because she realized it was the healthier way to live.

On the other hand, many people, even those who speak to Hussainbi respectfully, consider her privately to be a little bit crazy. For the old woman says quite openly that she has been for many years befriended by an invisible *jinn,* a supernatural spirit who regularly visits her in her little home. *Jinns,* as is well known in Islam, can be good or evil, male or female, Muslim or non-Muslim. This one happens to be good. The *jinn* has been given a special dais or low platform in Hussainbi's house, upon which no one else, no visitor, is ever allowed to sit.

Mariam and Abid once related to me another story about Hussainbi. It seems that in her dreams she has visited Mecca and has even had the privilege of seeing the very grave that has been prepared for her. "She just says this stuff out loud in front of other people," Mariam says smiling.

The conversation turns to burials at the cemetery we have just visited. One man I do not recognize says that once when a tomb was opened, the body of a man who had been buried long ago was dripping blood and had not yet begun decomposing. Another man said that in the same cemetery, just as the corpse of a moneylender, a man who had charged interest on his loans, was being lowered into the grave, flames shot out from the grave, a sure sign that hell awaited him. This was a story Mariam had heard as a girl. It terrified all the neighborhood children and made them even more fervent in their prayers.

In answer to a question about why Khatijah was not buried with her husband, Hussainbi replies that there must be a six-month waiting period between burials in the same grave, but not the full year that some people think.

Habib Mamu, Khatijah's brother, remarks that Afzal should not have burned incense at the gravesite this morning. Islam does not allow fire near a grave. That leads Abid to comment that even though many Muslims learn to sight-read the Qur'ān, most of them don't know the first thing about their religion. Abid is also disturbed that flowers and bowls of fruit are displayed in Khatijah's home during prayer rituals on her behalf. This, too, smacks of Hinduism. It is not the pure tradition of Islam. I wonder to myself just who God is for this otherwise gentle young man with a good sense of humor, a man who is, nonetheless, so often disturbed by even minor deviations from standard Muslim practice. Is God for him only a harsh lawgiver? Is there any place for a patient monarch? Perhaps even a forgiving Creator? It seems to me that in Islam what is important is not only to believe in one God. What is also important is the *kind* of God you believe in that will determine your peace and happiness. In contrast to Abid's God of rigid rules and unbending practices, Hussainbi's God is patient and merciful. And yet both are Muslim.

I came away deeply impressed by what I had experienced of the Muslim community during Khatijah's burial and the days that followed: their serene acceptance of death as a normal part of life, their fluency with death's rituals and their vibrant display of solidarity with the dead, their unquestioning trust in God as the just and merciful Judge on the Last Day, their overall dignified manner in living out their life of faith. I was grateful also that Mariam had been in India during the very time her mother suddenly passed away. This was an unexpected mercy.

Epilogue

Rethinking Jesus and the World's Religions

It was not long after I first arrived in India so many years ago that I began to realize how little my training in Catholic theology had prepared me to appreciate the other religions of the world. To be sure, I had expected to find goodness among the followers of other religions as well as a sincere search for spiritual liberation, but I was surprised to find just how much more was already there waiting to be discovered. What I did not know was that for centuries Hinduism, Buddhism, and Islam had produced a multitude of saints and holy sages, a wisdom of the greatest depth, and countless miracles. All this has become for me a sign that God is very much at work in those religions, using them as vehicles of His power and grace.

But my new awareness of the greatness of other religions has also raised many questions about the relation of those religions to Christ and to Christianity, questions having to do especially with Christ's universal lordship and authority, how to best express his salvific meaning, and the proper way to witness to him in my encounter with Hindus, Buddhists, and Muslims.[1] The more I have wrestled with these issues, the more certain I've become that witnessing to Christ must also involve my readiness to learn how God is already present and working in the lives of people of other faiths. I therefore think that what is most important in this era of human history, a time in which religious traditions are interacting with each other like never before, is that we open ourselves to the truth and beauty of other faiths in a living, respectful, and receptive encounter. Part of this encounter will involve dialogue, an exchange of convictions in charity and in openness to truth. It is here, when heart speaks to heart, that a fuller appreciation of other religions will be unveiled and a deeper understanding of Christ's meaning and significance will gradually shine forth. For we have not yet come to the end of our understanding of Christ.

What has especially fascinated me since my first visit to India is that so much holiness is possible in the different religions despite so much doctrinal discord. For example, when we look at Islam and Christianity, we notice immediately their total disagreement about the Trinity and Christ's divinity. And yet we find great spiritual and moral commonalities that unite Muslim and Christian saints. It is not difficult to recognize the similarity of holy men and women across this religious divide: whether Muslim or Christian they are imbued with a spirit of deep humility, they have given their lives over entirely to the will of God, they have made selfless love their highest aim, and they express that love in prayer and in service to others.[2] This common holiness is a fact that is still too little known among Christians. And holiness, from the Christian perspective, is always a fruit of the Holy Spirit. St. Paul, in his Letter to the Galatians 5:22–23, lists the transformative effects of the Spirit in the following way: "The fruit of the Spirit is love, joy, peace, patience, kindness, generosity, faithfulness, gentleness, and self-control." We are able to recognize these same fruits of the Spirit not only among Christians, but also among Muslims and members of other religions.

But it is also evident that religion in our time is often enough connected with what is worst in humanity: blind faith, stubborn rejection of science, territoriality, authoritarianism, sexism, oppression of the many by the few and the few by the many, interreligious violence. I might have written more forcefully about the treatment of women in Islam in various parts of the globe or about discrimination and violence toward low castes, outcastes, and tribals in Hinduism and some Indian

Christian communities or about the clericalism and authoritarianism that have reasserted themselves in recent decades in Catholicism, not to mention the horrors of child abuse. These issues are important, and I have touched on some of them in the pages of this book, but not extensively. Moreover, these abuses are already widely known. That was not the main purpose of this book. The primary purpose was to highlight the strength of other religions and of Christianity, especially their ethical ideals and spiritual strategies that lead to transformative spiritual experience and growth, and I wanted to do that in part by putting a human face on the religions I had encountered in India. I was thereby presenting religion at its best. My hope remains that my various accounts of the goodness and holiness found within other religions will inspire Christians to explore these religions themselves to see how enriching they can be.

At the same time that we recognize the destructive power of religion we might also discern that the opposite is surely on the increase today: complementarity (we can learn from each other), self-critique, movements toward democratization, a greater turn inward through the appropriation of various meditation and prayer techniques; ecumenism and interfaith dialogue, liberation theologies and praxis, a greater focus on ethics and service to humanity than on doctrines that divide, mass flight from fossilized institutional religion and rituals to spiritualities that are more nourishing and liberating; the humanizing of religion. All this signals a movement toward greater human unity and equality and a more mature and giving spirituality.

When we reflect more on what is positive about these modern religious developments, we discern something that is quite remarkable about the lives and teachings of today's saints and luminaries. We notice two features characteristic of them that are more prominent than among the saints of the past. First, the saint of today tends to have a greater appreciation of other faiths and shows a greater public recognition of the value of other religions, of the need for interreligious collaboration, often proclaiming the harmony of what is best in the religions and the necessity of all religions to work together. Second, today's saint is more likely to be aware of the need to change society and improve the lot of the poor and oppressed, not simply by giving alms, but also by working for justice. These two elements are often seen to be inseparable. The turn within often enough nurtures social engagement without. Thich Nhat Hanh, Martin Luther King Jr., the Dalai Lama, Thomas Merton, Mahatma Gandhi, Aloysius Pieris, Gustavo Gutierrez, and Krishnammal Jagannathan[3] are some excellent examples of people who have seamlessly woven together the cultivation of the inner life with social and political engagement on behalf of the oppressed. As mass movements, liberation theology in Christianity and socially engaged Buddhism have become especially renowned for uniting the inner life with efforts for social change.

From the Christian perspective, this modern transformation of the great religions is a sign of the presence of Christ's Spirit at work in them.

All my experiences in India would be for naught if I hadn't come away with a great appreciation for the value of other religions. What follows are some of the things that I've come to value in Buddhism, Hinduism, and Islam.

From Buddhism I've learned the importance of understanding and controlling the mind in all spiritual striving. I've come to appreciate the practice of meditation, and I now believe that much more can be accomplished in the spiritual life through effort alone than I had previously assumed.[4] I have also learned to appreciate the lofty ethical ideals articulated in various brands of Buddhism, culminating in the *bodhisattva* vow to work tirelessly for the liberation of all suffering beings.

Hinduism has shown me that there are many different paths of spiritual growth, each one tailored to suit individual needs, temperaments, and levels of awareness. It introduced me to new ways of thinking about the mystery of divine immanence and authentic selfhood. From Hinduism I have learned to value meditation and yoga. Also, I have come to appreciate the genuine love of God and trust in divine grace and mercy expressed in countless theologies and practices of Hindu devotion as exercised by the great majority of Hindus. I find that I now have a deeper awareness that the whole world and everything in it, including plants and animals, should be regarded as sacred. Finally, I have come to value the "four stages of life"[5] as a blueprint that honors life in the body and society while recognizing the need to finally transcend time and worldly life altogether so as to attain the eternal Divine. And much more.

From Islam I have come to appreciate the focus on the mystery of God's transcendence and otherness and simultaneously God's total claim on human life, as well as the readiness of so many Muslims to place the whole of their life under the guidance and direction of the divine will. Through the practice of Muslim daily prayer I am given an impressive example of the remembrance of God throughout one's day.[6] I also have come to value the spontaneous generosity of Muslims toward the poor. And in Sufism I find compelling examples of married saints who choose to remain in society rather than withdrawing from it, knowing that they are surrounded and embraced by divine love.[7]

Christians should take care not to contrast Islam and Christianity too strongly on the issue of God, pitting a Muslim God of wrath against a Christian God of love. It is easy to generalize about other religions and to compare what is worst in theirs with what is best in ours. The fact is there are many understandings of God in Islam, ranging from the strict legalistic and wrathful Judge of militant extremists to the many Sufi theologies and spiritualities of divine love and mercy at the opposite end of the Muslim spectrum. My experience with most Muslims is that they are somewhere in between; there is legalism to be sure, but also a sure sense of God's goodness and mercy. And, too, along with the many good and loving Christians in the world there are also plenty of angry and heartless ones, acutely afflicted with the demons of neurosis, anxiety, and hidden repression, people who have not yet been deeply touched and transformed by the experience of a God of love, mercy, and forgiveness.

Above all, I have learned to appreciate so much more in my own religion, Catholicism,[8] as a result of my exposure to other religions. Its sacramental life, its devotion to Mary, its rich heritage of saints and varieties of spiritual schools, its vast treasury of spiritual literature come immediately to mind, as well as its continuous emphasis on the dignity of the human person. Catholic reflection on the dignity of the human person has given rise to what I believe is the most developed social teaching among the world's religions, with its promotion of human rights and justice in all spheres of life—social, economic, and political.[9]

All these strengths derive from Christ, whose uniqueness I have also come to appreciate more and more. Even after all the comparisons have been made and the many commonalities with the saints and sages and holy ones of the world religions have been established, I find much in Jesus that remains unique and authoritative and that inspires me to discipleship. I find nowhere else anyone quite like Jesus, a man who is the embodiment of divine love in human form. He represents divine mercy taking on our human condition of vulnerability, suffering, and even death. His call to repentance, too, makes me take a deeper look into my heart and recognize how far I am from the holiness of God and how, in turning to God, I may receive the strength and freedom of forgiveness. And it is in Jesus's resurrection that I am given a glimpse of the mystery that awaits us all, the victory of love in a broken world, the rescue of the human by divine love, the full participation and liberation of the human family in the eternal mystery of the Divine.

Jesus, moreover, brings the poor and the oppressed into the center of our theology and spirituality. His Gospel ethic is simple: love God with your whole heart, mind, and strength, and your neighbor as yourself (Lk. 10:27). And to love your neighbor means to practice mercy and to act with justice. The followers of Jesus are called to see the human race as one family, transcending all religion, caste, ethnic, and political divisions and power relations. Jesus establishes a relation with God not limited by the dictates and laws of a particular religion or tribe or social class; it is a relation with God beyond all religious compartmentalism or division.[10] All are welcome into God's fellowship, both the saint and the sinner, female and male, those born as high caste and outcaste. Jesus is thus both within and beyond the religions. He proclaims a "people come first" religion.

At the center of Jesus's proclamation was not himself but God, the great mystery permeating all life, the source and end of all creation. Jesus's entire ministry was intended to mediate the merciful power of God's mysterious and self-giving love. We are made for union with such a God. It is only in such love that we will find our highest happiness.

This same God challenges us to come to the aid of the poor and oppressed and to not be entirely wrapped up in our own private "spiritual" relationship with God. In this bodhisattva-like selflessness we are called to live out God's "preferential option for the poor." Such an emphasis on justice and responsibility to our neighbor can make mystics preoccupied with their own private spiritual progress squirm uncomfortably under the will of God. For God desires total human liberation, societal as well as individual.

This God of love, who is at work in all the religions of the world, creates community, even across religious boundaries, even when our doctrines don't agree.[11]

And this God, finally, gives us a hope that all will be well, that we will be saved by the power of divine love. In short, God gives hope not only to the poor, but to all people. The tangible sign of this hope is not only Jesus's earthly ministry but also his resurrection appearances. Jesus's resurrection gives us a glimpse, a sign of what is to come: the completion of our lives in the freedom and love of the divine mystery.

Sanskrit Pronunciation Key

Sanskrit words and names in the translated verses are given in a phonetic spelling utilizing a macron for alternate pronunciations of the vowels *a, i,* and *u* (see the pronunciation table below for the distinct sounds these six vowels make). The standardized full transliteration system for the Sanskrit alphabet is utilized for Sanskrit words in the notes and other parts of this book. Below are the vowels and consonants that require clarification. Transliterated consonants not listed below are pronounced as in English.

Vowels

a	like *a* in *about*
ā	like *a* in *yacht*
ai	like *ai* in *aisle* (*ai* represents a single transliterated vowel)
au	like *ow* in *cow* (*au* represents a single transliterated vowel)
e	like *e* in *prey*
i	like *i* in *bit*
ī	like *i* in *magazine*
ḷ	like *lree* (this vowel is rarely found; it is pronounced by combining the English *l* and *r* with an *ee* sound following)
o	like *o* in *home*
ṛ	like *ri* in *rich*
ṝ	like *rea* in *reach* (this vowel is rarely found)
u	like *u* in *put*
ū	like *u* in *rude*

Consonants

c	like *ch* in *chart* (never pronounced like the English *k* or *s*)
d	like *d* in *lude*
ḍ	like *d* in *red*

g   like *g* in *gate* (the soft *g* as pronounced in the word *germane* is
        found only in the Sanskrit letter *j*)

h   like *h* in *hot* (standing alone or followed by a vowel, without
        following a consonant)

_+h   any consonant followed by *h* is merely aspirated, like the
        subtle aspirated breath sound naturally occurring in the
        word *pot* (whereas aspiration is naturally absent from *dot*);
        thus *ph* sounds like the letter in the word *loophole* (never an *f*
        sound as in *pharmacy*); and *th* sounds like the *t* in the word
        torn (never the *th* sound as in *thorn*)

ḥ   is the silent consonant often found at the end of words;
        when the word is at the end of a sentence, the short form
        of the vowel of the last syllable is duplicated: for example,
        rāmaḥ sounds like *rāmaha*, and *śaktiḥ* sounds like *śaktihee*
        (underscored letters indicate duplicated syllable)

j   like *j* in *joy*

ṁ   like *n* in the French word *bon*

n   like *n* in *soon*

ṅ   like *n* in *song*

ñ   like *n* in *staunch*

ṇ   like *n* in *sand*

ph   like *p* in *pan* (with aspirated breath; it never makes the
        sound of *f* as in English, for example, the *ph* in the word
        phase)

ṛ   (is a vowel; see *ṛ* in the section above entitled "Vowels")

s   like *s* in *suit*

ś   like *sh* in *shoot* (this sibilant and the following are commonly
        pronounced by English speakers without any discernable
        distinction)

ṣ   like *sh* in *shout*

t   like *t* in *tool* (with tip of tongue near the place where the
        teeth meet the roof of the mouth)

ṭ   like *t* in *lute* (with tip of tongue toward the middle of the
        roof of the mouth)

In most compound consonants, each consonant retains its original
sound in combination with the others. However, the combination
jñ as found in the word *jñāna* is often pronounced like the *gy* in the
English compound *dog-yard*.

Acknowledgments

I am grateful to Mickey Maudlin and Eric Brandt at HarperOne for initial conversations about the possible publication of this book when the manuscript was still in a very underdeveloped stage.

I am especially thankful to have had an editor to guide me who is as patient and wise as Kathryn Renz. She faced the formidable challenge of taking on a very long manuscript consisting of chapters of quite varying length on very disparate themes without much evidence of a logical order. Somehow she managed to fit the pieces together to form a unified whole. She also offered important suggestions toward improving both style and content. Her frequent expressions of enthusiasm for this project were gratefully received.

Thanks also go to Mindy Malik for reading through the yoga chapter and for offering suggestions and raising questions that I had not considered.

Notes

PROLOGUE

1. "We see that it is not the task of Christianity to provide easy answers to every question, but to make us progressively aware of a mystery. God is not so much the object of our knowledge as the cause of our wonder." Archimandrite Kallistos Ware, *The Orthodox Way* (Crestwood, NY: St. Vladimir's Orthodox Theological Seminary, 1979), p. 16.
2. See Kosuke Koyama, *Three Mile an Hour God* (Maryknoll, NY: Orbis, 1982), pp. 51–55. He goes on to say, "One-way-traffic Christianity is an ugly monster" (53).
3. The Second Vatican Council (1962–65) signaled a new and positive Catholic approach to world religions, one that is still too little known among Catholics today.
4. I am well aware that Buddhists will find language unacceptable that would refer to them as "children of God," but I am writing as a Christian. I do not mean to offend. It is my way of expressing my belief that Buddhists, like all people, are throughout their lives enveloped by God's love, providence, and care, even if they reject the notion of God.

CHAPTER 1: RETURN TO INDIA

1. A recent report (January 2011) published in Indian newspapers estimates that fifty-six thousand children die of malnutrition in Indian slums each year.
2. A bomb exploded in the German Bakery in Pune on February 13, 2010, not far from a Jewish center.
3. Īd-al-'Aḍhá ("Feast of Sacrifice") is one of two major Muslim feast days. It commemorates the readiness of Ibrahim to sacrifice to God his son Isma'il.

CHAPTER 2: A FIRST CONVERSATION ABOUT JESUS

1. Swami Ashokananda once remarked how Sri Ramakrishna (1836–86), one of the most well known and beloved of modern Hindu saints, "often praised the Muslims for their punctuality in prayer." See "Before You Sit in Meditation,"

in *Meditation* by Monks of the Ramakrishna Order (Mylapore, Madras: Sri Ramakrishna Math, 1984), p. 31.

2. Articles written by Mueller and Douglas on their Notovitch investigations were published in 1894–1896 in *The Nineteenth Century* magazine and can be found under "Some Articles on Notovitch, The Unknown Life of Christ" at www .tertullian.org/rpearse/scanned/notovitch.htm. See also George Gispert-Sauch, "Brahmabandhab Upadhyay on Notovitch," *Vidyajyoti* 71/8 (2007): 624–625.

3. See the excellent essay by Anantanand Rambachan, "A Hindu Looks at Jesus," in *The Hindu Vision* (Delhi: Motilal Banarsidass, 1994), pp. 39–46. Rambachan is one of the most creative Hindu thinkers today and has made significant contributions to Hindu-Christian understanding.

CHAPTER 3: FIRST ARRIVAL IN ASIA

1. The author was the famous Henri Troyat. The book, translated from the French in 1967, was called simply *Tolstoy*.

2. An excellent recent introduction to Catholic social teaching is Daniel Groody, *Globalization, Spirituality, and Justice: Navigating the Path to Peace* (Maryknoll, NY: Orbis, 2007).

3. Years later I would discover that Muslims similarly suspend all their activities to pray five times a day and put themselves in God's presence.

4. At the same time the great generosity of the German Catholic Church toward poorer Catholic countries around the world must be readily acknowledged.

5. Kasper stepped down from that position in July 2010.

6. The research was conducted in India, but the degree was given in Tübingen.

7. Due to ill health Rahner could not attend, but he sent his paper instead, which was read aloud. The paper, "Welt in Gott—zum christlichen Schöpfungsbegriff" ("World in God: On the Christian Concept of Creation"), showed Rahner's receptiveness to the possibility that the Hindu doctrine of nonduality might be useful in articulating the mystery of creation in a Christian context. It would, he hoped, help overcome some widespread Christian misunderstandings on the popular level about the world's relation to God. Rahner passed away a year later, in 1984. One can only wonder what impact he might have had on Catholic-Hindu dialogue had he lived long enough to immerse himself deeper in Hindu thought and spirituality.

CHAPTER 4: AN INDIAN VILLAGE

1. *Sannyāsi*s are renunciates, people who forsake the world in pursuit of spiritual fulfillment.

2. A *lunghi* (pronounced LOON-gee) is a wraparound skirt worn by both men and women in south India.

3. Their freedom has become somewhat restricted in recent years in the larger cities, due to the steady increase of traffic.

4. I will return to the issue of caste discrimination among Palayam Catholics in the chapter called "Crossover Communion."

CHAPTER 5: A CROSSROADS OF THE SPIRIT
1. The Sanskrit compound roughly translates as Knowledge-Light University.

CHAPTER 6: CROSSOVER COMMUNION
1. Pronounced pra-SAHD.
2. See Noel Sheth, S.J., "Hindu Prasāda, and Its Reception." *The Examiner* (Bombay), May 2, 1998, p. 12.
3. "Idol" is a standard term in Hindu parlance for any physical object into which the deity freely enters, for the purpose of drawing near to his or her devotees. The word, as used by Hindus, is devoid of the normal negative connotation found in the Bible and Christian theology. The deity, moreover, freely enters the idol at the conclusion of a sacred installation ceremony.
4. *Prasād* in Sanskrit originally means "grace."
5. See Noel Sheth, S.J., "Hindu Parallels to the Eucharist," *Vidyajyoti* 62/9 (September 1998): 679–699 and 62/10 (October 1998): 753–768. See also the same author's "Hindu Sacrifice and the Christian Eucharist," *Body, Bread, Blood: Eucharistic Perspectives from the Indian Church,* ed. Francis Gonsalves, S.J. (Delhi: Vidyajyoti/ISPCK, 2003), 64–85.
6. Differences have to do with the nature and degree of God's involvement in the material world and for what ultimate end or purpose. In Christian understanding, all of creation is being led by God toward a final transformation and integration into the divine life, to participate fully in God's infinity and eternity. The emphasis is not merely on the spiritual or inner dimension of created reality, but rather on creation in its totality. For the individual person the word for this transformation is *resurrection.*
7. According to Catholic teaching, at the end of her earthly life—whether or not she first passed through death—Mary was taken up or "assumed" into heaven, both body and soul.
8. The town's name is spelled in various ways.
9. Formerly Madras.
10. The other three major Marian feast days are Mary, Mother of God (January 1), the Annunciation (March 25), and the Immaculate Conception (December 8). See Richard P. McBrien, *Lives of the Saints: From Mary and St. Francis of Assisi to John XXIII and Mother Teresa* (San Francisco: HarperSanFrancisco, 2001), 332.
11. The number of visitors to the basilica is apparently on the increase. Some recent estimates have placed the larger gatherings at near two hundred thousand.
12. Sheth, "Hindu Prasāda," 13, writes, "How is it that, unlike Hindu *prasāda,* the Christian *prasāda* is not shared with others? The present Catholic understanding is that by receiving the Eucharist, people are not only expressing their faith in Jesus Christ as God, but are also united with the Christian community, sharing in the life, and accepting the basic doctrines, values, etc. of this community. Hence it would not be proper to offer Communion to non-Christians, for, in doing so, we would be forcing them to acknowledge Christ as God and also to accept our beliefs and doctrines. So one could tell our Hindu brothers and sisters that it is precisely out of respect for them that Communion is not given to them." But such an explanation was unfortunately not delivered to the Hindus gathered

at the Vailankanni basilica the day I attended. I doubt that it would have mattered, anyway.
13. Two well-known examples of doctrinal disagreement are reincarnation and resurrection. Reincarnation is normally accepted by Hindus and rejected by Christians, whereas the reverse is normally the case with regard to resurrection.
14. See my earlier remarks in "An Indian Village."
15. The Mass ends with the words of the priest, "Go in peace to love and serve the Lord."

CHAPTER 9: IN THE HANDS OF A SKILLED HINDU PHYSICIAN
1. More precisely, Dr. Nanal was a Gāṇapatya; that is, a Śaivite with a special devotion to Lord Gaṇesā.

CHAPTER 10: BUDDHIST VIPASSANĀ MEDITATION
1. *Vipassanā* is the Pali term; its Sanskrit equivalent is *vipāśyanā*.
2. Igatpuri is the city near to which Dhammagiri, the vipassanā center, is located.
3. There is an ongoing dispute as to whether the Buddha really ate meat. Some scholars today assert that the Buddha died from eating poisonous mushrooms.
4. The Dalai Lama has returned to eating meat, under doctor's orders. See vegetarianstar.com/2010/07/29/dalai-lama-says-eating-meat-not-always-against-monks-principles/ (July 29, 2010).
5. This claim has been challenged by Huston Smith and Philip Novak, *Buddhism: A Concise Introduction* (New York: HarperCollins, 2003), p. 205, note 5: "It appears that for many centuries meditation practice all but died out in the Southeast Asian lands of the Theravada tradition, and that the sangha was occupied almost exclusively with scriptural study, ritual performance, moral refinement, and the education of and assistance of the laity. What the world currently recognizes as 'Theravada meditation' and 'vipassanā' are products of rather recent rebirths of interest in meditation that can be confidently traced back only about 150 to 250 years." On this they refer to Robert H. Scharf, "Buddhist Modernism and the Rhetoric of Meditative Experience," *Numen* 42 (1995), especially pp. 246–259.

If such a view of the recent history of vipassanā is correct, then modern vipassanā might be regarded not as an innovation, but rather as a return to the original meditation method taught by the Buddha as described in the Pali canon. Goenkaji bases his meditation teaching on *The Discourse on the Grounding of Mindfulness* (*Satipaṭṭāna Sutta*) from that same early canon. According to Walpola Rahula, *What the Buddha Taught* (New York: Grove Press, 1977, [orig. 1959]), p. 69: "The most important discourse ever given by the Buddha on mental development ('meditation') is called the *Satipaṭṭāna-Sutta* 'The Setting-up of Mindfulness' (No. 22 of the *Dīgha-nikāya*, or No. 10 of the *Majjhima-nikāya*)."

See also the works of Glenn Wallis, who seems to want to bypass Buddhist religions and traditions in all their varied historical and cultural forms in order to return, at least to the limited degree that it is possible, to the pure original and simple teaching of the Buddha himself, by focusing in particular on the earliest layers of Buddhist scripture. See his *Basic Teachings of the Buddha* (New York:

Modern Library, 2007) and *The Dhammapada: Verses on the Way* (New York: Modern Library, 2007).

6. In due time, however, Goenkaji did refer to the Buddha's teachings of the Four Noble Truths, the Noble Eight-fold Path, the doctrine of impermanence, dependent coorigination or conditioned arising, and philosophy of mind. But in comparison to the time spent in the course in meditation, Buddhist doctrine was kept to a minimum.

7. Literally "mindfulness of inhalation and exhalation."

8. Heinrich Dumoulin, S.J., *Christianity Meets Buddhism* (LaSalle, IL: Open Court, 1974), p. 13.

9. See his introduction to the *Brahma-Sūtra-Bhāsya*.

10. See here the remarks of Bernard Senécal on Korean Buddhist meditation practice: "Christian religious often find themselves at a loss for words when asked by Buddhist counterparts how many hours a day they spend in meditation, and still more so when they learn that anything less than twelve hours is not taken seriously." "Korean Buddhism Today and Its Encounter with Christianity," in *Monasticism Buddhist and Christian*, ed. Sunghae Kim and James W. Heisig (Leuven–Paris–Dudley, MA: Erdmans 2008), p. 55.

11. On addressing this mental impasse, see Swami Ashokananda, "Before You Sit in Meditation," in *Meditation,* by Monks of the Ramakrishna Order (Mylapore, Madras: Sri Ramakrishna Math, 1984), p. 37, who remarks, "What should we do to conquer our desires and adverse impulses? Sometimes they succumb to direct attack, but a flank attack is usually better. Fighting a state of mind directly in order to conquer it can do more harm than good, for thereby the mind often becomes more and more entangled. The wise course is not to allow yourself to dwell on the condition of mind to be eradicated. Remember this psychological fact: the more you dwell on a mental condition, the more it is strengthened."

12. See Romans 7.

13. See S. N. Goenka, *The Discourse Summaries* (Onalaska, WA: Pariyatti Publishing, 2000) and William Hart, *The Art of Living: Vipassana Meditation as Taught by S. N. Goenka* (New York: HarperOne, 1987).

14. *Nibbana* in Pali.

15. In addition, our prayer can also benefit from meditation practice. Meditation can help us to settle into a deeper place within ourselves, from which we learn to pray more simply and purely.

16. This is a point made by Stephen Batchelor, who, as a practitioner of Buddhist meditation, is skeptical of most Buddhist doctrine, including reincarnation. See especially his *Buddhism Without Beliefs: A Contemporary Guide to Awakening* (New York: Riverhead Books, 1997) and *Confession of a Buddhist Atheist* (New York: Spiegel & Grau, 2010). In the latter book, pp. 25–26, Batchelor describes his ten-day vipassanā course with Goenka and the lasting impact it had on him. He writes appreciatively of this meditation course in which the student is not required to "master the intricacies of any doctrine or philosophy," unlike the Tibetan Buddhism in which he had immersed himself and to which he would give ten years of his life. In later interviews, he revealed that the Tibetan monks with whom he studied only reluctantly allowed him to integrate vipassanā into his

spiritual practice. The Tibetan focus was on texts and doctrines, and the monks did not seem to allow that the degree of mental calm and insight that vipassanā made possible in the brief space of ten days was even possible. Batchelor (p. 26) further notes that the Tibetan canon, "which, I had been assured, contained every single discourse the Buddha ever gave, lacks the majority of texts preserved in Pali, including *The Discourse on the Grounding of Mindfulness* (*Satipatthana Sutta*), on which Mr. Goenka based his teaching."

CHAPTER 11: YOGA

1. That is, they wear nothing at all.
2. See Geeta Iyengar's *Yoga: A Gem for Women,* various publishers and reprints.
3. From the Sanskrit root *yuj,* meaning to "harness," "yoke," or "unite." Gerald Larson, one of the most authoritative contemporary scholars of yoga, offers "concentration" or *samādhi* as an alternative original meaning of *yuj* in Patañjali's *Yoga-Sūtra.* Cf. *Yoga: India's Philosophy of Meditation.* Edited by Gerald James Larson and Ram Śaṅkara Bhattacharya; Volume XII of the Encyclopedia of Indian Philosophies (Delhi: Motilal Banarsidass, 2008), pp. 28–29.
4. This understanding of "Christian yoga" as a term synonymous with Christian spirituality is to be distinguished from the phrase "Christian yoga" as it was used some decades ago by a few Catholic scholars. In that more narrow understanding, "Christian yoga" simply meant adopting a few elements from classical Hindu yoga, especially postures, and integrating them into the framework of Christian spirituality. Cf., for example, Jean Dechanet, *Christian Yoga* (London: Search Press, 1970, [orig. 1956]).
5. The Indus Valley civilization was located in what is now Pakistan and western India.
6. The more critical recent scholarship places the *Yoga-Sūtra* between 350 and 500 CE. Some well-known translations with commentary on the *Yoga-Sūtra* include James Haughton Woods, trans., *The Yoga-System of Patañjali* (Delhi: Motilal Banarsidass, 1914); I. K. Taimni, *The Science of Yoga* (Wheaton, IL: Theosophical Publishing House, 1961); Gaspar M. Koelman, S.J., *Pātañjala Yoga: From Related Ego to Absolute Self* (Poona: Papal Athenaeum, 1970); Georg Feuerstein, *The Yoga-Sūtra of Patañjali* (Rochester, VT: Inner Traditions International, 1984); Usharbudh Arya, *Yoga-sūtras of Patañjali with the Exposition of Vyāsa: A Translation and Commentary.* Vol. I. (Honesdale, Pennsylvania: The Himalayan International Institute of Yoga Science and Philosophy of the U.S.A., 1986); *Patañjali's Yoga Sūtras with the Commentary of Vyāsa and the Gloss of Vāchaspati Miśra.* Translated by Rama Prasada (Delhi: Munshiram Manoharlal, 1988 [1912]); *Yoga: India's Philosophy of Meditation.* Edited by Gerald James Larson and Ram Śaṅkara Bhattacharya; Volume XII of the Encyclopedia of Indian Philosophies (Delhi: Motilal Banarsidass, 2008); Edwin Bryant, *The Yoga Sūtras of Patañjali* (New York: North Point Press, 2009). Klaus K. Klostermaier, *A Survey of Hinduism* (Albany: SUNY, 1994), pp. 401–407, presents an excellent summary of the *Yoga-Sūtra.* Also useful for yoga studies is Georg Feuerstein, *Encyclopedic Dictionary of Yoga* (New York: Paragon House, 1990) for analysis of key terms used

in texts from within classical and postclassical yoga traditions, both Hindu and non-Hindu, as well as related terms from the Upaniṣads.

7. From *aṣṭa*/eight + *aṅga*/limb.

8. See Bhagavad-Gītā 6:19, a passage that is sometimes used in yoga teaching.

9. Vegetarianism is propounded by classical yoga.

10. It must be conceded that this is a disputed point in contemporary scholarship. Bryant, for example, in his recent monumental study, *Yoga Sūtras* (see note 6 above), argues that Patañjali's *īśvara* should be regarded as belonging to the general Hindu understanding of a personal God and supreme being characteristic of most *bhakti* or devotional movements of Patañjali's time (cf. 88–89). He says, "one . . . cannot extricate and immunize Patañjali's *Īśvara* from the theological landscape of his time" (281). Moreover, Bryant goes so far as to suggest that Patañjali was "necessarily" a devotee of either Viṣṇu or Śiva (275). Scholars such as Gerald Larson strongly disagree with this understanding.

11. These five afflictions (*kleśas*) are ignorance (*avidyā*), egotism (*asmitā*), desire (*rāga*), aversion (*dveṣa*), and dread of death (*abhiniveśa*).

12. Cf. Larson's remarks on *īśvara* and note how his position contrasts with that of Bryant: "if God is a *puruṣa*, God can neither be personal nor any kind of cosmic absolute . . . The Yoga God is untouched (*aparāmṛṣṭa*) and, hence, uninvolved in the transactions of afflictions, action, and the karmic ripening of traces (YS I.24). Hence, God in Yoga becomes an impersonal, acosmic, detached presence whose inherent contentlessness can only show itself as what it is not." *Yoga: India's Philosophy of Meditation*, 49.

13. Bryant, *Yoga Sūtras*, 279, in addition to YS I.26 reads YS II:45 ("From submission to God comes the perfection of *samādhi*.") as teaching the grace of the Lord. But the text itself, in fact, says nothing about grace; it speaks rather of the yogi's practice. Grace is at best implied.

14. Here I agree with Larson, who states, "The term *praṇidhāna* is not *bhakti* or devotional theism in any conventional sense . . . it is a deep meditation on the nature of transcendence, not any sort of devotional theism." *Yoga: India's Philosophy of Meditation*, 50.

15. See Wade Dazey, "Yoga in America," *Theory and Practice of Yoga: Essays in Honour of Gerald James Larson*, ed. Knut A. Jacobsen (Leiden–Boston: Brill, 2005), pp. 409–424.

16. "*Samādhi* is both the technique for realizing this condition and the condition itself." Joseph S. Alter, *Yoga in Modern India: The Body Between Science and Philosophy* (Princeton and Oxford: Princeton University Press, 2004), p. 4.

17. This sexual exploitation of the defenseless by persons of high religious authority is, unfortunately, a problem all too well known in other religions, including my own Roman Catholicism.

18. In *śavāsana*, or the corpse posture, we keep our eyes closed while systematically examining and relaxing every part of our body, starting with our head and working our way down to our feet.

19. See Russill Paul, *Jesus in the Lotus: The Mystical Doorway between Christianity and Yogic Spirituality* (Novato, CA: New World Library, 2009), pp. 132–136.

20. Here I am not taking up the related and very difficult issue of trying to distinguish between the evil influence of the demonic on my mind and the darkness already lurking in my own subconscious.

CHAPTER 12: A CATHOLIC HOLY MAN

1. Bede Griffiths, *The Marriage of East and West* (Springfield, IL: Templegate, 1982), p. 8.
2. "The Sacred Mystery," in *Return to the Center* (Springfield, IL: Templegate, 1976), pp. 19–20.
3. See www.monasticdialog.com/a.php?id=361.
4. *The Cosmic Revelation: The Hindu Way to God* (Springfield, IL: Templegate, 1983), p. 7.
5. *The New Creation in Christ: Christian Meditation and Community*, ed. Robert Kiely and Laurence Freeman, OSB (London: Darton Longman and Todd, 1992), pp. 99–100. It should be added that people of other religions will be baffled by such christocentric language about grace. They will wonder why Bede would not speak of the grace of "God" present to all people instead of the grace of "Christ." To speak of the grace of Christ seems to imply that by virtue of Christ's death, resurrection, and sending of the Spirit, those people of other religions who do not know Christ or believe in him are still somehow beneficiaries of his work, that what God has accomplished in him has touched the lives of all. But what does that mean exactly? How has Christ's work concretely impacted the lives of those who do not know him or believe in him?
6. *Saccidānanda* is a medieval Sanskrit compound (from *sat + cit + ānanda*), still very much in use among contemporary Hindu monks to designate the supreme reality, *brahman*. Drawing on the terminology of the Upaniṣads (ca. 800–200 BCE), *saccidānanda* indicates—correctly, but analogically and therefore imperfectly— that the nature of the great Mystery, *brahman*, is infinite being, pure consciousness, and unalloyed bliss. In choosing this term as the name for the Catholic ashram they had founded in 1950 (the one in which Father Bede now lived), two French Catholic priests, Jules Monchanin and Swami Abhishiktananda (Henri Le Saux), were in effect professing that the term is a legitimate expression of the Holy Trinity, though not identical to the standard Christian understanding with its emphasis on divine love. The term *saccidānanda* was first adopted from its original Hindu context and inserted into a Christian framework at the end of the nineteenth century by the famous Catholic convert from Hinduism, Brahmabandhab Upadhyay (1861–1907).
7. For a more extensive account of life at Father Bede's ashram, see my "Editor's Introduction" to Sara Grant, *Toward an Alternative Theology: Confessions of a Non-Dualist Christian* (Notre Dame: University of Notre Dame Press, 2002), pp. xi–xii.
8. "The world," wrote Bede, "is looking not for words about God, but for the experience of God." This quote is from his "The Sources of Indian Spirituality," *Indian Spirituality in Action*, editor not given, preface by Joseph Cardinal Parecattil (Bombay: Asian Trading, 1973), p. 67.

As an Indian Jesuit novice master told me at Bede's ashram, "Theology is all right, but if you want to know God, you have to learn to transcend your mind." He meant we need to transcend the analytical thinking mind, so as to be still and receptive to the divine presence.

9. Seyyed Hossein Nasr, *Knowledge and the Sacred* (New York: Crossroad, 1981).
10. Griffiths is clearly a perennialist in the sense that he finds traces of shared universal wisdom in all the major religions, but he differs from most other perennialists in that he regards Christ as the place where God's will is definitively revealed and where God has become incarnate in a singular way.
11. See Pieris's *An Asian Theology of Liberation* (London–New York: T & T Clark, 1988).
12. The interview can be found at www.youtube.com/watch?v=wOAlyl7u2dw.

CHAPTER 13: MY MUSLIM FAMILY

1. Pronounce YAY-soo-dahs.
2. Not earlier than the year 57 CE. A Christian community had already been established in Rome by the time Peter arrived.
3. Christians overall constitute only a little more than 2 percent of the total Indian population.
4. A *haveli* is a two-story mansion with an inner courtyard.
5. Khatijah was the name of the Prophet Muhammad's first wife. Most Muslims today continue to give their children traditional names from the Qur'ān or from Muslim history.
6. *Mahārājah* in Sanskrit means "great king."
7. A Tommy helmet was made of steel and first used by British combat troops in World War I.
8. See "Muslims—India's New 'Untouchables'," *Los Angeles Times*, December 1, 2008, http://www.latimes.com/news/opinion/commentary/la-oe-nomani1 –2008dec01,0,4752.story.

CHAPTER 14: A SECRET LOVE

1. The word means "send back," meaning divorce.
2. I should add that when Mariam was growing up a Muslim, she had never been exposed to the great teachings about divine love professed by Sufism.

CHAPTER 15: TIWARI AND THE WEDDING INVITATION

1. See the biography of Yisudas written by his son, Ravi Tiwari, *Yisu Das: Witness of a Convert* (ISPCK, Delhi, 2000).

CHAPTER 16: WEDDING DAY FIASCO

1. Short for Mahatma Gandhi Road.

CHAPTER 19: SHIVAPUR AND THE MIRACULOUS STONE

1. A darvesh, or dervish, is a Sufi renunciant who has taken a vow of poverty.
2. The parallel to the *ora et labora* (pray and work) of Benedictine monasticism immediately comes to mind.

3. A subsequent visit to the shrine revealed that the smaller stone had broken in half some years before and is now housed inside the mausoleum.

4. *Ya!* means "Oh!" and *Darvesh* is pronounced "Dar-VAYSH."

CHAPTER 20: KHATIJAH'S DEATH

1. In this chapter I use the name "Khatijah" instead of "my mother-in-law" or "Mrs. Shaikh" in order to highlight her life in relation to so many people who knew her by that name.

2. Pronounced ahm-BAIR, it is also called Amer (ahm-AIR).

3. The Kachwahas belong to the *kṣatriya* or second-highest Hindu caste, the so-called warrior or ruling social group. The Kachwahas, moreover, trace their lineage all the way back to Kusha, son of Rama, the hero and avatar of the ancient epic Rāmāyaṇa.

4. The Qutb Minar is the highest brick minaret in the world at 238 feet. It was built over a span of almost two hundred years (1193–1386).

5. The temple is dedicated to the Hindu goddess Kālī.

6. *Foopoo* means "father's sister" or aunt.

7. Raksha Bandhan literally means "bond of protection" in Hindi. It is an annual pan-Indian Hindu festival celebrating a brother's promise to protect his sister. The two people need not be related by blood, however. The sister may adopt a nonrelative of her choice as her new brother. Tying the *rakhi* thread to the brother's wrist is a sign that the filial relationship is accepted by both, and the little ritual is repeated again the following year.

8. Śaṅkarācāryas are spiritual heads of Advaita monasteries in four areas of India. Each is a learned spiritual guide (*ācārya*) whose honorific title is named after Śaṅkara (ca. 700 CE), the founder of the four monasteries and the most authoritative teacher in the entire Advaita tradition. The word *advaita* itself means "nonduality" and refers to an understanding of reality in which the world and its source are regarded as not-two.

9. Though the majority of Muslims in the city visit the shrines of saints on a regular basis, they do not know the word *Sufi*, nor do they distinguish between Sufi saints and other Muslim saints.

EPILOGUE

1. "For a long time Christians have been willing to dismiss other religions as false religions. It has been said that Christianity is the one true religion, and Christians have not felt disturbed in any way. But when we begin to discover the truth in other religions, when we enter deeply into them, we realize how much God has given to them. Then the problems arise." Bede Griffiths, *The Cosmic Revelation* (Springfield, IL: Templegate Publishers, 1983), p. 109.

2. Thomas Merton, too, the great twentieth-century Catholic monk, has remarked on the sometimes strikingly similar qualities of holy people from different religions: "Without asserting that there is complete unity of all religions at the 'top,' the transcendent or mystical level—that they all start from different dogmatic positions to 'meet' at this summit—it is certainly true to say that even where there are irreconcilable differences in doctrine and in formulated belief, there

may still be great similarities and analogies in the realm of religious experience. There is nothing new in the observation that holy men like St. Francis and Shri Ramakrishna (to mention only two) have attained to a level of spiritual fulfillment which is at once universally recognizable and relevant to anyone interested in the religious dimension of existence. Cultural and doctrinal differences must remain, but they do not invalidate a very real quality of existential likeness." *The Asian Journal of Thomas Merton* (New York: New Directions, 1975), p. 312.

3. My thanks to Professor Catherine Punsalan-Manlimos of Seattle University for alerting me to the work of this inspiring Hindu woman.

4. I have also commented earlier on what I believe to be the limitations of effort-alone spirituality for Christians.

5. These four stages are being a student (*brahmacārya*), a householder (*gṛhastha*), retirement from social obligations (*vānaprastha*), and total renunciation (*sannyāsa*).

6. Two important modern Catholic figures in the Muslim-Christian encounter, Charles de Foucault (1858–1916) and Louis Massignon (1883–1962), recovered religious faith in part through the powerful witness to God displayed by Muslims in their daily spiritual practices.

7. Notwithstanding the fact that the Sufi saint I have written about in this book, Qamar Ali Darvesh, was unmarried, the great majority of Sufi saints have been married with families.

8. I restrict myself here to Catholicism instead of speaking of Christianity as a whole.

9. See http://www.osjspm.org/catholic_social_teaching.aspx. One might argue that Catholicism today is marked by three special strengths: its social teaching, its openness to other religions (after Vatican II), and its readiness to embrace scientific research. On this last point see http://en.wikipedia.org/wiki/Catholic_Church_and_science.

10. See, for example, the *Christbhaktas* (devotees of Christ), Hindu followers of Jesus in various parts of India, who do not identify themselves with any Christian church but who seek to live as disciples of Christ. See also the *ʿĪsā imandars* ("those faithful to Jesus") in Bangladesh, who likewise, as followers of Jesus, are not connected to any established institutional church but who maintain their traditional Muslim cultural and religious forms. I am grateful to Alison Fitchett Climenhaga for bringing this latter group to my attention.

11. I recall how some years ago a Hindu friend informed me, a Christian, that he would be praying for the health of my mother-in-law, a Muslim!